The Impact of UK Immigration Law

"This is a comprehensive, sweeping and yet forensic study of the UK's immigration laws and policies and how they have had an impact on social cohesion and the anti-immigrant narrative. Sheona brilliantly exposes how these laws have had such a detrimental effect on vulnerable people's rights. This book comes at an important time given the relentless assault on the Rule of Law by the Executive. Her recommendations need to be taken seriously and I wholeheartedly endorse this book."

—Toufique Hossain, *Director of Public Law, Duncan Lewis*

"This is a book that grapples with the legal developments in British immigration drawing on the expert legal analysis of author Sheona York. Her extensive experience in the field shines through the pages. A very important contribution."

—Dr. Devyani Prabhat, *Professor of Law, University of Bristol Law School*

"In this hugely ambitious undertaking, Sheona York brings together her decades of frontline experience and meticulous scholarship to examine the post-war history of immigration controls in terms of their detrimental impact on standards of public administration, the rule of law and democratic accountability. She exposes the consequences of an imperial, exclusionary ideology and a half-century of under-resourcing and over-legislating. She calls for a debate on citizenship and what it entails, which has never yet been conducted, and the need to build a system based on new forms of political solidarity. This book is an important resource for anyone wanting to understand the profound damage done to our legal, political and cultural infrastructure by an immigration system built on institutional racism."

—Frances Webber, *human rights lawyer, author of* Borderline Justice: The Fight for Refugee and Migrant Rights *(Pluto, 2012); vice-chair, Institute of Race Relations*

"The text is bursting with insights from York's half a century of immersion in immigration and nationality law as strategic litigator, student, academic, critic, and activist. It has the power to educate and inspire those who seek to understand and reform it from any of those perspectives. York explains how Britain's treatment of migrants exposes the very heart of what it means to be a British citizen and our ability to defend the rule of law."

—Sue Willman, *Senior Solicitor, Deighton Pierce Glynn; Assistant Director/Supervising Solicitor/ Lecturer, Kings College, London, Legal Clinic, Chair of the Human Rights Committee, Law Society of England and Wales; founding author in 2001 of* Support for Asylum-seekers, *LAG; and wild lawyer*

"Sheona's wide ranging work examines the failings in UK policy on immigration control and British nationality, comparing the overall success of the Home Office's EU settlement scheme with the lack of resources, lack of 'legal conscientiousness' and lack of competence in other areas of migration control. Her ambitious recommendations provide a positive framework for change. This well-researched work, building on Sheona's years of experience as a legal practitioner, should be read by policy makers who wish to improve the system, and by practitioners who need to question it."

—Judith Carter, *Solicitor and Lecturer, University of Liverpool Law Clinic (formerly of Islington Law Centre), Co-author of* Statelessness and Applications for Leave to Remain: A Best Practice Guide *ILPA 2016*

"Sheona York's accessible and wide-ranging study argues that post-colonial Britain has performed immigration control as political theatre at the expense of good administration and respect for the rule of law. So dysfunctional is the legal architecture of the system that it has become impervious to efforts to reform it. She argues that there can be no democratic accountability for the system of immigration control without a radically simpler legal framework and provides suggestions, born of many years' experience as a practitioner and academic in the field, as to what that might look like."

—Alison Harvey, *barrister, is a former General Secretary and then Legal Director of the Immigration Law Practitioners' Association, and a contributor to Fransman's British Nationality Law and to Macdonald's Immigration Law and Practice. Currently at no 5 Chambers, she has specialised in immigration, asylum, nationality, free movement and human rights for over 20 years, representing individuals and working on policy and legislation in both the UK and overseas*

Sheona York

The Impact of UK Immigration Law

Declining Standards of Public Administration, Legal Probity and Democratic Accountability

palgrave
macmillan

Sheona York
Kent Law Clinic
University of Kent
Canterbury, UK

ISBN 978-3-030-98720-6 ISBN 978-3-030-98721-3 (eBook)
https://doi.org/10.1007/978-3-030-98721-3

Cover illustration: Janine Wiedel Photolibrary/Alamy Stock Photo

This Palgrave Macmillan imprint is published by the registered company Springer Nature Switzerland AG
The registered company address is: Gewerbestrasse 11, 6330 Cham, Switzerland

To the thousands of individuals and families surviving the 'hostile environment' on no recourse to public funds, who have made Britain their home.

Foreword

Few subjects generate as many opinions as immigration. Debate is cyclical, rising and falling as a subject of public interest and political concern for the past several decades. It is an issue that can never be resolved because unrealistic expectations are often fostered by governments who often try to reduce anxiety at migrants' expense through over-complex and restrictive legislation that is subject to constant change. There has been resistance and some legal gains, including under the Human Rights Act, but they are fragile. In this context immigration law practitioners and academics are in an uneasy position. They see close up the damage that controls cause: the heartache, the loss of basic entitlements, the uncertainty, the lives put on hold, and the financial and other costs but they also know that there is not widespread popular support for the sorts of policies that would substantively change their position. The risk is therefore either idealistic calls for policy change that have little chance of being heard or fatalistic acceptance that little can be done.

Sheona York's book is written from an immigration lawyer's perspective and is a bold attempt to find a new way forward by focusing specifically on legal values. It is a valuable approach for two reasons.

Firstly, the book draws on her decades of experience as a lawyer acting for migrants in law centres, advice services and, more recently, at Kent Law Clinic. She understands not just what the law says but how it works, how poor administration or apparently minor points of process can make a vast difference to someone's life. The insights she brings cannot be learned from a textbook but have been achieved through years of dedication and experience and are combined with knowledge of the history of immigration control over decades and a deep understanding of law to create a unique perspective.

Secondly, her focus on legal values allows for a different, less confrontational and more productive approach to the question of what we want the immigration system to look like. Issues of justice, fairness and good administration command a consensus that the immigration question alone cannot and Sheona's argument is that this is where we need to focus our efforts. Improvements here would, in themselves, be a benefit, a step towards a system that is fairer and works better. They would also do more. The book shows repeatedly how bad laws and poor administration are themselves causes of many of the problems that are laid at the feet of migrants. We need to reverse the mind set whereby all the costs of the immigration system, personal, social and financial, are dumped on migrants and their families because that causes many of the problems that we want to solve: irregularity, lack of employment, exclusion, visibility. If the immigration system worked properly without long delays and decision-maker errors, if the application process was transparent, affordable and fairly administered, if people knew that they could progress predictably through the system or, alternatively, that this was not an option for them, confidence in the government's ability to manage migration flows would increase. There would be short term costs because, for example, fees would need to moderate and staff would need to be recruited and trained but the long-term benefits would include not only a better experience for individuals but a de-escalation of tension and the opportunity for a more sober and realistic assessment of the benefits and costs of immigration.

Immigration and immigration controls are going to be part of our world for the foreseeable future. Sheona's perspective, as expressed in this work, is an invaluable contribution to our understanding of how we can do it better.

Dr. Helena Wray
Editor, Journal of immigration,
Asylum and Nationality Law,
Associate Professor of Migration
Law and Director of Research,
Law School
University of Exeter
Exeter, UK

The law stated in this book is accurate as at 22/12/21.

Acknowledgements

To John Fitzpatrick, Emeritus Professor of Law, University of Kent, former Director of the Kent Law Clinic 1992–2018: friend, colleague and inspiration in immigration and asylum work from the beginning of Hammersmith and Fulham Community Law Centre in 1979: and with particular gratitude for reviewing earlier drafts of this work and helping me to sharpen its focus;

To Sue Willman, International Human Rights Lawyer, Senior Consultant at Deighton Pierce Glynn and Clinic solicitor at Kings College, University of London: law centre colleague, friend and long-time inspiration through her own indomitable determination to make legal work make a difference;

To colleagues from Hammersmith and Fulham Community Law Centre, Immigration Advisory Service, Rights of Women and Kent Law Clinic; to colleagues from the Immigration Law Practitioners Association (ILPA) since 1984; to fellow-contributors to the Refugee Law Group; to barristers I have worked with, especially from Garden Court, Doughty Street, 1 Pump Court and no 5 Chambers; to colleagues on the editorial board of the Journal of Immigration, Asylum and Nationality Law; to immigration law colleagues at university law clinics around the country: *recognition and acknowledgement of the value of their contributions to immigration law practice and to access to justice for our clients;*

To David Lerner, retired CEO of the Samuel and Bella Sebba Trust, for proposing the funding of my Kent Law Clinic post in 2012 and for his full support thereafter;

To Kent Law School, University of Kent, for awarding me study leave for the academic year 2019–20, without which this book could not have been written;

Permissions

Thank you to Mr. Abidoye and his solicitors DJ Webb & Co, for giving permission to look at and quote from his court papers.

I am very grateful to the following copyright holders for permission to reproduce extracts and ideas first developed in detail in previously published material, in particular in articles I have published in the Journal of Immigration, Asylum and Nationality Law. That journal is published by Bloomsbury Professional, an imprint of Bloomsbury Publishing Plc 50 Bedford Square, London WC1B 3DP. The Birkbeck Law Review is published by The Birkbeck Law Review, 14 Gower St London WC1E 6DP.

York, Sheona. (2020). Privatisation, *'mission creep' and lack of Home Office legal conscientiousness in the immigration application process*—Journal of Immigration, Asylum and Nationality Law, 34 (1).

York, Sheona. (2018). *The 'hostile environment': How Home Office immigration policies and practices create and perpetuate illegality.* Journal of Immigration, Asylum and Nationality Law, 32 (4). ISSN 1746-7632.

York, Sheona. (2017). *Deportation of Foreign Offenders—A critical look at the consequences of Maaouia and whether recourse to common-law principles might offer a solution.* Journal of Immigration, Asylum and Nationality Law, 31 (1). ISSN 1746-7632.

York, Sheona. (2017). *The Law of Common Humanity: revisiting Limbuela in the 'Hostile Environment'.* Journal of Immigration, Asylum and Nationality Law, 31 (4). pp. 308–329. ISSN 1746-7632.

York, Sheona. (2015). *Revisiting removability in the 'hostile environment'.* Birkbeck Law Review, 3 (2). pp. 227–257. ISSN 2052-1308. E-ISSN 2052-1316.

York, Sheona. (2015). *Immigration Control and the Place of Article 8 in the UK Courts—An update.* Journal of Immigration, Asylum and Nationality Law, 29 (3). pp. 289–307. ISSN 1746-7632.

York, Sheona. (2013). *The end of legal aid in immigration: A barrier to access to justice for migrants and a decline in the rule of law.* Journal of Immigration, Asylum and Nationality Law, 27 (2). pp. 97–194. ISSN 1746-7632.

About This Book

The postwar UK system of immigration and asylum control has been charged with facilitating regulated immigration for the general economic and cultural good of the UK and upholding an historic commitment to accepting refugees, while at the same time addressing the concerns of those who fear the impact of immigration on their livelihoods and their cultural well-being.

The system which has emerged to manage this complex set of conflicting needs and aims is widely considered, by all sides, to be dysfunctional.

This study concentrates on the *legal* changes in immigration control in response to the major arrivals of migrants into the UK since the Second World War, and the *consequences of those changes.* It focuses on something that has not received the attention it deserves: *the grievous collateral damage inflicted by the system on the maintenance of high standards of public administration, on respect for the rule of law, on social cohesion and on democratic accountability for the whole system.* The study argues that the system should be assessed in the light of that collateral damage.

Following the Introduction, Chapters 2, 3 and 4 discuss and analyse the UK immigration control system's development and responses to the three main cohorts of new arrivals to the UK: British subjects, Commonwealth citizens and their families; asylum-seekers; and labour migrants, including the postwar European resettlement schemes, work permit holders and EU nationals enjoying free movement. Chapters 5 draws out the impact of decades of poor government policy choices on the norms and practice of public administration, and Chapter 6 exposes a parallel pervading and corroding indifference to rule of law principles. Chapter 7 argues for a fundamental discussion of the *meaning and purpose of citizenship*, to underpin development of an immigration policy aimed at social cohesion rather than concentrating on the forlorn hopes of enforcement and exclusion. Chapter 8 emphasises the importance of democracy: of democratic accountability for changes in immigration law, and also the need for wider public debate on the detrimental social consequences identified as having been wrought by the system. The study concludes by setting out proposals for legal and administrative change.

December 2021 Sheona York

Personal Acknowledgements

To my son Alex, always ready for searching debates whether on maths or music, politics or football;

To friends David and Ruth, companions on scores of mountaineering expeditions in Scotland and further afield, on which they have indulgently listened to critiques of the latest Home Office unlawful decision, administrative incompetence or 'new plan'….

Contents

About the Author

Sheona York is a Reader in Law, University of Kent Law School, and solicitor in Kent Law Clinic. She practised for nearly 30 years at Hammersmith & Fulham Community Law Centre, specialising in immigration, asylum, asylum support and public law, taking a number of reported cases alongside anti-deportation campaigns and policy interventions. Then as Principal Legal Officer at the Immigration Advisory Service she specialised in public law immigration and asylum cases including conduct of several reported cases dealing with removability and 'Dublin' returns. Following the 2011 demise of IAS she worked at Rights of Women, providing legal advice and running workshops for women with insecure immigration status. Since joining Kent Law Clinic in 2012 she has supervised students' work on immigration and asylum cases where legal aid is not available, specialising in family migration, fresh claims for asylum and refugee family reunion. Her casework includes the celebrated 'Afghan Atheist' case of 2014, and the withdrawal of a deportation order and grant of leave to a British-born stateless foreign prisoner with no country to which he could be expelled.

Sheona's previous landmark casework includes the two major pieces of litigation against withdrawal of support for asylum-seekers, in 1996 and in 2003, and a homelessness case which won in the House of Lords in 2000. In 1985 she brought the first legal case ever, anywhere, to rely on DNA fingerprinting, as dramatised in 2015 in ITV's *Code of a Killer*.

Sheona is a keen mountaineer and climber—she has 'compleated' 2 rounds of the Scottish Munros, and in 2017 participated in a mountain crossing of South Georgia to commemorate the 100th anniversary of Sir Ernest Shackleton's famous boat journey from the Antarctic.

Abbreviations

A8 countries	The eight largest 'accession' countries which joined the EU on 1/5/2004
BIA	Borders and Immigration Agency (1/4/2007–1/4/2008)
CA	Court of Appeal
CAB	Citizens Advice Bureau
CBI	Confederation of British Industry
CJEU	Court of Justice of the European Union
CPGB	Communist Party of Great Britain
CUKC	Citizen of the UK and Colonies
DHSS	Department of Health and Social Security (Now Department of Work and Pensions)
DP	Displaced Persons
DVLA	Driver and Vehicle Licensing Agency
ECHR	European Convention on Human Rights
ECtHR	European Court of Human Rights
EEA	European Economic Area
EEC	European Economic Community
EU	European Union
EUSS	EU Settlement Scheme
GLD	Government Legal Department (Previously Treasury Solicitors)

HAC	Home Affairs Committee (of the House of Commons)
HGV	Heavy Goods Vehicle
HOPO	Home Office Presenting Officer
HSMP	Highly Skilled Migrant Programme
IAT	Immigration Appeal Tribunal
ICIBI	Independent Chief Inspector of Borders and Immigration
IHS	Immigration Health Surcharge
ILPA	Immigration Law Practitioners Association
IND	Immigration and Nationality Division; Immigration and Nationality Directorate (of the Home Office, up to 2006) *(Both these terms used, even by government officials and members of parliament)*
IOM	International Organisation for Migration
IPPR	Institute of Public Policy Research
IT	Information Technology
JCWI	Joint Council for the Welfare of Immigrants
NACAB	National Association of Citizens' Advice Bureaux (now Citizens Advice)
NAM	New Asylum Model
NAO	National Audit Office
NASS	National Asylum Support Service
NGO	Non-Governmental Organisation
NHS	National Health Service
NRPF	No Recourse to Public Funds
ONS	Office of National Statistics
PEP	Political and Economic Planning (Since 1978 the Policy Studies Institute)
ss	sections (of an Act of Parliament)
SSHD	Secretary of State for the Home Department
TUC	Trades Union Congress
UK	United Kingdom
UKBA	UK Border Agency (1/4/2008 to March 2013)
UKIAS	UK Immigration Advisory Service, Later Immigration Advisory Service
UKSC	UK Supreme Court
UKUT	Upper Tribunal, Immigration and Asylum Chamber
UKVI	UK Visas and Immigration (from 2013)
UNHCR	United Nations High Commissioner for Refugees
UNRC	UN Convention on Refugees
WRS	Workers Registration Scheme

1

Introduction, Conclusion and Recommendations

In addition to securing the country's borders, the United Kingdom's system of immigration and asylum control has been expected to facilitate regulated immigration for the general economic and cultural good of the UK, and to uphold an historic commitment to accepting refugees. At the same time, it has been expected to address the concerns of those who feel threatened by the economic and cultural impact of immigration on their livelihoods and their well-being generally.

The system which has emerged to manage this complex set of conflicting needs and aims is widely considered, by all sides, to be dysfunctional.

This study does not attempt to assess the success or merit of the system as regards the delivery of much-needed migrant labour, or a more open, diverse and internationalist society, or the protection of jobs, wages and access to hard-pressed social services, or an enduring sense of belonging 'somewhere' among those with shared values. Those are all political questions, which fall to be resolved through wide public debate.

Instead, it analyses the *legal* changes and developments in the *system* of immigration control in response to the major arrivals of migrants into the UK since the Second World War, and the *consequences of those changes*. It

S. York, *The Impact of UK Immigration Law*,
https://doi.org/10.1007/978-3-030-98721-3_1

focuses on something that has not received the attention it deserves: *the grievous collateral damage inflicted by the system on the maintenance of high standards of public administration, on respect for the rule of law, on social cohesion, and on democratic accountability for the whole system.* The study argues that the system should be assessed in the light of that collateral damage. It concludes with proposals for legal and administrative change. It demands wider public debate on the detrimental social consequences identified as having been wrought by the system.

Insofar as migrants and their rights and entitlements are concerned, this study focuses on those who are already present in the UK, and on those wishing to enter and remain under applicable laws – viewed as actually and potentially part of our society and who potentially could become part of the *demos*. It considers the terms on which new arrivals had originally entered, and how their respective rights and status have been eroded over time. It identifies the pervasive administrative incompetence of the system, focusing on delay, mistakes and lack of legal conscientiousness. It records the often unintended and unexamined consequences of complex laws on individuals, families, communities. It shows how this treatment has affected the fragile social solidarity that exists in a society that is already under threat from economic change and is increasingly bereft of collective and communal organisations and institutions.

The study locates these developments in the context of changing political forces which have, over time, led or driven changes in immigration legislation, rules, policies and procedures towards quick, poorly-thought-out, performative and always restrictive measures to the point of legal confusion and even administrative collapse. It also identifies one remarkable and crucial feature of the political landscape against which these developments have occurred—the absence of any extensive or thoroughgoing public discussion about the meaning and purpose of citizenship.

This study only briefly engages with those strands of migration theory which posit migrants not yet on the territory as possessing abstract 'rights' whether arising from international conventions or more generally from universalist philosophical or religious propositions, or from recent critiques arguing for reparations for the depredations of Empire. It does insist on an acknowledgement of what faces any such migrants arriving on a cold northern beach. Such migrants must contend with the democratic decisions of a specific host population. If those decisions embody indifference or opposition, that can only be changed by new democratic decisions following the widest political debate among the receiving country's residents.

This study sets out to scrutinise and assess the UK system of immigration control against three basic analytical frameworks: good public administration, the rule of law and democratic accountability. The study's examination of UK immigration control concentrates on the system's response to the three main categories of new arrivals into the UK since the 1940s – Commonwealth citizens and British subjects and their families; asylum-seekers; and labour migrants. The object of this study's analysis is the system itself: the relevant laws, policies, procedures, legal precedents. I first give an historical account of the above, set in the context of the relevant political and economic background. In that account I discuss the relevant legal developments in such a way as to draw out how the official responses to the arrival of each cohort of migrants, whether administrative, legislative or procedural, support and lead to the conclusions of this study. The second part of the study provides a detailed analytical discussion of each of those conclusions in turn, presenting an account of how these developments influenced each other, and how they underpin the study's legal and political recommendations. This study's definition of good public administration, discussed in Chapter 5, is uncontroversial: the implementation of democratic decisions as legislated by Parliament, by bureaucracies operating procedures which are legal, transparent and consistent, for which the political administration is accountable, including for avoiding delay, waste or corruption. In Chapter 6 the study uses Lord Bingham's rule of law principles[1] and Simon Halliday's discussion of 'legal conscientiousness' in the public administration of rights and entitlements,[2] as a guide to my conclusion that UK immigration control falls below democratic requirements of legal probity. I draw on Peter Ramsay's presentation of the weakness of the modern state, forced to legislate to protect the population 'from harm',[3] to evolve my own concept of *relegislation*, in which governments performatively reintroduce criminal measures in particular, to give the illusion of being in control of immigration. I analyse the effect on migrants of the Home Office's use of outsourcing to deliver immigration functions as *legal distancing* migrants from their legal remedies, as not parties to the relevant contracts. Finally, the study's assessment of democratic accountability firstly rests on identifying the extent to which many significant changes in immigration, asylum and nationality law have never been placed before Parliament: or (as with British citizenship) placed before Parliament but barely subject to public discussion: placed before Parliament in sections of Bills added at the last minute and barely debated; or, as with the Immigration Rules, placed before Parliament in negative resolutions only. The study further argues that the consequences of UK immigration control policies such as placing the burden of proof on the applicant, the reliance on retrospective effects of policy changes or the impacts of the hostile environment, as well as specific instances of the disarray caused by overlapping and contradictory legal measures, are barely subject to public scrutiny or debate, while underpinning significant social corrosion.

This is a legal study: a study of laws and their legal and bureaucratic implementation, which have resulted in the deterioration of substantive and procedural legal rights and entitlements, and in a deterioration of the operation of the rule of law and good public administration, not only with respect to immigration control. I examine fundamental legal concepts, including the burden and standard of proof, legitimate expectation, retrospectivity and *res judicata*, as applied in immigration and asylum law and as transformed by the system's operation of them in that legal arena. And I conclude by making proposals for legal changes, without which things cannot improve whatever policies may be introduced.

The study addresses the immigration and asylum system in its modern form as it has developed from just after the Second World War up to the present. It is presented in two parts. Chapters 2–4 examine how a system of control developed in response to the three main categories of arrivals in the UK from post-war to the present day: British subjects and Commonwealth citizens and their families from wartime through to the 1980s (Chapter 2); asylum-seekers from the 1980s onwards (Chapter 3); and labour migrants, from the post-war European resettlement schemes, through work permits and Commonwealth work vouchers, to Labour's points-based system and the advent of large-scale EU migration after 2004 (Chapter 4). Through a discussion of these three migration categories, the study traces the emergence of four fundamental consequences of the measures taken in response to these arrivals.

Those chapters identify how modern UK immigration control was conditioned from the beginning by Britain's post-war need to deal with economic weakness and the decline of Empire: and was deeply inflected by assumptions of racial superiority. Discussions about immigration control often foundered on the conflicts between those arguing the need for immigration to fill acute labour shortages, those fearing a return to unemployment as the million men still under arms were demobilised, and those scared that the British Isles would be overwhelmed by millions of black and Asian people with the right to enter. The early controls were accompanied by a strong reluctance to confront racism in British society or to argue for a solidarity-based vision of British citizenship, a reluctance moreover that extended to progressive, left wing and labour institutions. The fear of public debate over these issues cannot be separated from the British state's formal resistance to its colonies' demands for independence, a resistance which included deploying British troops to stamp out rebellions all over the Empire. These political conflicts are demonstrated most starkly by the passing of the British Nationality Act 1948, with almost no consideration even in Parliament of what British citizenship could or should mean, and certainly no consideration of what the Act itself would mean or the implications of granting the rights it accorded. That Act was conceived as a way of cementing *relationships between governments* in the dissolving Empire. Instead, a full debate on this crucial matter among the entire populations of the Empire and Colonies, at that moment, must surely have hastened and transformed the struggles for independence throughout the Empire, probably paralleled by demands in the UK for a UK-based citizenship as a recognition of rights and duties accruing to residents of that territory. As it was, the passage of that Act represented a crucial early step in governments' and politicians' determination to keep issues of immigration control away from public debate.

Chapter 4 confronts the basic issue facing any labour migration policy—'*we wanted workers, but people came*'.[4] Any labour migration policy which does not include a path to settlement and integration amounts to treating the rest of the world's workers as a 'reserve', to be exploited without taking any responsibility for their upbringing, education, family support, training, healthcare or retirement. Of course, the irreducible background to UK labour migration policies must be sought in the Empire: in the way Britain's capitalist development was underpinned by the colossal, worldwide exploitation of people for work, from slavery through indentured and bonded labour schemes, to clearances and race-based settlement policies. UK Labour migration policy also suffers from a lack of or shallowness of democratic debate. Chapter 4 discusses the main postwar legal frameworks for UK labour migration in the light of that simple contestation, that complex, deplorable history and that poverty of public discussion.

The second part (Chapters 5–8) proceeds to examine in detail the deterioration in standards of public administration and a diminishing respect for the rule of law and good practice across the whole gamut of immigration control, from the design of legislation, rules and policies through application and enforcement procedures to the conduct of litigation. I look at the corrosive effect of immigration laws on social solidarity; and the abiding 'democratic deficit' in the discussion and development of both immigration and nationality law. Chapter 8 concludes with some proposals for democratic discussion, and makes specific recommendations about public administration and legal probity.

Chapter 5 shows how the decline in standards of public administration first emerged in the 1960s with the failure to provide adequate resources to handle spouse applications from the Indian subcontinent. The 1980s and 1990s saw further delays, and a corrosive interplay between the build-up of queues of spouses and families seeking entry, and the use of that phenomenon by right-wing politicians and racist groups to whip up 'concerns' about 'too many migrants'. The relentless expression of those 'concerns' in turn led to introductions of further restrictions and legal requirements on applicants which themselves added to the administrative burden. In the 1980s asylum backlogs grew rapidly, as until the early 1990s the Home Office made few administrative or legal changes to its operations in response to the increasing numbers of asylum-seekers. Then a period of public expenditure cuts and expensive and unsuccessful

IT contracts in the 1990s led to administrative chaos: and the entire immigration function was declared 'not fit for purpose' (2006) and 'not good enough' (2013). The quality of decision-making has over decades received formal criticism, and the proportion of allowed appeals has steadily grown, standing now at 50%. The post-2010 policies bearing down on family migrants, 'illegals' and foreign criminals, including the formal hostile environment measures in the Immigration Acts of 2014 and 2016, confirm that, rather than increasing resources, simplifying legal requirements or improving administration, the response of every government since the 1970s to complaints of 'lack of control' has largely been to further restrict rights and entitlements, curtail access to legal remedies, criticise lawyers and judges and stigmatise applicants. The March 2021 *New Plan for Immigration* and current (December 2021) Nationality and Borders Bill exemplify all these features. Chapter 5 concludes with a brief account of the EU Settlement Scheme—which, in granting status to over five million people in just two years, shows what can be achieved with a shared burden of proof, simplified legal requirements and a clear intention to grant leave.

Chapter 6 draws together the ways in which the system of immigration and asylum control has failed to meet acceptable standards of legal probity. This is demonstrated throughout the period, from the 1960s Commonwealth Immigrants Acts which hid their true purpose, to signal instances of failure to follow rules, guidance or binding precedents, acts of bad faith in specific cases, and indifference to the retrospective effects of legal changes operating in a climate of lengthy casework delays. The Commonwealth Immigrants Acts were consciously drafted and discussed to use ostensibly neutral criteria, such as 'skilled workers' or 'those with a parent or grandparent born in the UK' to achieve an explicitly racist aim. Terms such as 'genuine' as in 'genuine spouse', 'genuine student' were consciously introduced to implement the colonial-style presumption that Commonwealth and Colonial men were simply deceitful economic migrants. Outstanding examples of failure to follow binding precedents took place during the 2000s in relation to cases dealing with the right to marry as well as cases from the European Court of Justice on free movement of third-country nationals.

The much-criticised 'culture of disbelief' of Home Office decision-makers is shown to rest on the *placing of the burden of proof on the applicant*. This was first demonstrated in the 'virginity testing' and 'primary purpose' rules for spouse entry, and more recently by purporting to require 'proof' of homosexuality, and proof from Windrush residents for every single year of their residence. An account of the impact of the 2014 and 2016 hostile environment measures shows how, far from reducing the numbers of 'illegals', those measures have *created and perpetuated illegality*. The study makes clear that the principle of a hostile environment was in no way new. The Thatcher governments of the 1980s and 1990s began limiting migrants' access to welfare benefits and social housing, explicitly using terms like 'gatecrashers' and 'benefits tourists'. Just as now, those measures caused hardship to others, including many who were no longer or who had never been migrants, but British subjects with full rights on arrival. It has been argued that the motivation of the Thatcher government was primarily to cut welfare spending. In contrast, in 2013 Theresa May advocated the modern hostile environment explicitly to drive out unlawfully-present migrants by making it impossible for them to survive here—but with the same result. Lawfully-present migrants, settled people and even British citizens and their families are caught by and suffer from those measures.

And, just as for poor standards of administration, these legal failings and poor practices have become institutionalised.

Chapter 7 considers the third important 'immigration' issue in the UK today—the effect on social cohesion. This study argues that an examination of this problem must start with a look at *citizenship*. The chapter examines how, in the UK, legislation on citizenship took place without much public discussion or formal consideration of legal, political or philosophical underpinnings of the concept. The analysis must begin, as this study does, with a critical look at the impact of the British Nationality Act 1948, passed with virtually no public debate, quickly followed *not* by any discussion of the meaning and purpose of citizenship, nor by revised and reconsidered legislation on *citizenship*, but by *immigration* laws aimed at denying the rights accorded in that Act, and a subsequent Nationality Act whose impact on citizenship itself was again barely discussed but whose purpose was to sort out the mess of immigration control. Official studies and proposals on the values, meaning and purpose of citizenship, in the late 1980s and early 2000s, were not widely publicised and had little influence, leaving the legal status of citizenship to perform a purely immigration control function. The chapter then notes that, meanwhile, official concentration on controlling entry and enforcement, without remotely achieving the stated policy aims, has left Britain with some two to three million residents with insecure immigration status—whether on time-limited visas or without any legal status—facing the snakes and ladders of long 'routes to settlement', high fees and requirements increasingly difficult to meet—and declared by law to be 'precarious'. These residents, many of them 'essential workers', find themselves unable to contribute to or participate fully in British society because they lack recognition and status, and any prospect of permanency. This briefly came to public attention during the first Covid lockdown in 2020 when it became clear how many 'essential workers' were on time-limited visas, and for a brief period public demands were made for citizenship, residence, access to social benefits and reduced visa requirements for those risking their health on the front line.

Chapter 8 discusses the final and fundamental issue arising today: democratic accountability for the character and conduct of the UK's system of immigration and asylum control. It first considers this from the perspective of the 'abstract migrant' not yet on the territory. Such an approach is valuable, in that it highlights the gap between aspirations based on every human being having equal moral value, and the reality facing displaced people all around the world. But generally, that perspective is advanced without engagement with the views of any host population. Whereas *their* voices, indeed their democratic rights, cannot be ignored, especially when they need to sound more loudly than ever in defence of their interests (and indeed those of immigrants) in the context of the financial crash of 2008, the ensuing austerity and the developing post-Covid economic disruption.

A second perspective is considered, more central to this study. It focuses on the primary legislation, and just as importantly on the Immigration Rules, procedures and guidance that constitute the UK system of control. Many measures have been introduced and changed with little publicity or parliamentary scrutiny. Neither has there been much formal discussion of the corrosive consequences of measures that have proved controversial. And underlying all this has been the lack of public discussion about the values, content and purpose of citizenship.

It is argued that a necessary condition for improving social cohesion is that those living and working and even just surviving in the UK but who are not citizens must be given a secure, affordable path to settlement, just as it is argued that refugees need 'safe and legal' routes to asylum. It is pure fantasy for any government to act as if all 'illegals' could be removed, or to expect long-resident work and family migrants to simply 'go home' if they cannot meet some future onerous requirement for settlement. Chapter 8 presents propositions for wide discussion, including a regularisation scheme for unlawfully-present migrants, a simple and cheap settlement scheme for those on 'routes to settlement', a consideration of labour migration policies which would take into account impacts on the wider economy and society, and more generous policies towards accepting asylum-seekers whether by resettlement or in relation to spontaneous arrivals. A more sustained public discussion would enable residents, citizens or not, to see and evaluate the true cost of the divisions in society exacerbated by current immigration controls, and might provide a real basis for improving social solidarity.

1 Conclusion

An important aim of this study has been to highlight the consequences for public administration and legality generally of a large department of state being tasked with the supervision of a politically controversial set of rights and entitlements without the resources to manage that efficiently—and being resolutely unwilling, except in relation to EU nationals, to simplify requirements, procedures or processes in any way which might grant anyone more rights. Already, since the public expenditure cuts which followed the 2008 financial crisis, intensified by the Covid emergency, aspects of the criminal justice system and welfare benefits administration show similar deterioration. It is hoped therefore that this study will catch the attention not only of academic and practising lawyers, officials and judges working in immigration and asylum issues, but also of any person who holds that democracy requires sound public administration and adherence to the rule of law.

Chapter 8, and the whole study, concludes with specific recommendations for legal and administrative reform. These recommendations are offered firstly as practical measures that seek to address the immediate circumstances of those who wish to enter or remain in the UK, and secondly to prompt the engagement of the public in a discussion about the meaning of citizenship and the integration of immigrants where that is desired. It is only on the basis of fuller participation by the *demos* and those seeking to join it, can longer term improvements be pursued successfully.

2 Recommendations

a. The introduction of a shared burden of proof in the immigration and asylum jurisdiction
b. The eradication of retrospective effects from immigration control legislation, rules and procedures
c. The provision of sufficient resources for the immigration and asylum function in public administration, without reliance on prohibitive fees or exploitative and malfunctioning outsourcing contracts
d. A restatement of the entire legal architecture of control, whatever its substantive content, in a form that is simple, coherent and transparent
e. A generous scheme for the regularisation of long-resident irregular migrants and their children, based on a shared burden of proof and adequate administrative resources.
f. An official campaign to encourage immigrants, including labour migrants, to seek permanent residence and eventual citizenship, emphasising 'common purpose', with simple requirements and without prohibitive fees.

Notes

1. Bingham, Tom. 2011. *The rule of law* London: Penguin 2011 [88].
2. Halliday, Simon. 2004. *Judicial review and compliance with administrative law* London: Bloomsbury Publishing.
3. Ramsay, Peter. 2012. *The insecurity state: Vulnerable autonomy and the right to security in the criminal law* Oxford: Oxford University Press.
4. From Max Frisch, a Swiss writer, reflecting on labour migration in Switzerland.

2

The Postwar Arrival of British Subjects—The Drive for Control Leads to Poor Public Administration and an Unequal Burden of Proof

1 Introduction

This chapter begins by reviewing the British Empire's legacy of enforced and 'free' population movements and its culture of *racial thinking*, which profoundly influenced both postwar migration to the UK and official and public attitudes to this. The early conflict between the British Nationality Act 1948's statement of citizenship rights and their rapid restriction by immigration control is shown to have driven the future development of UK immigration and nationality law. The Immigration Act 1971 was intended to terminate 'primary immigration'. Procedural and processing issues led to the build-up of delays and queues especially for spouse visas. A 'culture of disbelief' rapidly became prevalent. Against sustained right-wing campaigning, racial unrest and racial violence, laws and official practices turned their attention to internal controls. Immigration and race issues caused turmoil on the Left, often torn between campaigning for colonial independence and combating racism in the UK, while vacillating on immigration controls. The slow official move from dealing with 'immigrants' to adapting to a politically significant new settled population led to a concomitant transformation of anti-racist

S. York, *The Impact of UK Immigration Law*,
https://doi.org/10.1007/978-3-030-98721-3_2

campaigning from independent political and street action to a more legalistic central government and local authority 'race relations' operation, and to campaigners' reliance on litigation to oppose egregious state activities. This fed in to a generally weakened understanding of how social solidarity is constituted.

2 Empire's Shadow: Capitalist Exploitation and Racial Thinking

Britain finished the Second World War exhausted, indebted and shabby. Its immediate postwar economic and political problems brought 'immigration' onto the political scene in two distinct ways. With a million men still under arms, some fighting colonial wars, an acute labour shortage led to two separate, significant, streams of immigration. The first was the planned recruitment of displaced servicemen and refugees from continental Europe. This, the beginning of formal labour migration to the UK, will be discussed in Chapter 4. The second, of British subjects from the colonies and independent Commonwealth countries, took place at the same time as Parliament was considering legislation on British citizenship—a question so little considered in Britain that an Act, the British Nationality Act 1948, was passed with no public debate and almost no thought to its consequences. This lack of democratic discussion about British citizenship will be discussed in Chapters 7 and 8.

As those holding rights under that Act began to enter in numbers without any restrictions, political hostility to 'coloured immigrants' drove a series of poorly-conceived measures to control and stop them. Campaigns for trade union and political solidarity, whether with European resettled workers or British subjects from the Colonies and Commonwealth countries, were impeded by two sets of influential political forces. First, a specific Empire-based form of nationalism had developed in the late nineteenth century, influencing many working-class politicians in Britain and elsewhere to adopt race-based and pro-Empire policies. Secondly, *racial thinking* pervaded all levels of British society.

In this study the term *racial thinking* is used to refer to popular, elite, scientific and academic views that human beings are biologically divided into identifiable races, with distinct behavioural characteristics believed to be natural and heritable and only with difficulty amenable to social influence. And in this study the British Empire is analysed as founded largely on private capital, relying on large scale enforced international population movements, driven by capitalist exploitation based on burdensome commercial contracts and treaties, and administered through bureaucratic structures underpinned by racial thinking. Precise racial stratifications in the Empire's different colonial societies had led to local conflicts between the colonial rulers, the various displaced populations and the original local inhabitants. The postwar arrival in Britain of people from all these strata—returning expatriates, displaced workers expelled by newly-independent self-determining polities, colonial subjects seeking a better life in the 'mother country'—inevitably brought with them the habits, hopes and expectations of the colonial society, and the experience of oppression there. The impact of their clashing experiences, intensified by the difficult postwar economic conditions, in turn strongly influenced British debates on immigration, the precise structure of modern immigration control and the speed with which the law changed.

The Empire's population movements had involved millions of people. The slave trade forcibly moved over 12 million people over 400 years. And by the end of the First World War, some 5 million indentured labourers had been moved from India and China to work elsewhere in the Empire.[1,2,3] British overseas interests and possessions had long provided destinations for British unemployed and landless people of all classes, either into colonial administration or to work in companies such as the East India Company or the growing overseas banking, mining and agriculture sectors. This 'free' emigration peaked in the beginning of the twentieth century at just over 300,000 a year.[4]

After the Second World War, the Dominions, especially Australia, were still encouraging British emigration, not discouraged by Britain despite Britain's acute labour shortage[5]: and in the 1950s and 1960s British people continued to emigrate to South Africa and Rhodesia (now Zimbabwe). Those emigrants generally accepted the racial stratification of colonial life and the relatively luxurious standard of living this provided. This emigration created small but powerful white settler populations opposed to racial equality, some later mounting formal opposition to decolonisation based on majority rule. Many of those who returned to find black and Asian people living and working in the UK were attracted by campaigns to curb immigration.

3 Background to British Emigration and Immigration at the End of the War

Before these developments, growth and changes in the British population had previously been discussed by governments in terms of population pressures in growing urban areas especially from the feared 'underclass', and problems of poor physical health and mental unfitness. Since the late nineteenth century these issues had led to consideration of policies ranging from social assistance to eugenics.[6]

The absence of formal immigration controls in the nineteenth century, anachronistically described as 'free movement' by some modern writers, was simply part of the free trade policy of the dominant world economy. As soon as economic conditions changed, policy changed very quickly. The 1880s Great Depression led eventually to such alarm about impoverished Jewish people arriving in Britain that the Aliens Act 1905, representing a radical change in policy towards foreigners, was quickly introduced. On the outbreak of the First World War the Aliens Restriction Act 1914 (passed in one day) gave unlimited control over aliens' entry and presence in the UK. The Aliens Restrictions (Amendment) Act 1919, which had to be renewed every year, somewhat relaxed the wartime internal controls, and for the first time limited the prerogative power to deport to those cases in which the Secretary of State 'deems it to be conducive to the public good'.[7] Those controls remained in force until 1971.

The prevalence of racial thinking and xenophobia, and the weakness of the commitment to assisting refugees, were demonstrated by successive governments' attitudes to the entry of Jews fleeing from the Nazis.[8] Racial thinking combined with unemployment after both world wars had led to poor treatment of the small groups of black and Asian people living in the UK. Many were deliberately given papers describing them as 'aliens' despite their being British subjects.[9] Men from the West Indies and other colonies arriving during the Second World War to work in industry and serve in the RAF faced racial discrimination and abuse. Anti-colonial campaigners criticised Labour's failure to confront these issues. Gopal (2019) recount how, between the wars, a few MPs from the Independent Labour Party, including Fenner Brockway but in particular Shapurji Sakatvala, Indian-born MP for Battersea, campaigned relentlessly inside and outside parliament for colonial liberation, along with major international black intellectuals including CLR James and George Padmore, with significant audiences of black and white political and trade union activists.[10] But these campaigners made little headway on issues of racism in Britain.

4 Broken Promises?—From '*Civis Britannicus sum*'[11] to Comprehensive Immigration Control

As the *Empire Windrush* sailed across the Atlantic, the British Nationality Bill 1948 was going through Parliament. This Bill aimed to ensure that, as the newly-independent Dominions and Commonwealth countries developed their own citizenship laws, the status of British subjects would remain coherent throughout the Empire and Commonwealth. The parliamentary discussion comes from a bygone age.[12]

Section 4 of the Act provided that *every person born within the United Kingdom and Colonies after the commencement of this Act shall be a citizen of the United Kingdom and Colonies by birth.* However, the rights conveyed in these magnificent and inclusive propositions were barely discussed during the passage of the Act. They formed no part of any demands of any of the subject peoples. In 1946 the first Pan-African conference was held in Manchester, and Indian independence and Partition took place the following year. Their battle-cry was '*We won't beg for what we deserve, but demand what is ours*'—independence.[13]

The parliamentary debates on the British Nationality Act 1948 notably failed to consider the questions of *membership* of a nation-state and *substantive entitlement* to the civil, political and social rights attached to membership (Marshall [1950]).[14] These issues are at the crux of what happened in Britain. In 1958 a Home Office Minister of State noted that '*we have always allowed any of the people in what was the Empire and is now the Commonwealth to come to this country … as they please. That was not due to a deliberate act of policy … It is simply a fact which we have taken for granted from the earliest days in which our forebears ventured forth across the seas*'.[15]

Crucial also was the divergence between formal entitlement and mutual social acceptance.[16] '*We are seafaring men that have served this Country faithfully… either in the services of his Britannic Majesty or in the Merchantile Marine. The places of our birth are surely British possessions… and here in Great Britain we are badly treated by British People. Every morning we go down to shipping offices to find ourselves work … and are bluntly refused on account of our colour…*'.[17]

4.1 The Arrival of Commonwealth and Colonial Citizens: Racial Unrest and Political Responses

Though the passengers on the Empire Windrush were not the first citizens of the colonies to arrive in the UK, 'Windrush' is the name now given to the unplanned arrival in Britain of British subjects and Citizens of the UK and Colonies (CUKCs) who were 'freely landed'—not subject to any control on entry. They could work, settle and bring their families.

This immigration rose from 3,000 in 1953 to 46,800 in 1956 and thence to 136,400 in 1961, principally from the West Indies, India and Pakistan.[18] Many were recruited by new public bodies such as the National Health Service: others made their own way. No resettlement resources were provided. Widespread racial prejudice led to concentrations of newly-arrived people in already poor areas. Overcrowding, and noise from people excluded from pubs and working-men's clubs and so obliged to do their socialising on the street, caused tensions with the existing populations.

Public pressure for controls started to grow. However, for over ten years none of the political parties publicly addressed these issues. While commitments were repeatedly made to ending race-based political and economic structures *in the colonies*, the increase in racial discrimination and even violence against black and Asian people in the UK was not discussed. Both Conservatives and Labour were disconcerted by the impact of the new arrivals.[19] Secret official discussions on controlling Commonwealth immigration foundered on the great economic need for migrant labour and the determination not to control immigration from the old white Dominions. One report, clearly showing the persistence of racial thinking, said: '*There may be more general problems of social assimilation... On present evidence, a trend towards miscegenation can neither be forecast nor excluded*'.[20] Even the 1958 unrest in Notting Hill and Nottingham did not lead to any practical proposals to address problems such as the impact of rent decontrol or slum clearance programmes. Above all, neither the Conservatives nor Labour considered exploring the electorate's views, let alone that government had any political role to play in changing the terms of the discussion.

4.2 The Position of the Trade Unions and Left Organisations

In 1955 the Communist Party of Great Britain (CPGB), then a significant force in several trade unions and represented by two MPs, published a '*Charter of Rights for coloured workers in Britain*'.[21] The Charter called for racial discrimination to be made a criminal offence, no immigration controls, equal treatment in wages and conditions for all workers, and full encouragement for new arrivals to join their trade union and exercise their trade union and political rights. But that party lost influence among UK-based black workers, who increasingly resented being organised into 'national' sections corresponding to 'their own country' while their immediate experiences in Britain were ignored.[22]

The 1958 Notting Hill and Nottingham riots led to a similarly narrow response from the Trades Union Congress (TUC):

> …the most serious social problems facing immigrants to Britain were those which had faced working people for many years and caused hardship to substantial sections of the British public as a whole … immigrants could best serve their own interests by taking part on an equal footing with other members of the trade union movement…[23]

This response did not formally confront racist and prejudiced attitudes among the white workforce—nor did it challenge the intellectual bases of racial thinking.

On behalf of the extraparliamentary Left, David Widgery (1976) apologises that his book *'reflects the pre-1968 Left's complete lack of interest in the particular situations of women and immigrants'*.[24] He sums up the period by noting that *'immigration from the West Indies reached a peak in 1958–1960 and for Asians in 1963–1964, almost precisely in time with the jobs available'*. He continued succinctly: '*the appetite for labour was keen enough to bring women workers and immigrants into the workforce from their sinks and villages*'.[25]

As for Labour, the debate on the Commonwealth Immigrants Act 1962 showed that some in the Labour hierarchy had been considering restrictions for some time.

4.3 The Commonwealth Immigrants Act 1962: Turning Commonwealth Citizens into Labour Migrants

The Conservatives won the 1959 general election, and very soon proposed a Bill to restrict entry of Commonwealth citizens. The Bill proposed restrictions on entry both of citizens of independent Commonwealth countries ['Commonwealth citizens'] and certain CUKCs. For *Commonwealth citizens* the restrictions operated through the grant of work vouchers. Skilled workers and those with job offers, expected to be from the white Dominions, were prioritised, while few vouchers were offered for unskilled work. The Bill also introduced measures allowing for Commonwealth citizens to be deported. For CUKCs, the control mechanism was the place of issue of a person's passport—if London (generally, people who were born in the UK) they faced no restrictions, but if issued by a colonial authority in their own colony the holder had to obtain a voucher. This distinction became important in the 'Kenyan Asians' crisis of 1968.

Thus, instead of directly confronting the consequences of drawing British citizenship to include all the subjects of Empire, the UK Parliament decided that some people with formal membership rights of that polity should be denied substantive rights only recently confirmed in the 1948 Act. The conditions were explicitly drawn to exclude black and Asian people not already present on the territory. Home Secretary R A Butler referred to the '*cherished tradition of the Mother Country*' that '*throughout the continuous evolution of the Commonwealth, citizens of Member States have always been free to come here ...[but]... 'a sizeable part of the entire population of the earth is at present legally entitled to come and stay ... Most people, I think, would agree that eventually an influx on the present scale would have to be controlled*'.[26]

Patrick Gordon Walker noted the hypocrisy of demanding equal rights in the black-majority colonies while passing discriminatory legislation in the UK. He recommended instead that government should disperse the immigrant populations, take steps to prevent overcrowding of property, take active measure to '*combat the colour bar*' and prevent people '*stirring up race hatred*'.[27] Sir Hugh Gaitskell, closing for the Opposition, concluded that '*the introduction of this Bill as a method of dealing with the problems of racial friction arising from 400,000 or even 500,000 coloured immigrants in this country is an appalling confession of failure by the Government...*' Opposed by most senior Labour politicians, the Act came into force on 1 July 1962.

In 1966 academic Beryl Radin commented: '*The introduction of measures to curtail immigration in the Commonwealth Immigrants Bill in 1961 was criticised as 'though not a racial measure in form...its operation is bound to weigh against Commonwealth citizens who are coloured*'.[28] Whether that legislation was racial in form, content or intention has since been extensively discussed.[29] In March 2020, in the official *Windrush Lessons Learned Review*, the author notes that '*the root causes [of the Windrush debacle] ... can be traced back to the legislation of the 1960's, 70's and 80's, some of which, as accepted at the time, had racial motivations*'.[30]

Labour's 1964 election manifesto accepted the need for immigration control. The Conservative manifesto said nothing whatever about immigration, but immigration and race were major issues during the campaign. The Conservative candidate for Smethwick, Peter Griffiths, campaigned against the sitting MP Patrick Gordon Walker, with frankly racist slogans.[31] Griffiths won the election. After the election Labour prime minister Harold Wilson referred to him as a 'parliamentary leper'.[32] At the same time Labour took further steps to limit immigration.

4.4 The Labour White Paper 1965—The Turn to Control

Labour's 1965 White Paper *Immigration from the Commonwealth*[33] proposed cutting Commonwealth work vouchers, plus limiting lengths of stay and easier deportation procedures, while proposing separate legislation to outlaw racial discrimination. The parliamentary debates on the White Paper are notable for speeches on both sides congratulating themselves and each other for taking race and immigration 'out of politics'. Following the 1966 general election, the academic journal *Race* noted the relief of Labour campaigners: '*they've stopped talking about it in the clubs*'.[34] Widgery[35] says that under Wilson, [Labour] '*was able to proceed along a programme at least as right-wing as Gaitskell's but untroubled by the traditional Left's objections. The party's quite explicit retreat from its internationalist neo-principles on immigration policy went unmarked*'.

Labour's semi-formal immigration policy was effectively enacted by the later Conservative government in the Immigration Act 1971. Labour legal academic Cedric Thornberry criticised the 1965 White Paper as removing Commonwealth citizens' essential legal rights, reducing them to the status of (undesirable) aliens.[36] However his 1964 Fabian pamphlet *The stranger at the gate*[37] had proposed a very similar structure of control. And the 1971 Act, in curtailing 'primary immigration', did precisely reduce the position of both Commonwealth citizens and aliens to 'undesirables', albeit with published criteria for entry and a right of appeal. Thornberry makes no critique of any reasons for imposing immigration control, nor provides any economic or political analysis of the underlying motivations for migration, or of the causes of racism and discrimination in the host country. But he concludes: '*Noone suggests that the pattern of wholly unrestricted entry and unqualified asylum of before 1905 should be resurrected*'.[38]

4.5 The Commonwealth Immigrants Act 1968—Keeping Citizens Out

This Act, passed in three days, restricted the future right of entry of CUKCs to those born in the UK or who had a least one parent or grandparent born there, setting the framework not just of future immigration policy but the future structure of British nationality law.[39] Following independence in Kenya (1963) and Uganda (1962) the new governments adopted 'Africanisation' policies, curtailing economic and other rights of the descendants of indentured and other workers from India who had chosen to keep their CUKC status. In 1968, Kenya's 'Kenyanisation' policies had a catastrophic impact on them. Many fled to the UK. Because their CUKC passports had been issued in London after independence, they gained entry.

On 27 February 1968 Home Secretary James Callaghan stated[40]: '*There are at least 1 million persons living in various parts of the Commonwealth overseas who are ... potentially able to come to these islands free of control... It would be irresponsible not to legislate on ... the prospect of an invasion of a size which I have indicated, even though it is not likely*'. Entry was to be controlled by issuing vouchers, at a rate of 1500 per year. The applicants were expected to '*form an orderly queue*', with no discussion of how they were to survive meanwhile. Once here, it is '*essential that ... they should be treated in every way as equal before the law...*'. He promised further race relations legislation.

Quintin Hogg, Conservative shadow Home Secretary, replied: '*I view the idea of devaluing a British passport with the utmost abhorrence*'. The Bill was described as '*white man's treachery*', while others discussed the tension between ensuring equal rights and a reasonable standard of living for those already in the UK and allowing entry to all those to be affected by the Bill. '*I have yet to see a coloured man as a shop steward, let alone a foreman ... a house near to where I live was up for sale, and the degree of apprehension in the neighbourhood had to be seen to be believed. The working-class people ... see immigrants... as increased pressure on housing, schools and the health service, and additions to the unemployment figure of 600,000*'.[41] Other MPs complained about the lack of support for local authorities experiencing pressure on housing, welfare and education. The debate was closed by Home Office Minister David Ennals[42]: '*The debate has not been on party divisions: thank heavens that it has not... the Bill is one that no one in this House would willingly have wanted to introduce. However the Bill is necessary...*' The Act came into force 3 days later.

The hardships endured by the CUKCs stuck in Kenya and elsewhere following that Act are well-documented.[43] In 1973 the European Commission on Human Rights published its report on the cases cited as *East African Asians v UK*.[44] It concluded that the 1968 Act discriminated on grounds of colour or race, amounting to degrading treatment in the sense of art 3 ECHR. But the Commission ducked the fact that there had been a clear undertaking made to those CUKCs. That had been discussed in Parliament during the passage of the 1968 Bill, and Duncan Sandys, then Colonial Secretary, was strongly criticised for denying it.[45]

A short Immigration Appeals Act 1969 introduced a system of adjudicators and an Immigration Appeal Tribunal for those facing a decision to deport, believed to be politically essential before rendering Commonwealth citizens liable for deportation. This Act also implemented a proposal from 1965 Labour White Paper, requiring spouses and dependants to obtain prior entry clearance before travelling to the UK. This caused enormous hardship, as queues were allowed to build up.

5 The Foundation of Modern UK Immigration Control—The Immigration Act 1971

Labour lost the general election held in 1970. The Conservatives had promised[46] '*a single system of control of all immigration from overseas*' and an end to permanent settlement for workers. An existing Commonwealth resident would be allowed to bring *'his wife and young children'* into the country.

The Immigration Act 1971, repealing all previous immigration legislation, provided a concise description of what immigration controls should contain: controls on entry, conditions and restrictions under which people could remain, powers to deport and remove, and the basic criminal offences of entering or remaining without leave, assisting others to enter or remain without leave, and using false documents, deception, etc., to enter or remain without leave. The Act required the Secretary of State to bring in Immigration Rules setting out requirements for different categories of migrant, at least including visitors, students, workers and family members.[47] This structure, now vastly complicated by further complex legislation and scores of changes to the Immigration Rules, still today provides the architecture of UK immigration control.

The Act was also used to deal with the aftermath of the *'spectacularly false'* assumption made in 1948 that only a *'post-independence residual'* of non-British-born CUKCs would retain a right to enter the UK.[48] Contrary to British expectations, several African countries had been unwilling to accord citizenship to minority populations.[49] The Act introduced the concept of 'patrial', an invented word defined as those with a parent[50] born in the UK, was intended to distinguish between those from the white Commonwealth and the rest. The provisions were decried as a racist and cowardly stopgap introduced to avoid white Commonwealth opposition.

Labour opposed the Bill, identifying several objectionable legal and political features. The Bill breached the undertaking to preserve the statutory rights of Commonwealth citizens to bring in their family members. On Home Secretary Reginald Maudling's defence that those rights were to be preserved in the Immigration Rules, Callaghan and others presciently highlighted how weak a protection that was likely to be. The Bill was criticised for dealing with immigration control rather than the underlying problems created by the British Nationality Act 1948's very wide definition of British citizenship. Some British subjects would be able to vote, though present on time-limited visas, obliged to report to the police and liable to deportation, while others such as 'Anglo-Indians' would be able to enter and remain but not allowed to vote—a bizarre picture of the rights and duties normally considered to attach to citizenship.

Callaghan and others noted that the real problems ostensibly to be addressed by the Bill lay in people's social conditions. Not enough was being done on 'urban renewal' or to help 'disaffected black youth'. The result of the Bill would be racial. Requirements for Commonwealth citizens to register with the police only made sense if those breaching their conditions were to be followed up, which would lead to social conflict, since 'the coloured community' would need to be investigated. Peter Shore, a Labour MP opposed to Britain's joining the Common Market, highlighted the fact that Commonwealth and colonial citizens would unacceptably have fewer rights than nationals of Common Market countries—a criticism which 40 years later contributed to the demand for Brexit.

6 1971–79—The Consequences of Continued Anti-Immigration Pressure

The passing of that Act did not reduce demands for further immigration controls. Not just Enoch Powell (best known now for his 'rivers of blood' speech of April 1968, but by then estranged from the Conservative Party leadership over joining the European Economic Community), but also Conservatives belonging to the Monday Club[51] continued to campaign for *'Halt Immigration Now!'*; including repatriation programmes for black and Asian migrants and the repeal of the Race Relations Acts. A far-right organisation, the National Front (NF), had been founded in 1967. They espoused views based on biological racism, arguing that only white people should be citizens of the UK, and all others deported. Their support grew precisely during the period of the 'Kenyan Asians' debacle, and was briefly boosted again during the 'Ugandan Asians' rescue, described below. They briefly obtained support especially in East London, attracting votes in local council elections. In the early 1970s the NF were attracting Tory voters. They tried to draw the influential

Tories in the Monday Club towards their demands. However, they were not successful, and it could be argued that, despite the presence of some Monday Club members in the Cabinet, the Heath government met their first major immigration issue more honourably than did the previous Labour government.

6.1 The 1972 'Ugandan Asians' Debacle; Small Labour Reforms

Uganda had become independent in 1962. In 1971 Idi Amin, then Commander of the Army, launched a coup against President Milton Obote and took power. He launched an 'economic war' against Asians and Europeans, expropriating property and businesses and ordering those who were not Ugandan citizens to leave within three months. Many thousands were CUKCs and had no other citizenship. They could not freely enter the UK, as excluded under the 1968 Act unless had a parent born in the UK. However, the Conservative government noted what Callaghan had said during the debate on the 1968 Act: *'[we would have] a publicly acknowledged obligation to receive such individuals if they were expelled with no prospect of any alternative refuge'.* Over 23,000 'Ugandan Asians' were airlifted direct to the UK, and a further 17,000 were distributed between other Commonwealth countries. That quick decision was contrasted with the fate of the 'Kenyan Asians', reduced to queuing over years for an entry voucher.

Heath's Conservative government then faced sterner challenges in the 1973 oil crisis and world recession, which led the government to declare a 3-day working week with minimum lighting in premises open to the public and a 50mph maximum road speed limit. A strongly supported and effective coal miners' strike led Heath to call an election in February 1974 on the theme 'who governs Britain?' No party won an overall majority, and Harold Wilson became prime minister in a Labour minority government supported by the Liberals. After having negotiated a 'social contract' with the trade unions, Wilson was confident enough to call a second general election in October 1974, which Labour won with a bare majority. The economic situation remained fraught, with growing numbers of unemployed and a series of strikes culminating in the 1979 'winter of discontent', in which uncollected rubbish lay piled up in the streets.

Under Wilson in 1974, Roy Jenkins became Home Secretary. He has a reputation as a liberal, having previously provided formal government support in the 1960s to homosexual law reform and to the Abortion Act 1967. The 1974–1979 Labour government is widely viewed as a reforming government. However, though pressed to repeal the Immigration Act 1971, that was not even contemplated. Some small ameliorating administrative decisions were taken. First, vouchers for 'British Asians' marooned in Africa were increased from 3500 to 5000 per year.[52] Husbands and fiancés were permitted to join British and settled women. Grandparents and other distressed family members were permitted to come. A decision was made to speed up applications from family members in India, Pakistan and Bangladesh. However, when Callaghan took over from Wilson as Prime Minister In 1976, Minister of State Alex Lyon was dismissed for being too radical, and immigration policies tightened noticeably. This may well have been a response to the wide public opposition to letting in the 'Malawi Asians' and to the rise in support for the National Front, who had just won 19% of the votes in a Leicester ward in local elections.

6.2 May 1976—The 'Malawi Asians' in the 4-Star Hotel; 'Back Door' Immigration

May 1976 saw a further crisis when the Malawi government under Hastings Banda, another authoritarian post-independence ruler, declared some British passport holders originally from Goa in India to be prohibited immigrants. Around 250 of them arrived in the UK. Some were homeless on arrival. One family was accommodated by the receiving local authority (near Gatwick Airport), and, because of shortage of temporary accommodation, were placed in a hotel. This episode was reported thus: '*SCANDAL OF £600 A Week Immigrants In A Luxury Hotel", screamed the Sun. "Asian Influx Will Swamp Us", claimed the Express. "Immigrants - How Britain Is Deceived", added the Mail'.*[53]

In the House of Commons on 17 May, Foreign Office minister Evan Luard located the origins of this crisis in the practices of the Empire. He said:

> ... we are now talking about a group whose forebears were taken to Africa from Asia at the will of the British Government. It was on these grounds that it was decided by a Conservative Administration that they should have the right to acquire British passports and the right to come here at the appropriate time...[54]

Jonathan Aitken MP[55] embarked on a critique of 'back door' immigration, implying that the real figures were being deliberately hidden from the public. On *illegal immigration* he contrasted the 188 arrests of 1975 to the '*over 300,000 sealed containers*' entering through Dover each year. On *dependants* he rejected the government's statement that the queue is 'very limited' at around 150,000, and 'finite', as applying only to those covered by the transitional provisions of the Immigration Act 1971: and on *students* he complained that many did not leave at the end of their studies.

He found support on both sides of the House. Bob Mellish, Labour MP for Bermondsey, said:

> We cannot go on like this ... People born and bred in their own constituencies have been on the housing waiting list for as long as six years ...People cannot come here just because they have a British passport—full stop.[56]

Enoch Powell, by then an Ulster Unionist MP, continued the discussion of *dependants* '*including second or third wives*', immigrant tax frauds and the admission of people who cannot speak English, moving seamlessly into a discussion of assaults on the police and where, '*in daylight, let alone after dark, ordinary citizens are unwilling and afraid to go abroad*' [col 53]. He concluded by comparing the situation in mainland British cities to Belfast, which at that time was under formal military occupation by the British army.

Joan Lestor, Labour, Eton and Slough, intervened to point out that campaigning against immigrants because they don't belong amounts to a 'self-fulfilling prophesy':

> [they] tell those youngsters that they do not belong and that they are not wanted; they thus alienate them from the very processes of integration. We want to see such youngsters accepted in Britain and integrated.
>
> ...
>
> Every time they see a face which is identifiable by colour, they say "Is he here legally or illegally?" Many people deliberately try to create and foster this feeling. [76]

The debate shows the anti-immigrant lobby basing their campaign on two 'concerns'—that the people weren't being given proper information about immigration, and that the government was not listening to the concerns of ordinary people. Those 'concerns' remain to this day.

6.3 Gender Bias, Unacceptable Practices and the 'Culture of Disbelief'

The queues referred to in the above debate arose from the Immigration Appeals Act 1969 requirement that a wife and children under 16 had to obtain an entry certificate before travelling to the UK. This required applicants to attend the relevant High Commission in person for an interview and to show their birth and marriage documents. In Bangladesh in 1974 the average waiting time for such an interview was 38 months, in India in 1975–6 it was 16 months,[57] and in Pakistan in 1980 was 23.75 months.[58] Until 1974 women could not sponsor their husbands to enter. Labour changed this in 1974. However in 1977, asserting that men were using marriages of convenience to enter the UK and look for work, Labour introduced the **'primary purpose'** rule: '*that it is not the primary purpose of the intended marriage to obtain admission to the UK*.[59] Men granted entry clearance were given leave enter for only 12 months, with a requirement to reapply for indefinite leave. That application was subject to intrusive investigation.[60] Those rules, which were tightened further in 1980, were challenged in the European

Court of Human Rights (ECtHR) and in 1985 found to be discriminatory. In *Abdulaziz, Cabales and Balkandali*[61] the plenary court of the ECtHR judged that the old rules for the admission of husbands discriminated against women. The government promptly tightened the Immigration Rules so that wives and fiancées also had to meet the rules on maintenance and accommodation.

The official suspicion that marriages were 'sham' was not new. The British Nationality Act 1948 had removed the entitlement to British nationality for a foreign wife, on the basis that some were marrying for money.[62] Register offices had long since been drawn into investigations into marriages of British citizens with foreigners. A Joint Council for the Welfare of Immigrants (JCWI) enquiry later revealed that there had been formal liaison between the Home Office and the Registrar-General since 1925, and that Dr Shirley Summerskill, Labour Home Office minister in the 1974 government, had found the arrangement 'valuable' and had had no intention of terminating it.[63]

'Virginity testing' was only the grimmest example of the 'culture of disbelief'. Fiancée applicants were subject to compulsory internal examination to see if the hymen was intact.[64] Alex Lyon had ordered in 1975 that the practice be stopped, but that it had nevertheless continued for some years. The British government was condemned by the Indian representative at the UN Commission on Human Rights. Merlyn Rees stated that the tests were not 'normal practice', had only happened on 'rare occasions', and were technically legal, as medical examinations were permitted. But none of the grounds for medical examinations could justify a gynaecological examination. A Commission for Racial Equality (CRE) investigation[65] showed that despite lack of evidence, immigration officers believed many fiancées to be 'bogus', and that South Asian women were 'meek, submissive, and tradition-bound' and therefore would always be virgins before marriage. They did not seem to know that not every woman has a hymen.

Value-laden requirements in other immigration categories also led decision-makers to resort to the culture of disbelief. A visitor had to be 'genuine'. The visitor and student rules' requirement that the applicant must have an 'intention to return' was and still is effectively interpreted as 'incentive to return'. Applicants owning no property in their home country, having no dependant family, no permanent job or evidence of annual leave from their employment still find it hard to demonstrate 'intention to return'. Visitors would be subject to baggage searches for documents such as job offers or letters from family advising them to bring their educational qualifications. This treatment of visitors was reserved for black and Asian visitors. For young people from the white Commonwealth there was a special working holiday rule,[66] not extended to 'new Commonwealth' citizens until 1994.[67]

7 Internal Controls, Enforcement and Deportation

Once all new immigration was controlled by strict entry requirements, immigration could only be further attacked by internal controls, detention and deportation.[68]

The 1971 Act provided a framework of powers for internal control. It gave wide powers to immigration officers and 'any other person' to search people, seize and copy documents and detain an applicant. This opened the way to the outsourcing of those responsibilities which began under Margaret Thatcher. The obligation to register with the police was extended to all Commonwealth and colonial citizens not resident before the commencement of the Act. The police were given power to arrest without warrant anyone 'reasonably suspected' of being an illegal immigrant. The criminal sanctions in the Act provided for a 3-year time limit for prosecution rather than the 6 months normal for summary offences. Court interpretation of the criminal offences gradually led to the burden of proof being placed on the immigrant to prove he or she had leave to enter or remain.

Under its general powers to impose conditions of stay, the Act permitted the introduction of rules restricting immigrants to remain in particular jobs. The Act had increased control over Commonwealth and colonial citizens to those similar to aliens, providing for settlement only after 4 years, and then only upon application. Deportation could now be applied to any Commonwealth or colonial citizen who had not become settled on the commencement of the Act, including members of their families. Finally, the Act together with s7 Ministry of Social Security Act 1966 extended the powers of the Supplementary Benefits Commission to reduce or withhold benefits from a family where an applicant is refusing work (forcing them to take low-paid or strike-breaking jobs), and to pay the fare home of an immigrant family, forcing them to accept voluntary repatriation.

Instances of internal surveillance had already been instituted. In 1972 the police had set up their own Illegal Immigration Intelligence Unit, mainly to search for seamen deserters, absconders or people with deportation orders, on being notified of them by the Home Office. This unit carried out fishing raids on workplaces, looking for 'illegals', including people such as visitors or students who had leave to be in the UK but who were working illegally. It was reported that in Leicester around 200 women attending for ante-natal care had been refused treatment until they showed their passports—a practice which was stopped after a comment by Dr David Owen, the then Minister of Health, that '*no other section of the public is expected to [prove their eligibility]*.'[69,70] Even Home Secretary Merlin Rees described internal controls as 'repugnant' and 'objectionable in principle'.[71]

Nevertheless, enforcement powers were developed under Labour. In 1978 the Select Committee on Race Relations and Immigration stressed the need for '*substantially more resources to tackle all aspects of illegal immigration*', '*effective controls on unauthorised employment backed by sanctions to be introduced as a matter of urgency*' and measures to tighten up the issue of new national insurance numbers.[72] Increasing number of illegal entrants were removed without a formal deportation order.[73,74]

Breaching conditions of stay or entering without leave amounted to criminal offences which led to liability for deportation. The Act provided a right of appeal but no legal aid, and few received any legal advice at all. Section 23 Immigration Act 1971 provided for '*grants to any voluntary organisation which provides advice or assistance for, or other services for the welfare of, persons who have rights of appeal under this Part of this Act*'. The Home Office set up the UK Immigration Advisory Service (UKIAS),[75] which provided advice and representation on the day at the immigration tribunals. Between 1977–79 fewer than 12% of appeals were allowed, while the Home Office was winning over 50% of Immigration Appeal Tribunal appeals against adjudicators' decisions.[76]

After the Act came into force, deportations amounted to between 4–500 a year until 1977, when it jumped to over 1,000 a year, and continued to rise slowly until reaching around 2,000 a year in 1982.[77,78] The figures expose a move towards more restrictive immigration operation under Callaghan, and after the Tories gained power in 1979, the further intensification of all these operations.

7.1 'Mission Creep' and Retrospective Changes in Definition of 'Illegal Entrant', 'Settled', 'Deception'

A tightening of Home Office decision-making followed by restrictive interpretation of the law led to an expansion of the meaning of 'illegal entrant' and an increased reliance on a widened interpretation of 'deception'. An illegal entrant had been understood to refer to a person who entered the UK without presenting to an immigration officer. Through a series of court cases culminating in *Zamir*,[79] an illegal entrant was defined in addition to refer to anyone who had entered the UK, obtained leave to remain or even British nationality, through 'deception'. 'Deception' was defined in *Zamir* to include a failure to provide information to an immigration officer, even when not asked. Even the definition of 'settled' was eroded in this way. In the case of *Azam*,[80] in a dissenting judgment, Lord Salmon said:

> To give s33(2) an extended meaning would enable the executive, in the future, to seize and imprison a Commonwealth citizen long resident in the country and leading a blameless life, because of a summary offence ... for which he may long ago have been tried, convicted and punished. It seems incongruous to describe such a man as being here in breach of the immigration laws...

That retrospective effect is now contained in part 5 Nationality, Immigration and Asylum Act 2002 s117C (1): *The deportation of foreign criminals is in the public interest*. That provision, passed as s19 Immigration Act 2014, was part of almost a decade of legal attacks on foreign criminals, discussed in Chapter 6.

More formal examples of mission creep concerned the treatment of spouse applicants, discussed above, and of visitors. Most Commonwealth and colonial citizens wishing to visit did not at that time require a visa, but increasingly people would be stopped at the port or airport and denied entry as not meeting the requirements of the Immigration Rules. Conventionally, an MP could intervene on behalf of a constituent, or a relative or friend of a constituent (as in relation to an administrative act of any other government department) and ask the Minister's office to look into the matter. An MP could request a 'stop' on an enforced return, removal or deportation and that the applicant be granted 'temporary admission' into the UK while their case was investigated. In 1988, MPs' ability to demand a 'stop' on a removal or deportation was significantly restricted to cases showing *exceptional and compelling circumstances.*[81]

7.2 The Emergence of Home Office Internal Policies

In Ian Macdonald's first immigration law textbook[82] he notes that so much immigration decision-making *'depends on the exercise of someone's discretion, either at an airport or inside the Home Office itself'... [that] even those dealing daily with immigration cases are unable fully to fathom what these practices are'*. In the first edition of his standard textbook he refers to 'secret' policies, and to less secret policies which were openly referred to but which were not part of the Immigration Rules; to adjudicators' recommendations in appeals; and to the discretion exercised when there was no rule covering the circumstances.[83] He discusses to what extent these policies, all of which operated under the inherent discretion of the Home Secretary, were reviewable by any court. While a decision based on the Rules was open to challenge on *Wednesbury*[84] grounds, where a decision relied on Home Office policy the court declined to interfere with the Secretary of State's discretion, except to say that representations should be considered *honestly and fairly.*[85]

Gradually, such policies became discernible. Evidence of exercise of discretion would appear in Home Office letters to applicants or their representatives, or in letters written by a Home Office minister to an applicant's Member of Parliament. As legal representation in immigration cases developed through the 70s and 80s, these examples of discretion were shared among immigration lawyers, submitted in other applications, in appeals and, increasingly, in applications to the High Court for judicial review. Courts began ordering the Home Office to produce evidence of internal policies.

Under Labour, Home Office internal policies were formally published and could be relied upon in statutory appeals and judicial reviews. But during the 1970s and 1980s, with scarce legal advice and little formal litigation, it was a matter of luck for an applicant to find out if there was a policy applying to his or her situation.

8 Control by Impoverishment and Poor Administration

The Conservatives under Thatcher won the 1979 general election. Cuts were proposed to public services and a programme of privatisation was planned. In relation to immigration, a 1979 White Paper proposed prohibiting entry of spouses where the couples have not met, further limitations on parents, grandparents and children over 18 wishing to join their families in the UK, and a ban on visitors and students changing the basis of their stay while inside the UK, where such a change might lead to permanent settlement in future. The drive to halt 'abuse' also lay behind the decision to enable the refusal of anyone who has previously overstayed or used 'deception' to obtain entry—a clear case of legislation with retrospective effect.

The attack on 'abuse' included restrictions on access to public funds. Those sponsoring relatives would henceforth be expected to provide an undertaking that they would accommodate and maintain those relatives. These moves to formal retrospective and after-entry control had emerged from a previous development in Tory anti-immigrant rhetoric discussed next—the charge that immigrants were 'liars', 'scroungers' and 'gatecrashers', however long they had lived here.

8.1 Curtailment of Immigrants' Rights to Benefits and Services

The 1979 Conservative manifesto did not include any proposals to curtail migrants' access to welfare benefits or public services. However, in a World in Action interview in 1978, Thatcher had said[86]:

> ... if we went on as we are then by the end of the century there would be four million people of the new Commonwealth or Pakistan here... people are really rather afraid that this country might be rather swamped by people with a different culture ...

The first Statement of Changes in the Immigration Rules, proposed in 1979,[87] provided that those entering the UK under the immigration rules (as spouses, workers, students) would be granted leave to remain on a condition of no recourse to public funds.[88] 'Persons from abroad'[89] were also excluded from regular entitlement to benefits, though applications could be made for 'urgent cases' payments, at 90% of income support, for example for students facing a temporary lack of funds from abroad.[90] Very quickly, those internal controls began to affect a far wider group than ostensibly intended—a process entirely familiar to us since the 2013 formal declaration of the hostile environment. People who did not understand their immigration status were denied benefits from not knowing what they had to prove; the Department of Health and Social Security (DHSS) did not sufficiently understand immigration law to administer the system accurately; it made decisions which amounted to changing the law, causing people to lose benefits until a binding judgment was eventually made; people were denied benefits because of long delays in Home Office decision-making, or in returning the person's passport.[91] Close links developed between the Home Office and the DHSS, referring cases to each other so that benefits could be stopped and alleged illegal entrants could be picked up. Advice agencies and community groups reported that requesting passports was widespread—and very largely confined to black and Asian people. In response to complaints the DHSS referred to the regulation which requires a claimant to *'furnish such certificates, documentation and evidence … as may be required by the Secretary of State'*. Sponsors, having to show that they could support their dependants, faced enquiries about their own finances. The DHSS manual required staff to ask all new claimants who had entered the UK since 23 May 1980 to show whether they had been sponsored. If so, the information was passed to the Liable Relative Section of the DHSS, who would then check whether that sponsor can maintain them. *'Sponsorship … creates a class of people who are lawfully in the country, and settled here, but who are treated differently from the rest of the settled population'.*[92]

On 3 October 1979 the DHSS issued a circular to inner London hospitals entitled *Gatecrashers*,[93] instructing hospitals to check people's entitlement to be in the UK before treating them. Powers to charge for access to health services for 'overseas visitors', defined as those not 'ordinarily resident', had been introduced through the NHS (Amendment) Act 1949, but were not enacted until 1982.[94,95] Local authorities and education authorities also began requesting passports for housing applications and school admissions. Several local authorities refused housing to applicants on the grounds that they could return home.

8.2 The Year 1988 and Onwards—Further Restrictions and Bad-Faith Measures

The Immigration Act 1988, debated in November 1987, contains some provisions which caused great hardship. The Act repealed s1(5) Immigration Act 1971, which preserved the right of Commonwealth citizens settled before the Act to have their families join them. Persons claiming the right of abode in the UK thereafter had to produce documents proving this before entry. The Act overturned a court judgment finding that overstaying was not a continuing offence, which had limited the period during which the overstayer could be prosecuted. Finally, the Act provided for fees for applications for indefinite leave to remain.

A new consolidated set of Immigration Rules were introduced: HC 388.[96,97] These Rules were debated in the House of Commons on 20

June 1989. The main changes were the prohibition on visitors from applying from inside the UK to remain as students, stated in the House to be *'directed against bogus students from West Africa'*, and the extension of the visa regime to Turkey, from where many Kurdish refugees were fleeing, precisely to prevent those people from entering the UK.

The parliamentary debate revealed two instances of deterioration in legal procedures. Firstly, *administrative custody* was being used as a form of detention without trial for migrants. Students accused of breaching the conditions of their stay would face *'a deportation order and custody, or an unwinnable appeal'* following the new Rules' restrictions on appeal rights. Secondly, examples were given of *entrapment*. Mr. Harry Cohen (Leyton):

> ...The immigration officer may ask, "Would you like to study?" The immigrant may reply, "Yes, I would. I would not mind if I had the chance." That person is trapped, whether he intended to study or not.

The **1993 Asylum and Immigration Appeals Bill** proposed abolishing the right of appeal for those refused a visitor's visa, and for those entering as students unless they had prior entry clearance. As a consolation, the Bill provided for the setting up of an independent monitor on entry clearance decision-making, who would present an annual report to parliament.

Since the abolition of visitor appeals mainly affected the family members of British and settled people, it had to be approached in a different way. Opening the debate,[98] Home Secretary Kenneth Clarke said:

> With a backlog of 23,000 undecided cases in the immigration appeal system—well over a year's work—it cannot be sensible to continue to treat all immigration decisions as if the issues that they raise are of the same importance. [32]

Shadow Home Secretary Tony Blair replied:

> [43] … It is a novel, bizarre and misguided principle of the legal system that if the exercise of legal rights is causing administrative inconvenience, the solution is to remove the right.

Roy Hattersley, by then on the back benches, notes the responsibility of Empire:

> [50] …Now that the queue for applications to visit is growing unacceptably long, it is not tolerable for the Government to abandon the appeal system because only black and Asian British are affected.
>
> [51] …
>
> Our immigration relationship is different from that of the rest of Europe as we have an imperial inheritance, the responsibility of empire and a duty to Commonwealth citizens who came to this country 30 or 40 years ago. at the invitation of the Government, and who are denied the right for their families to visit them.

In what was already a famous critique of entry clearance officers' decision-making:

> Mr. Piara S. Khabra (Ealing, Southall)
>
> The entry clearance officers over there, who I have been told are bloody minded, already ask totally unreasonable questions. They ask applicants how many cows they have in the village or how many cows the family has.[99] … In effect, the entry clearance officers have already decided that they will reject such applications.

Keith Vaz, Chair of the House of Commons Home Affairs Committee, referred to the bureaucratic 'shambles' of the Home Office:

> Our immigration service has been in a shambles and a crisis for the past 13 years. Even the Select Committee on Home Affairs, of which I was a member until recently, produced an all-party report which described the shambles at Lunar House[100] when 250,000 unopened letters were discovered some years ago.

8.3 The Immigration 'Shambles' and the Citizen's Charter

Those short interventions by Piara Khabra MP and Keith Vaz MP highlight the failure and deterioration of the immigration control system already evident by the early 1990s. This is exposed in the period under discussion through reports emerging as part of a new public service management style to be applied to all public sector departments. An important aspect of the Thatcher-Major years was the ideological and organisational transformation of the public sector from the provider of public goods and services to the population at large to a set of market-orientated organisations dealing with the public as *consumers*. Business rhetoric and methodology began to be applied to services and functions directly carried out by the state.

In 1991 Prime Minister John Major introduced the Citizen's Charter,[101] whose principles now pervade most areas of public administration. These include published standards of service, treating users of public services as paying consumers, and providing better information and greater responsiveness when things go wrong. Major's principles were barely applied to the Home Office's immigration and nationality work, though targets and performance measures were introduced. Chapter 6 discusses how the choice of targets led to unintended consequences,[102] such as where prescribing fixed response of case conclusion times led to the archiving and neglect of old or complex cases. A subtle and complex aim such as improving the quality of decision-making can never be captured or driven by easily-measured performance indicators. The choice of targets is always likely to reflect anterior political stances and choices. For example, a view that most asylum-seekers are just illegal migrants will lead to targets for removals—which eventually caused the downfall of a Home Secretary as part of the 2018 Windrush debacle.

From January 1991 the Home Office, along with all other Government departments, was required to produce an annual departmental report.[103] That first Report discusses the importance of performance targets and indicators, and states: '*The most vivid illustration of failings in the IND [Immigration and Nationality Division] lies in large backlogs and waiting times...*'.[104]

On 7 December 1992 the House of Lords debated[105] the report *A Charter for all? CAB evidence on immigration and nationality.*[106] Applications (from inside and outside the UK and including nationality applications) were taking an average of 27 months. The proposer, Lord McIntosh of Haringey, referred to a Home Affairs Committee report from 1990 telling of 250,000 unopened letters, including some containing marriage certificates and passports. He continued:

> ... we are profoundly dissatisfied with the resources and policy directives which have been given to the Immigration and Nationality Directorate in the past but because we envisage that the asylum Bill will make the situation even worse.
> § Nor is it simply a matter of delays and the lack of consultation, the lack of compensation and the lack of an effective complaints procedure. The suspicion must be that there is an element of racial discrimination in the way in which the department works. [my emphasis]

He referred to figures showing that an Asian applicant for entry clearance was more than 8 times likely to be refused, and an applicant from Jamaica was 30 times more likely to be refused, than someone from the USA. The '250,000 unanswered letters' arose from a backlog of nationality applications from before 1987, the closing date for Commonwealth Citizens to register as British under the transitional provisions of the British Nationality Act 1981. It is interesting now to read the 2020 *Windrush Lessons Learned Review*'s note that the Home Office had resisted carrying out a campaign on this, so as not to '*stimulate a flood of enquiries*'.[107]

Lord Meston highlighted how *unusual* the situation was, in UK public administration. He considered whether the delays and backlogs were part of government policy:

> The delays are clearly excessive and beyond anything that would be expected or tolerated in any other bureaucratic exercise. Yet those delays have to be tolerated by applicants seeking to enter this country who, not surprisingly, have no bargaining strength whatsoever. As the report says —and it is not the first to say it—delay has come to be seen as a method of control. Paragraph 4.7 of the report describes how the very

existence of queues of applicants creates the impression of a clamour to enter this country which in turn reinforces the feeling that controls should be increasingly strict. [78] (my emphasis)

The Government spokesperson Earl Ferrers,[108] replying, took a defensive line, stating that the report *'did not...paint... an accurate or a fair picture'*. He outlined the proposed increases in staff, expressed a determination to improve, and maintained that the introduction of new legislation (the Asylum and Immigration Appeals Act 1993) would reduce backlogs and delays. However, Tony Blair's intervention in the Asylum and Immigration Appeals Bill debate, quoted above, shows that the principal methods of workload reduction already consisted of reducing applicants' avenues of redress.

9 Civil Unrest, Confrontation and Colonial-Style Cooption

9.1 Unrest and Confrontation

Underneath the general economic and social hardship of the 1970s and 1980s, shown by the major industrial battles and government crackdowns under both Labour and Tory governments, a separate set of struggles were taking place. Black and Asian workers, mainly unsupported by white workers and the trade union movement, often working on segregated shifts and sometimes in segregated workplaces, were beginning to organise for themselves, and it took a decade before mainstream working-class organisations and political groups paid much attention. During the same period, the economic problems facing people living in the inner cities continued to deteriorate, with poor housing, low educational expectations and lack of job opportunities disproportionately affecting black and Asian people, who were generally concentrated in the most deprived areas. Episodes of violent unrest took place which called for formal political responses. Reports were published about conditions in the inner cities including problems of racism and discrimination, and the impact on access to good jobs, levels of unemployment, average wages, access to local authority housing and school attainment. A Political and Economic Planning (PEP) report from 1976 noted the disadvantage experienced by every minority group in each of these fields.[109]

These issues, events, episodes and reports all show the clear shift of emphasis from the 1960's discussion of immigrants as new arrivals finding it hard to fit in, to a formal, official acceptance that Britain by then had a substantial black and Asian population who belonged here; whose children and even their children had been born here and who even the Conservatives officially regarded as having equal political and social rights.

Those reports however did not generally consider how the continuing rhetoric against 'liars, scroungers and gatecrashers' and concomitant increase in internal controls militated against access to those equal rights, never mind the 'quiet enjoyment'[110] of them. Nor was there much discussion of the prevalence of racial thinking, as racism was generally equated with *acts* of violence, abuse or discrimination, while what lay behind those acts was ascribed either to 'Nazis' such as the National Front, or to tabloid journalism. There was not much enquiry into why such ideas, or such journalism, struck such a deep chord among people.

During the 1970s and 1980s a series of strikes by Asian workers took place which show a limited change in working class, trade union and political attitudes to those workers. However following the eventual failure of the Grunwicks strike, there was criticism from the black and Asian communities, accusing the official trade union movement of *'steering the black workers away from community support'* and towards the unions, '*who finally betrayed them*'.[111]

Meanwhile, left organisations were concentrating on 'fighting fascism', in the form of the National Front. The Anti-Nazi League and Rock against Racism, the left's major campaigns 'against fascism' in the UK, claimed success, in that the National Front did poorly in the 1978 council elections and the 1979 general election.

Despite that political activity and the plethora of reports, the rising incidence of racial attacks received little official attention. Peter Fryer, in *Staying Power,* published in 1984, charts a number of racist attacks starting with Kelso Cochrane in Kensington in 1959, and a riot in Middlesbrough in August 1961 when thousands of whites 'chanting '*let's get a wog*' smashed black people's windows. He notes that '*between 1976 and 1981 thirty-one black people had been murdered by racists*', in different towns all over England, and '*for every black person murdered, scores of others were attacked, beaten, kicked unconscious, places of worship, shops, centre, homes attacked*'.[112]

Uprisings in Brixton, Toxteth and other places, which saw the full deployment of hit-squads by the police and the first mainland use of CS gas,[113] were among the violent events of the most confrontational period in British politics since the General Strike of 1926. April 1981 saw the deaths of Irish nationalist hunger strikers in jail in Northern Ireland, and in 1982, fervently supported by Labour leader Michael Foot, Thatcher embarked on the Falklands War.[114] At the time, the British economy was still in depression, with official unemployment at 3 million (implying a real level of around 4 million): about 10% of the labour force. The year 1980 saw the greatest-ever one-year decline in British output: manufacturing production fell by 13.5%, a greater fall than in the Great Depression of 1930–1931. Inflation had fallen from 20% pa but was still higher than before Thatcher came to office.[115] Despite this, after the Falklands war concluded, the polls registered support for the Tories at 50%. Thatcher used the Falklands victory to win the 1984 general election. '*Her "authoritarian populism" strikes a chord... Although [her] domestic policies have ensured a degree of social and economic fear amongst the working classes unequalled since 1945, she has also managed to address some of the aspirations and beliefs which the electorate hold*'.[116]

9.2 Imposition of Visa Requirements on Commonwealth Citizens

Thatcher's reference to the striking miners as the 'enemy within' is well-known.[117] 'Immigrants' were also treated as a potential 'enemy within'. After imposing visas on Commonwealth citizens for the first time in 1985, explicitly to keep out Tamil asylum-seekers, visa requirements were imposed in September 1986 on other 'new Commonwealth' countries. Hundreds of families arrived at Heathrow just before the date and had to sleep on the floor, detained in the airport until they could be processed.

Separately, a special investigation squad was set up to track down 'illegals' from those countries.

This discriminatory and expensive[118] bureaucratic procedure was introduced on the basis of a 'growing pressure' from people regarded as not eligible, from 0.21 to 0.25% of all visitors. Contemporary statistics on refusals showed that refusal of white Commonwealth citizens was far lower than those for citizens of 'new Commonwealth' countries. Visitors from the 'white' countries had hardly ever bothered to apply for entry clearance, while it would be '*highly unsafe*' for a would-be visitor from Bangladesh to set out without it.[119]

9.3 Government Responses to Racism and Unrest—Cooption of Communities

Labour MP Roy Hattersley had declared, '*without integration, limitation is inexcusable; without limitation, integration is impossible*'.[120] Labour's view was accepted by the Conservatives and developed into a twin-track strategy of strict immigration controls and heavy policing on the one hand, and 'integration' on the other. During the 1970s all the main political parties took account of an identifiable, growing, black electorate. By the late 1970s many Labour boroughs and local authorities had sizable black and Asian representation in their council chambers, and several black and Asian Labour candidates had been elected to parliament.

By s11 Local Government Act (LGA) 1966 Labour had provided funds to local authorities facing particular burdens from recently-arrived immigrants, to spend on such as additional language teachers, community workers and so on. After the riots of 1981, the Conservatives introduced further similar measures, speaking about the need to identify and cohere a group of black people who could help keep the lid on inner-city unrest. Sir George Young, minister responsible for race relations, said:

> We've got to back the good guys, the sensible, moderate, responsible leaders of ethnic groups. If they are seen to deliver, to get financial support from central government for urban projects, then that reinforces their

> standing and credibility in the community. If they don't deliver, people will turn to the militants.[121]

There are clear parallels with how the British used to govern colonial possessions—by identifying 'native leaders' to cohere, neutralise or ward off black dissent. There developed, and still exists, a vast race relations industry made broadly of two strands: formal equal opportunity policies, racial awareness training programmes and so on, and provision of grant aid to cultural and community centres, including a small amount of education and legal advice provision.

The provision of financial grants, made under s11 LGA 1966 and subsequent Urban Programme policies and Inner City Partnerships, comprehensively drew local community organisations and campaigning groups into formal relationships with local authorities and central government entities; obliged them to constitute themselves formally with management committees, charitable status and audited accounts; obliged them to produce regular reports about the impact of their activities, numbers of individuals benefiting and so on. Grant-funded organisations were encouraged or obliged to join with others under the umbrella of Community Relations Councils in formal and informal consultation with local authority and central government officials, generally a time-consuming and wearying process out of which very little changed.

A group of academics active in the Labour Party in the 80s have written 'more in sorrow than in anger' about both of these strands of race relations policy.[122] After discussing the different types of organisations involved in anti-racist activity (black and left-wing political organisations, community groups and more formal pressure groups) they describe how those groups experienced *marginalisation*, arguing that the funding for 'initiatives' rather than an in-depth examination of mainstream service provision was '*inconsistent, gestural and borne of panic*'.[123] Black and minority anti-racist groups and self-organisation in general became *institutionalised*[124] as many activists moved towards and into the Labour Party and became part of local and central government. Marc Wadsworth, a well-known black left activist, said: '*we do not have black MPs. We have Labour MPs who happen to be black*'.[125]

The introduction and development of equal opportunities policies included ethnic monitoring of workforces, housing provision and take-up of most public services and the policing of the information revealed by ethnic monitoring. Then, and certainly now, the development of ethnic monitoring and equal opportunities policies was regarded as progressive.[126] However this did little to challenge the basis on which mainstream services were to be allocated, and to whom, or to challenge the racial thinking engendered by equal opportunities policies, nor the racial thinking already becoming evident in the next round of the Thatcher government's attacks on immigrants' rights. In this, a new, more atomised, cohort of migrants—asylum-seekers—were to be stigmatised and demonised as cover for a general attack on welfare and working-class living standards.

Notes

1. Campbell, Persia Crawford. 1923 reprinted 1971. *Chinese coolie emigration to countries within the British empire* London: Frank Cass & Co 1971 [169] [172].
2. University of Minnesota Immigration Research Centre *Coolie trade in the nineteenth century* 16 June 2015 https://cla.umn.edu/ihrc/news-events/other/coolie-trade-19th-century accessed 23/6/19.
3. Hui, Ong Jin. 1995. *Chinese indentured labour: Coolies and colonies.* In *Cambridge survey of world migration* ed Robin Cohen, 51–56 Cambridge: Cambridge University Press.
4. Mitchell, B.R., and Dean, Phyllis. 1962. *Abstract of British historical statistics* Cambridge: Cambridge University Press [50].
5. Political and Economic Planning (PEP). 1948. *Population policy in Great Britain—A report by PEP.* London, PEP.
6. Stepan, Nancy1982. *Idea of race and science in Britain 1800–1960* Macmillan.
7. In *R v Inspector of Leman St Police Station, R v Secretary of State for Home Affairs, ex p Venicoff* [1920] 3 KB 72 the court decided that the word 'deems' did not entitle the applicant to any hearing.

8. London, Louise. 2001. *Whitehall and the Jews, 1933–1948: British immigration policy, jewish refugees and the holocaust* Cambridge: Cambridge University Press.
9. Fryer, Peter. 1984. *Staying power* London: Pluto Press.
10. Gopal, Priyamvada. 2019. *Insurgent empire* London: Verso.
11. *'I am a British citizen'.*
12. See for example *HC Deb 07 July 1948 vol 453 cc385-510 col 398.*
13. Gopal 2019 n10.
14. Marshall, TH 1950. *Citizenship and Social Class* Cambridge University Press.
15. HC Deb 05 December 1958 vol 596 cc1552-971 [552].
16. Brubaker, Rodgers. 2010 *Migration, membership and the modern nation state: internal and external dimensions of the politics of belonging.* Journal of Interdisciplinary History, 41 (1). pp. 61–78.
17. Fryer 1984 n9 [298].
18. *HC Deb 19 March 2003 vol 401 cc270-94WH, Andrew Turner (Isle of Wight).*
19. Hennessy, Peter. 2006. *Having it so good—Britain in the 50's* London: Penguin Allen Lane.
20. *Colonial Immigrants: Report of the Committee of Ministers* CP (56) 145 22/6/1956 National Archives CAB 129/81/45.
21. Smith, Evan. 2018. *British Communism and the Politics of Race.* Chicago: Brill Historical Materialism series, Haymarket [60 fn 173].
22. Ibid.
23. Radin, Beryl. 1966. *Coloured Workers and British Trade Unions.* Race vol 8, 1966, Institute of Race Relations.
24. Widgery, David. 1976. *The Left in Britain 1856–1968.* Harmondsworth. Penguin Books 1976, [15].
25. ibid [157].
26. HC Deb 16 November 1961 vol 649 cc687-819 c687.
27. Patrick Gordon Walker, Labour, Smethwick, at col 708, 712, 716. Gaitskell's speech is at col 797.
28. Radin 1966 n22.
29. Most recently in Patel, Ian Sanjay. 2020. *We're here because you were there: immigration and the end of Empire* London: Verso.

30. Williams, Wendy. 2020 *Windrush lessons learned review* HC 93. Laid before Parliament 20/3/20.
31. See for example Jeffries, Stuart. 2014. *Britain's most racist election: The story of Smethwick, 50 years on* https://www.theguardian.com/world/2014/oct/15/britains-most-racist-election-smethwick-50-years-on accessed 20/11/21.
32. Ibid.
33. *Immigration from the commonwealth* 1965 (draft available online at http://filestore.nationalarchives.gov.uk/pdfs/small/cab-129-122-c-109.pdf accessed 20/11/21.
34. Deakin et al. 1966. *Colour and the 1966 general election, Race* vol 8.
35. Widgery 1976 n23 [199].
36. Thornberry, Cedric. 1966. *Note on the legal position of commonwealth immigrants* Race, vol 7.
37. Thornberry, Cedric. 1964 *The stranger at the gate* Cedric Thornberry, Fabian research series 243.
38. Ibid [25].
39. A new, detailed background to the 'Kenyan Asians' and 'Ugandan Asians' crises is given in Patel, n28.
40. *HC Deb 27 February 1968 vol 759 cc1241-368, col 1246.*
41. Charles Pannell, Labour, Leeds West (voted in favour).
42. David Ennals, Labour, Dover.
43. Cable, Vincent. 1969. *Whither Kenyan migrants?* Young Fabian pamphlet 18 https://digital.library.lse.ac.uk/objects/lse:tel582mib accessed 20/11/21.
44. *East African Asians v UK* [1973] ECHR 2.
45. Hansen, Randall. 1999. *Kenyan Asians, British politics and the commonwealth immigrants act 1968* Historical Journal; Shepherd, Robert. 1998. *Open letter from Iain McLeod to Duncan Sandys 23 February 1968.* The Spectator 25/4/1998.
46. http://www.conservativemanifesto.com/1970/1970-conservative-manifesto.shtml accessed 20/11/21.
47. Immigration Act 1971 ss1(4), 3(2).
48. Hansen, Randall. 2000. *Citizenship and immigration in post-war Britain* Oxford: Oxford University Press.

49. Ibid.
50. Those with grandparents born in the UK were included in the 1973 immigration rules.
51. see https://truepublica.org.uk/contributor-news/meet-the-conservative-monday-club-racist/ accessed 20/11/20.
52. HC Deb 24 May 1976 vol 912 cc33-104 col 100.
53. Kimber, Charlie. *Scapegoating led to murder.* Socialist Worker 14/4/2000 https://socialistworker.co.uk/art/36122/Scapegoating+led+to+murder accessed 20/11/21.
54. HC Deb 17 May 1976 vol 911 cc964-74 at 968.
55. HC Deb 24 May 1976 vol 912 cc33-104.
56. ibid.
57. Hansen 2000 n47.
58. ibid [229].
59. Immigration Rules HC 251 para 47(a).
60. Young Justice. 1993. *The primary purpose rule: A rule with no purpose* London: Justice.
61. *Abdulaziz, Cabales and Balkandali. 9214/80, 9473/81, 9474/80.*
62. *HC Deb 07 July 1948 vol 453 cc385-510 Col 396.*
63. JCWI bulletin vol 1 no 6 Oct/Nov 1983, cited in Gordon *Policing Immigration* n68 below [no date given for Dr S letter].
64. Travis, Alan. *'Virginity tests for immigrants 'reflected dark age prejudices' of 1970's Britain* Guardian 8/5/2011 https://www.theguardian.com/uk/2011/may/08/virginity-tests-immigrants-prejudices-britain accessed 20/11/21.
65. Commission for Racial Equality *Immigration control procedures: Report of a formal investigation* London, CRE 1985.
66. Restricted in the March 1980 Rules from five to two years.
67. *Statement of Changes in Immigration Rules*—HC395 May 1994.
68. Gordon, Paul. 1981. *Passport raids and checks* Runnymede Trust pamphlet, later reproduced as *Policing immigration: Britain's internal controls* 1985 Pluto Press; *Deportations and removals* 1984 Runnymede Trust.
69. Gordon, Paul. 1985. *Policing immigration* London: Pluto Press.

70. Cohen, Steve. 2001. *Immigration controls, the family and the welfare state: A handbook of law* London: Jessica Kingsley Publishers. The passport checks for health care were reinstituted in 1979.
71. Quoted in Gordon 1985 n68 p(i). See also Alex Lyon speaking in the Commons debate about illegal immigrants cited at n72 below.
72. Gordon 1985 n68 [(i)].
73. Parliamentary answers from 1972 stated that 13 people had been successfully prosecuted in the previous 12 months for facilitating illegal entry and 10 people had been treated as illegal entrants. https://api.parliament.uk/historic-hansard/written-answers/1972/may/11/immigrants-illegal-entry#S5CV0836P0_19720511_CWA_65 accessed 2/10/19.
74. Gordon 1985 n68 [21].
75. UKIAS was the predecessor of Immigration Advisory Service and the Refugee Legal Centre, latterly Refugee Migrant Justice.
76. Macdonald, Ian A.1983. *Immigration law and practice in the United Kingdom* London: Butterworths [4].
77. Tompson, Keith. 1988. *Under Siege,* Penguin Special, table 7, [170].
78. Shukra, Kalbir. 1995 *The changing pattern of black politics in Britain* PhD thesis, University of Kent.
79. *Zamir v SSHD* [1980] AC 930.
80. *Azam and others v SSHD* [1974] AC 18 (UKHL 11/6/1973.
81. See Home Office minister Timothy Renton's intervention at *HC Deb 10 November 1988 vol 140 cc518-44* col 521.
82. Macdonald, Ian. 1972. *The new immigration law* London: Butterworths.
83. Macdonald 1983 n74 [26].
84. *Associated Provincial Picture Houses Ltd. v Wednesbury Corporation* [1948] 1 KB 223 (the precedent for the standard public law review test: whether a decision is so unreasonable that no reasonable public official could have made it).
85. *Birdi v SSHD,* (1975) Times 11/2/75, cited in Macdonald n74, xxi.
86. https://www.margaretthatcher.org/document/103485 accessed 20/11/21.

87. Statement of Changes in the Immigration Rules HC 169 1/1/1983 [reprinted in Macdonald 1983 n74.
88. 'Public funds' were not defined in the Immigration Rules until HC 306, 24/3/1994.
89. 'Persons from abroad' were defined as those with 'limited leave to remain', overstayers, those subject to deportation orders and those deemed to be illegal entrants.
90. Patterson, Terry. 2002. *From safety net to exclusion: Ending social security in the UK for 'persons from abroad'*. In *From immigration controls to welfare controls* eds Steve Cohen, Beth Humphries and ed Mynott, Routledge [157].
91. Gordon, Paul and Newnham, Anne. 1985. *Passport to Benefits? Racism in social security.* London: CPAG and Runnymede Trust, ch 1.
92. ibid [35].
93. Quoted in Tompson 1988 n75, Cohen 2001 n68 and other books of the time, all of which report different examples of people being denied treatment to which they were entitled.
94. National Health Service (Charges to Overseas Visitors) (No. 2) Regulations 1982 SI 1982/863.
95. National Health Service (Charges to Overseas Visitors) Regulations 1982 no 795.
96. Hansard debate on statement of changes in the Immigration Rules following the Act https://api.parliament.uk/historic-hansard/commons/1988/jul/27/immigration#S6CV0138P0_19880727_HOC_236.
97. Statement of Changes in the Immigration Rules HC 388, 8/7/1989.
98. HC Deb 02 November 1992 vol 213 cc21-120.
99. Lal, Sushma, and Wilson, Amrit. 1986. *But my cows aren't going to England": A study in how families are divided* Manchester: Manchester Law Centre (out of print).
100. Lunar House, in Croydon, is the operational headquarters of what then was called the Immigration and Nationality Directorate of the Home Office.

101. Major, John. 1992 Speech to The Economist Conference *Streamlining the Public Sector* 27/1/1992.
102. Boswell, Christina. 2018. *Manufacturing political trust—Targets and performance management in Public Policy* Cambridge: Cambridge University Press.
103. Home Affairs Committee 6th report *form and content of the Home Office annual report* HC 464 session 1989–1990.
104. Ibid para 18.
105. *HL Deb 07 December 1992 vol 541 cc75-84.*
106. *A Charter for all? CAB evidence on immigration and nationality* 1992, National Association of Citizens Advice Bureaux.
107. *Windrush lessons learned review* n28 [12].
108. Shirley, Robert, 13th Earl Ferrers, Minister of State at the Home Office.
109. Smith, David J. 1976. *The facts of racial disadvantage—A national survey* PEP Vol XLII Broadsheet no 560.
110. By analogy with a tenant's common law right of 'quiet enjoyment' of their tenancy.
111. Smith, Evan 2018 n20 [169].
112. Fryer 1984 n8 [380], [396].
113. Barnett, Anthony. 1982. *Iron Britannia: Time to take the great out of Britain* London, Allison and Busby Ltd [17].
114. 2/4/82 to 14/6/82 https://www.opendemocracy.net/en/opendemocracyuk/falklands-syndrome-30-year-legacy-of-iron-britannia/.
115. Singh, Ajit. *Full employment capitalism and the Labour Party* Socialist Register 1981 [12], cited in Barnett n112.
116. Barnett 1982 n112 [80].
117. Thatcher, Margaret draft speech: *'from the dark cloud falls an acid rain that eats into liberty'* The Times https://www.thetimes.co.uk/article/conference-attack-on-the-miners-was-silenced-by-brighton-bomb-prrd32vf3kt accessed 21/11/21.
118. Since July 1985 fees for entry clearance had been introduced, by statutory instrument under the Consular Fees Act 1980 [SI 1986/1881)] (Cited in Macdonald, Ian A. 1987). *Immigration Law and Practice 2nd edition* London: Butterworths [33].
119. Macdonald 1983 n74 [149].

120. https://hatfulofhistory.wordpress.com/2015/03/16/integration-and-limitation-labour-and-immigration-1962-68/#_edn22 (now New Historical Express), accessed 21/11/21.
121. Tompson 1988 n75 [91].
122. Ben-Tovim, Gideon et al. 1986. *The local politics of race* London: Macmillan.
123. Ibid [117].
124. Shukra 1995 n76.
125. Interview with Shukra, cited in Shukra 1995 n76 [339].
126. See accounts from Tompson 1988 n75, Cohen 2001 n68 and Gordon and Newnham 1985 n90; also *Race, government and politics in Britain* ed Zig Layton-Henry and Paul B Rich London: Macmillan 1986; Spencer, Ian R.G. 1997. *British immigration policy since 1939—The making of multi-racial Britain* Abingdon: Routledge; Paul, Kathleen. 1997. *Whitewashing Britain—Race and citizenship in the postwar era* Ithaca and London: Cornell University Press.

3

The UK Immigration Control Responses to Asylum: Exclusion, Disbelief, Stigma and Neglect

1 Introduction

Facing increasing asylum arrivals from the mid-1980s, the UK determined to apply the UN Convention definition of 'refugee' strictly. Wider groups 'of concern' were stigmatised as 'economic migrants' or 'bogus asylum-seekers'. UK asylum law emerged through reactive measures, often amounting to 'relegislating'—a performative reformulation of measures already in place, to give the illusion of control. The 'culture of disbelief' was fully embraced in asylum claim processing. So also was the use of destitution as a deterrent, shown in the first attempt (1996) to deprive asylum-seekers of accommodation and support based on the timing of their claim. Labour further limited asylum-seekers' access to legal processes and social support; and presided over the second attempt (2003–2005) to deprive asylum-seekers of support based on the timing of their claim. Again, mass litigation was effective, but again showed that political opposition was reduced to relying on the law. Continued poor public administration led to the first (2006) collapse of the Home Office immigration and asylum function, leading to the Legacy programme, fresh claims for asylum, and growing numbers of

S. York, *The Impact of UK Immigration Law*,
https://doi.org/10.1007/978-3-030-98721-3_3

'failed asylum-seekers' difficult to remove. The chapter concludes by analysing the UK's response to the 'landings on the beaches', as set out in the March 2021 *New Plan for Immigration*—more relegislating, stigma and curtailment of legal rights.

2 The Construction of Asylum-Seeking as Essentially Bogus: Choice of Destination, Credibility and Refugees 'Of Concern'

From the mid-1980s a new type of migration, asylum, led to a wholly different response from both main political parties, in both the pace of legal change and in the intensity of restrictions. These covered not just immigration-based rights, duties and administrative functions but restrictive changes in housing and social security law. The contemporaneous conceptualising of public service applicants as consumers failed to ensure a reasonable standard of public service from the government's fraying and under-resourced immigration bureaucracy, affecting asylum-seekers and other migrants alike. This chapter concentrates on Britain's response to asylum-seekers as a receiving state and a receiving polity, showing how the government's actions and inactions led to further deterioration in legal standards and norms of public administration in the wider realm of immigration control.

Governments constantly repeat the claim that Britain '*welcomes refugees*'. However, right from the early modern period, Britain's 'welcome' has been qualified by wider geopolitical considerations as well as concern about internal social and economic stability: and hostile environment-style measures have been imposed as necessary.[1]

The concept of the refugee became internationally codified and recognised in the 1951 UN Convention on Refugees.[2] During the Cold War, the Convention was used to give succour to well-known Soviet defectors. The outspoken, identifiable 'political refugee' from a regime deplored by the West has acted as a paradigm against which everyone seeking refuge, and every other category of refuge-seeker, has since been measured.

The limitations of this concept have been exhaustively analysed in academic writings and before the courts. It has taken decades for it to be formally accepted that the Convention applies where persecution is meted out by 'non-state agents'[3]; where (generally women) are subject to sexual oppression as a way of making them obey[4]; that persecution can take place where political opposition can be 'imputed' to a family member,[5] and can be feared where opposition can consist in failure to conform (as for secret atheists, closet homosexuals and silent political opponents),[6] and where children face being trafficked for sex, crime or domestic servitude, or face forced recruitment to extreme organisations or illegal armies.[7] It is strongly resisted that the Convention might consider that famine and starvation could amount to 'persecution' or that the Convention should apply to those fleeing civil war. There is no formal international appetite for accepting peoples forced to move by climate change as *refugees*.

In the UK, the 1985 arrivals of Tamils fleeing communal violence in Sri Lanka—the first asylum claims from Commonwealth citizens—provoked quick rule changes requiring them to obtain a visa before seeking entry. Uniquely, Tamils were permitted to apply for asylum *inside* the country of persecution.[8] However they had to show severe hardship *and* a close connection with the UK, the underlying assumption being that, otherwise, *they did not need to come to Britain.*

This is the nub of the construction of the asylum-seeker as 'bogus'. The overwhelming numbers of refugees in the world survive in neighbouring countries, some with protection and assistance from the UN High Commission on Refugees (UNHCR). The remaining displaced people survive with difficulty in the face of meagre help, indifference or even hostility from the authorities of that neighbouring country and its residents. For European receiving states, asylum-seekers from other continents represented a *threat*. Having claimed asylum, applicants could not be 'refouled' until an individual determination had been made. Receiving states quickly realised that such migrants could not easily be expelled.

The European states' pre-emptive response was to stop them arriving, and, failing that, to discredit their claims from the start, both in their formal legal proceedings and in the eyes of the public. For those states, an applicant's very journey all the way to Europe surely demonstrates a *choice of destination.* Therefore they could not be 'genuine refugees', but merely looking for economic betterment. And because the Refugee Convention and UNHCR Handbook place the burden of proof on the applicant,[9] 'credibility' became the major legal issue in asylum determination. This is examined further in Part 5 below, and more broadly in Chapter 6.

Macdonald, writing in 2001, suggests that it is '*the mismatch between Convention refugees and actual or de facto refugees which has allowed western European governments to enact ever more restrictive measures against refugees, often irresponsibly described as 'bogus' or 'abusive' Over the past decade the word 'asylum ' has almost lost its meaning under the weight of political scaremongering…*'.[10]

He contrasts this with the Convention concerning the Specific Aspects of Refugee Problems in Africa 1969, proposed by the Organisation of African Unity (OAU), whose definition of 'refugee' embraces '*those compelled to leave their place of habitual residence through 'external aggression, occupation, foreign domination or events seriously disturbing public order in either part or the whole of the country*'. International bodies have always been clear that, while UN Convention definition of 'persecution' does not include the far greater number of people forced to flee their own country by reason of war, civil strife or generalised repression, international human rights imperatives also require assistance for those others. This was made clear in the UN formulation '*refugees within the mandate [of the Convention] and those [to be protected] under the UNHCR's 'good offices*'. After 1965, 'good offices' were understood to cover '*groups of refugees of the High Commission's concern*'. From 1972, this was applied to internally-displaced people, and after 1982 this was applied to those displaced in a situation '*analogous to refugees*', thereafter referred to as displaced persons.[11] The later drafting of regional refugee conventions such as that of the OAU accepted this. Such cases could be dealt with by relying on objective evidence about country conditions, not requiring individual evidence of persecution. This approach can be glimpsed in Europe in the granting of temporary status to asylum-seekers from Somalia, the former Yugoslavia, Iraq and Afghanistan, discussed below; and secondly in the much later definition of article 15c of the

European Union's Qualification Directive,[12] implemented in 2004 as part of the European Union's drive for a common asylum policy. That offered protection to those who faced:

> (c) serious and individual threat to a civilian's life or person by reason of indiscriminate violence in situations of international or internal armed conflict.

Needless to say, very few places have been accepted by the Home Office or in UK tribunal 'country guidance' cases to fit that definition, even where 'international or internal armed conflict' is visibly taking place.

Even official UNHCR pronouncements sometimes elide the difference between the protection needs of those fleeing countries in turmoil and 'economic migrants'. For example, Thorvald Stoltenberg, in his Statement 22 February 1990 to the 46th Session of the UNHCR, referred to the *'optical [difficulty] of an association between refugees seeking asylum and unauthorised border-crossers of whatever other character... Refugee arrivals become, from this perspective, a problem of irregular migration...'*[13] He did go on to say that '*those who leave because of ethnic and social unrest are precarious because outside the Refugee Convention definition, ... [and] do need 'multilateral action within a human rights framework'.*

In 1986, under its presidency of the European Commission, the UK took the lead in constituting an Ad Hoc Group on Immigration under the European Economic Community (EEC)'s Trevi programme, which reported in November 1986.[14] Its terms of reference were *'to end the abuse of the asylum system'*, making it clear that their aim was to declare all asylum-seekers from outside Europe ineligible for asylum in Europe.[15] First, this proposed an EEC-wide programme of imposing visas on nationals from an agreed list of third countries, to be followed by sanctions on airlines bringing in people with false or no documents. These measures were quickly introduced in the UK.

Fear of 'asylum shopping' led to what in 1990 would become the Dublin Convention.[16] Those found to have been documented in another EEC Member State would be returned there for processing. The proposed common fingerprint database (later EURODAC), and proposals on 'manifestly unfounded' claims and 'safe third countries' rested on the view that *'intercontinental movements are seldom necessary for protection'*. It was suggested that only those refugees fleeing *persecution* (for which read 'individual persecution') should be granted in Europe. Those fleeing wars and civil strife who were currently being granted 'tolerated' status *'should be excluded'*. In the UK these included Somalis, Iraqis and Afghans, who were generally being granted 'exceptional leave to remain' in the UK.[17]

3 UK Responses to the First 'Asylum Crisis': Exclusion, Stigma, Disbelief and Control

The UK responded to the question of choice of destination in four ways. First, the categories of refugee and economic migrant were treated as mutually exclusive, leaving no intellectual or legal place for migrants fleeing 'generalised violence'. Even the UNHCR Handbook's notes on economic migrants make no mention of those fleeing generalised violence.[18] Secondly, asylum decisions tended to reify what applicants said in their first contact with authority as 'the person's true reasons' for entering the country. Thirdly, the well-foundedness of an applicant's fear of persecution is conflated with their motives and methods of escape. Finally, all the mainstream UK political parties accepted that an essential response to uncontrolled arrivals was to increase internal controls: and all accepted that this could not be done without the risk of blurring any distinction between 'genuine refugees' and the rest, or, even, without the risk of blurring the legal distinctions between migrants and settled people.

From the mid-1980s, as soon as a country showed signs of political instability, and certainly once the number of asylum applications from a country were seen to increase, the Home Office imposed entry visa requirements. The Immigration (Carriers Liability) Act 1987 provided for charges for carrying *'a person who required leave to enter but who fails on arrival to produce a valid immigration document showing his nationality and identity and also a valid visa*'. The Home Secretary stated in that debate that whereas '*two years ago, only 10% of those seeking asylum in the UK claimed at a port of entry, now some 50% were so applying*'. They '*could not be genuine asylum-seekers*' as had travelled too far or had no documents and therefore had to be bogus. In the House of Lords, Earl Ferrers, in a debate on the Immigration Bill 1988, said: '*The Act was ... aimed at a new phenomenon ... migrants from a number of under-developed countries [who] avoided removal from the United Kingdom by ... claiming asylum*'.[19]

Guy Goodwin-Gill, in an introductory article to the first edition of the Journal of International Refugee Law in 1989, said:

> ...state practice supports a group or category approach... excluding by reference to pure economic motivation or pure personal convenience. [Asylum] is a fundamental human rights issue. ... [despite this], apologists for unbridled State action fail to acknowledge ... that the ultimate destination of their argument against refuge is that people must be repelled by force: and short of killing those in flight, they would justify every other indignity in the name of self-preservation, community identity or ... narrow chauvinism.[20]

Thus, while it was accepted that States have a legitimate interest in controlling irregular migration, States risked breaching international conventions where such measures hinder access to asylum and access to status determination.

3.1 The Slow Development of UK Asylum Law, Rules and Procedure

For some time, UK immigration law and rules said little or nothing about asylum. The House of Lords first considered the Refugee Convention in 1987 in the case of *Bugdaycay*.[21] For three of the appellants the question was the status of the Convention in UK law, and in particular whether the Convention's requirement of an adequate determination procedure necessitated a right of appeal from inside the UK. The House of Lords said No:

> [this would] override the express terms of section 13(3) of the [1971] Act, which prohibits an appeal against refusal of leave to enter so long as the intending appellant is in the United Kingdom. ... It is equally plain that a person who has secured entry illegally can be in no better position in this regard than a person refused leave to enter. ...

Their Lordships also wielded against refugees the strict interpretation of 'deception' applied in immigration cases:

> The first three appellants ... each committed an offence under section 26(1)(c) by misrepresenting to an immigration officer on arrival in this country the true nature and purpose of his visit...

The question of an in-country right of appeal had been considered in 1985 by the Race Relations and Immigration Sub-Committee of the Select Committee on Home Affairs.[22] The government was strongly against this. It feared that a delay of even a few days before removal would make it impossible to remove without lengthy negotiations with their country of origin. They also believed that the mere existence of an in-country right of appeal would act as a pull factor. The Home Secretary noted that *'more than 28,000 people were refused at our ports [in 1986] and it would take only a small proportion of those to claim asylum—that would be an obvious move for them, if there were an independent right of appeal—to overwhelm any appeals system'.*[23] At that time, remedies for applicants who had been refused entry at a port were, firstly, a reference to a UKIAS adviser stationed at the port, who would consider the case and make representations to the Secretary of State; secondly, a request to an MP to put a 'stop' on removal, and finally an urgent application for judicial review.

In a memorandum for the House of Commons in 2003,[24] the Information Centre about Asylum and Refugees in the UK (ICAR) provided figures showing asylum applications made in the UK from 1985 to 2002. The first striking fact is that only a few thousand asylum claimants were needed to whip up a sense of urgency in the government responses of 1985 and 1987 (though the numbers arriving in other European countries at that time were far higher). But secondly, although there is a fall in numbers in 1988 (ascribed by Earl Ferrers to the passing of the Carriers' Liability Act in 1987), numbers rose significantly after that, suggesting that the great pressure of war and turmoil in 'asylum-producing' states overcame the difficulties imposed by that piece of legislation. It is also noticeable that the proportion of refusals increased sharply after Labour came to power in 1997. Labour policy is discussed below.

The political panic about asylum numbers was not followed by any changes to administration or policy. The process of making an asylum application was envisaged as an applicant's simply telling an immigration officer or Home Office official that he or she was afraid to return to their country of origin, or, at best, getting help from a UKIAS adviser to present that claim in more formal terms.[25] Those representations would then be considered by an immigration officer and a decision made while the applicant was detained in the airport. Obtaining more time, whether to contact witnesses or obtain documents, could only be achieved by issuing an urgent judicial review challenging removal, or contacting an MP to stop removal. Until 1987 an asylum-seeker was simply interviewed at the airport and a report (not provided to the applicant) sent to the Home Office. A person who claimed asylum after entering the country, whether immediately after having passed through immigration control on their false papers, or already in the UK as a student or work permit holder who feared returning home, would be sent for an interview at Lunar House in Croydon. No written reasons were provided for refusal, and there was no right of appeal.

Not until the Immigration Rules HC 251,[26] by which time asylum claims had reached over 26,000 in the year, do we see any acceptance that by virtue of being a claim under an international Convention signed by the UK, an asylum claim must trump normal immigration procedures, if only at the moment of entry. However, those rules simply transferred discretion from a Chief Immigration Officer to a Home Office official in Lunar House. *Bugdaycay* had shown that as far as rights of appeal were concerned, an asylum-seeker had no greater rights than any other migrant, as provided for in the Immigration Act 1971.

Those Rules do not describe any procedural measures. Asylum is briefly covered in paras 75–77. Para 75 says:

> ... Every such case is to be referred by the immigration officer to the Home Office for a decision regardless of any grounds set out in any provision of these rules which may appear to justify refusal of leave to enter. The Home Office will then consider the case in accordance with the provisions of the Convention... (my emphasis)

In 1991, following a decision in the Court of Appeal[27] the Home Office began providing a questionnaire for applicants to complete, giving a copy of interview notes to the applicant, providing a 'minded to refuse' letter and asking for a response.

By the early 1990s the asylum system was beginning to crack. Macdonald noted in 1994 the *'considerable delay in processing pre-1993 cases – some have lasted for years. The Home Office now aim to provide decisions in post '93 cases in under 6 months'.*[28]

4 The Asylum and Immigration Appeals Act (AIAA) 1993 and the Statement of Changes in the Immigration Rules 1994: Restrictive Legislation Amidst Administrative Turmoil

In line with the policies agreed with the EEC, the Conservatives in 1992 had introduced an Asylum Bill proposing reduced legal rights and introducing new enforcement measures. But, for the first time, a right of appeal was granted to a special adjudicator, with onward rights of appeal to the Immigration Appeal Tribunal and, with permission, to the Court of Appeal.

The Lords debate on the Bill noted what the UNHCR's Director of International Protection had written about pull factors:

> *The majority of people coming as asylum seekers into Europe are not refugees but economic migrants"* ... [who] clog up the asylum procedures which cannot function normally any longer. This, in turn, *"proves to be an attraction to many destitute persons abroad, who feel that, if they apply for refugee status in a Western country, they will be taken care of by the social welfare*

> *system of that country for a year or two, or even longer, while their claims are being examined.*[29]

The government fell before that Bill became law, but the Conservative manifesto for the 1992 general election determined to reintroduce the measure straight away.[30] Kenneth Clarke, Home Secretary, introducing the new Bill, began with 'bogus' asylum-seekers[31]:

> ... About five years ago, many people suddenly discovered that it was possible to get through our port controls simply by asserting a claim to political asylum. Even when people were already resident and had been required to leave, the ordinary controls could be avoided by making a claim to asylum at that stage. [26]

He highlighted the pressure on the Home Office bureaucracy:

> ... When my predecessor introduced the original Asylum Bill 12 months ago, the rate of applications was running at 10 times the level of that in 1988. Backlogs were spiralling out of control. The time taken to decide applications stretched into years. Since then, we have done all that we can to seek improvements through administrative changes without changing the law ...
> The backlog now stands at more than 60,000 cases awaiting decision and the need for reform remains as pressing as ever. [31]

The ensuing debate, as all subsequent debates about asylum, clearly exposed the legal and political challenges posed by the new immigration. Mayblin (2019) shows that proposing the Convention definition of 'asylum' as an either-or principle of selection draws the argument directly into what is meant by a 'genuine refugee' and what to do about those who may not fit into the Convention definition but who are nevertheless at risk and therefore 'of concern'. It then determines the details of selection procedures, and, having downgraded the value of the claims of those 'of concern', also downgraded are the rights accorded to all applicants while their applications are being considered.[32] Additionally, the existence of even a small number of claimants who were definitely not genuine refugees, i.e. unabashed economic migrants without visas, dominated the treatment of everyone else, and so, over time, the policy options became limited to the provision of deliberately basic reception facilities, the barest acceptable legal procedures, and increased internal controls to mop up those who get in anyway. And as the deteriorating bureaucratic machine failed to deal with growing backlogs of applications, further restrictive measures eventually become merely performative—panic measures brought in by a weak state in the face of an intractable situation.

Meanwhile, having accepted the narrow Convention definition of 'genuine refugee', the opponents' options are politically limited to pointing out the inhumanity or indeed the stupidity of a specific measure, supporting their position by pointing out that, in fact, not many of the world's refugees arrive in the UK, and suggesting that Britain is in no way taking 'its share'.

In the new Act, for the first time in legislation, asylum-seekers were distinguished from the general population in **access to housing**. An asylum-seeker could not be accepted as homeless if it was 'reasonable to continue to occupy' their current accommodation, 'however temporary'.[33]

Credibility, discussed more fully in part 5 below, was the main issue dealt with in the new Part 11 of the Immigration Rules on asylum.[34] Para 340 contained the following list of 'credibility' factors: failure to promptly disclose information, failure to attend an interview, failure to present to be fingerprinted, failure to claim asylum 'forthwith', making false representations, destroying passports, travel documents or travel tickets, acting inconsistently with declared beliefs, acting in ways calculated to create the basis for an asylum claim, making more than one claim concurrently. Para 346 stated that a person who had previously been refused asylum, anywhere, will be refused, ruling out any fresh claim based on change of country conditions. But for the first time the Rules contained details of decision-making procedures, including informing applicants about rights of appeal.

Precisely because the asylum rules define 'a claim for asylum' strictly by reference to the Refugee Convention, the granting of any leave to remain to a person 'of concern' to the UNHCR, i.e. fleeing war or civil unrest, could only be at the discretion of the Home Secretary, decided on the basis of policies which had not yet formally emerged.

5 The Asylum and Immigration Act 1996—'Relegislation', 'Destitution by Design'[35] and Continued Administrative Turmoil

On 11 November 1995 Michael Howard, Home Secretary, opened the debate on a further asylum and immigration bill.[37] As many MPs noted in the debate, it was almost as if the Asylum and Immigration Appeals Act 1993 and the new Immigration Rules of 1994 had not been introduced. Howard stressed the same themes, of too many applicants, too many incentives for people to come here, abuse of the system, the system's inability to cope. The debate on this Bill demonstrates the emergence of a new phenomenon of *relegislation*—the performative response of repeating or intensifying specific legislative measures to show that something is being done. The Bill also further pursues the forlorn hope of dissuading future applicants; and turns the screw of internal controls by removing asylum-seekers' access to housing and benefits.

> Britain has a proud record of giving refuge to those fleeing genuine persecution, but we cannot ignore the fact that our procedures are being abused. Only 4 per cent. of those claiming asylum are deemed by the Home Office to be genuine refugees and just 4 per cent. of appeals are upheld by independent adjudicators.

This shows the government's reliance on a narrow interpretation of the Refugee Convention definition. Anyone beyond 'the 4 per cent' must be bogus. Behind the scenes, large numbers of applicants from countries stricken by war and civil unrest were still being granted exceptional leave to remain.

New Immigration Rules, introduced in August 1996 shortly after the Act became law, continued the tinkering with definitions of deception, fraud and so on, but did introduce one reform. Following the Court of Appeal decision in *Onibiyo*[38] a new Para 346 set out the basis for making a fresh claim for asylum. Fresh claims, discussed below, became important as the delays and backlogs continued to grow under Labour.

In a truly rare example of a minister accepting the scale of the Home Office 'shambles', Charles Wardle, replying in the same debate, says:

> Most practitioners in the Home Office's middle ranks would, I think, tell senior officials and the Ministers whom they advise that to process the queue of 75,000 asylum applicants will take additional resources, manpower and facilities—within the asylum division and the appellate section of the Lord Chancellor's Department—of substantially more than the £37 million announced by the Home Secretary.
>
> ... My estimate is that it will probably take £150 million a year for two years, including set-up and temporary redeployment costs, to reduce the queue to a manageable work-in-progress level of three months. .... Once the queue is removed, the very attraction of the bogus application is destroyed.

Briefly set out in ss 9-11 were measures excluding all 'persons subject to immigration control' (PSIC) (as defined by the Immigration Act 1971) from entitlement to all social benefits including child benefit, and from access to any social housing. The speed with which these measures were introduced, and their effects, will be discussed in section 6 below.

The link between internal controls and race emerged in this debate, as did the questions of delay and the ineffectiveness of relegislating. Jack Straw argued that the proposed employer checks would be burdensome and lead to racial discrimination. Roy Hattersley announced that he was '*sick and tired of people saying repressive legislation is good for race relations*'. Jim Lester spoke about the probable effect of denying support to asylum-seekers:

> ...for the first time in this country, we will create a sub-culture of totally dispossessed people, who will have no mechanism and no rights. In other countries, they talk of "illegals". We have not had that system here.

Roseanna Cunningham [Perth and Kinross]

> In effect, it appears that the Government intend to starve them out of the country.

However Labour not only did not later repeal any of the measures it opposed, but continued the process of intensifying internal controls, relegislating offences and limiting appeal rights.

6 Legal Failings and Critiques: The Issue of 'Credibility' and the Overburdening of Proof

The responses of various governments to the delays and backlogs also drove another emerging trend—a degradation of legal principles, practices and procedures in respect of migrant applicants. One of the biggest legal issues in immigration control is that of credibility. The legal point is a simple one. In the absence of the most scrupulous institutional adversary, and especially in the context of hostile political and public opinion, placing the burden of proof wholly on an applicant inevitably leads to what has variously been termed a 'refusal culture' or a 'culture of disbelief'. Though in immigration cases the formal standard of proof is the normal civil standard of the balance of probabilities, and in asylum cases the lower standard of 'real risk',[39] applied with 'anxious scrutiny', i.e. slightly more generous to an applicant, the fact that the *burden* of proof lies on the applicant has inexorably led to a standard of proof nearer to the criminal standard of 'beyond all reasonable doubt'. The broader legal implications of this are explored further in Chapter 6.

The Refugee Convention clearly places the burden of proof on the applicant. The UNHCR Handbook[40] says:

> 196. It is a general legal principle that the burden of proof lies on the person submitting a claim.

However, that paragraph immediately continues:

> … while the burden of proof in principle rests on the applicant, the duty to ascertain and evaluate all the relevant facts is shared between the applicant and the examiner … there may also be statements that are not susceptible of proof. In such cases, if the applicant's account appears credible, he should, unless there are good reasons to the contrary, be given the benefit of the doubt.

During the 1980s few asylum claimants had access to formal legal advice, and at first those refused were not even provided with written reasons for refusal. As numbers of asylum-seekers grew, private solicitors, Law Centres and other charitable advice centres had begun assisting asylum applicants. A representative body of immigration practitioners, the Immigration Law Practitioners Association (ILPA), was formed in 1984. Practitioners comparing notes through ILPA and other networks began to see the tendency for quick refusals solidifying into a *culture* of refusal. After the introduction of a right of appeal, a refused applicant would receive a formal letter setting out 'reasons for refusal'. Some refusal letters simply stated that an applicant had not advanced a Convention reason for claiming asylum. Detailed 'reasons' fell into the following broad categories: not from the country claimed; from the country claimed but not judged to be sufficiently at risk; account not convincing because relies on 'what your mother told you' rather than on original documents; inconsistencies and 'discrepancies' in the account mean that it cannot be believed; not from the named political group; not an adherent of the declared religion because didn't know enough about the Bible; not a homosexual because hadn't had any homosexual encounters; haven't lost touch with family; wasn't raped because did not declare this immediately on claiming asylum; there is a safe place in the country in which the applicant could have taken refuge; should have claimed in the first (or another) safe country. Claims of escapes from prison, escapes over an armed and guarded border, or long treks on broken limbs, were met effectively with 'you couldn't have done that'. (In one case I filed a copy of the *Colditz Story*, then popular on TV, and in another a copy of *Touching the Void:* rather childish attempts to shame the decision-maker into not using those arguments.)

And the 'reasons' did not stop there. The Home Office often showed a cavalier attitude to objective country evidence. Decision-makers would often make assertions of his or her own, *as if based on some alternative evidence,* but in fact based on the decision-maker's own opinion, a throwaway idea or free-floating proposition. It is the *applicant* who must prove the contrary. Decision-makers would assert that an applicant had 'lied'. Judicial determinations are seen which make negative findings of fact which are themselves inconsistent, leaving an applicant caught in a tangled, knotted skein of 'findings' and who can then never either be granted leave nor removed, whatever subsequent evidence they provide.

In 1994 the Tribunal case of *Chiver*, still frequently cited, held that *it is perfectly possible for an adjudicator to believe that a witness is not telling the truth about some matters, has exaggerated the story to make his case better, or is simply uncertain about matters, but still to be persuaded that the centrepiece of the story stands.*[41] Formal complaints began to be made about the poor quality of decision-making, including references to the wrong country, insertion of stock paragraphs with blanks where details should have been inserted, or letters that were straightforwardly illiterate.

The reliance on 'credibility', and on alleged contradictions and discrepancies, was pervasive. In 1995 the legal charity Asylum Aid published its report, *No Reason at All.*[42] Their report quotes from *Jeyakumaran*[43]*: 'while I am conscious of the administrative problem of numbers seeking asylum, it cannot be right to adopt artificial and inhuman criteria in an attempt to solve it'.*

The report uses examples from refusal letters to show: the Home Office's misapplication of binding caselaw, whether on the burden of proof, standard of proof or otherwise; ignorant and illogical Home Office reasoning such as juxtaposing two unrelated facts and claiming inconsistency; the dismissal of later evidence as necessarily being less reliable; asserting there are safe areas in the person's country to which the person could return but without identifying such; rejecting people on the grounds that their (illegal) political activities were illegal, and therefore would be at risk of punishment rather than persecution; asserting implausibility, as in 'it is unlikely that your friend would have assisted you to escape without payment...'. Asylum Aid was tempted in the same way as I was, referring to *Schindler's Ark* to support that person's case.

Some applications are refused because: '*the threats against you were not carried out...*' (in other words, they fled before suffering harm), while others were refused because they *'did not leave at the earliest opportunity'.* Failure to declare rape and sexual abuse immediately on making the claim was fatal. Small errors (in dates, spellings of names) are fatal. The use of country evidence was seen to be shameless, relying on selective quotations and the most optimistic interpretation.

Then the report notes 'technical' obstacles to acceptance: not claiming asylum immediately on arrival; not claiming in the first safe country; the use of their own genuine passport, or alternatively the failure to produce any national documents.[44]

Only two years after the right of appeal was introduced, the report identified a Home Office lack of legal conscientiousness in relation to appeals, including bringing up new issues not stated in the refusal letter, and not clearly stating what parts of the story are accepted. The report notes the result of Home Office policy changes: significant increase in numbers of refusals, from 14% of applications before the Act to 76% afterwards; people who applied before 1993 were still waiting, and the backlog had increased from 42,170 in March 1993 to 52,760 in September 1994.[45] Appellants were waiting at least six months for an appeal hearing. While refusals were expected to reach 17,000 per year, the capacity of the appeals system was 5000 per year[46]: there was no legal aid, and the only organisation available to assist was the Refugee Legal Centre, (a segment of UKIAS which by then had set up separately to specialise in asylum claims) who could take only 3500 applicants a year.

Unsurprisingly, and again typical of all future Home Office responses to criticism, the Home Office response to the report, contained within the report itself, was that the cases referred to 'were not typical', that there are policies on dealing with asylum claims, there is extensive staff training and quality control. It is not surprising either that the same criticisms have been made many times over the decades since then. Not only has nothing changed, but new immigration rules and then legislation has been introduced to formalise many of the assumptions and procedures complained of. The broader legal implications of all this are explored further in Chapter 6.

7 The 1996 Housing and Benefit Restrictions: Immediate Impact and Litigation Response

The Conservative Party had shown earlier that they had the welfare system in its sights. They started by limiting migrants' access to social assistance. At the 1992 Conservative Party conference, Social Security minister Peter Lilley, in a celebrated speech[47] rails against '*bogus asylum-seekers*', '*claiming using a dozen different invented names*'. In 1993, he had announced in a press release *New Rules to Curb Abuse by People from Abroad*[48] that 'urgent cases' payments were to be terminated for 'persons from abroad', except for some asylum-seekers.[49] In 1994, a new 'habitual residence test' targeted European national 'benefit tourists', a measure which also affected British citizens returning from long periods abroad.[50]

In his 1995 conference speech, Peter Lilley again attacked 'bogus asylum-seekers'. The government introduced regulations[51] denying benefits to those who applied 'in-country' rather than on arrival, a bizarre reversal of the assumptions behind the Carriers' Liability Act.[52] The parliamentary Social Security Advisory Committee viewed this as a poor Home Office response to its own institutional inability to respond to formal requests made under international law,[53] instead employing stigma and destitution to influence migrants' behaviour.

Challenging the Regulations, the Joint Council for the Welfare of Immigrants (JCWI) issued judicial review proceedings against the Department of Health and Social Security.[54] JCWI argued that the right to claim asylum, and to appeal against a refusal, had been brought into UK domestic law by the Asylum and Immigration Appeals Act (AIAA) 1993, which had made no distinction between on arrival and in-country claims. In the Court of Appeal, Simon Brown LJ accepted that the Secretary of State had the right to discourage economic migrants by restricting access to benefits. However, the regulations would also harm genuine applicants. He said:

> Parliament cannot have intended a significant number of genuine asylum seekers to be impaled on the horns of so intolerable a dilemma: the need

either to abandon their claims to refugee status or alternatively to maintain them as best they can but in a state of utter destitution. Primary legislation alone could in my judgment achieve that sorry state of affairs.

The government promptly legislated to deal with this legal setback, introducing a new part of the Asylum and Immigration Bill, headed *'Persons subject to immigration control' (PSIC)* which excluded asylum-seekers from access to public sector housing and social security benefits, apart from those who had claimed asylum on arrival, or who had dependent children.[55]

These provisions were accompanied by the Housing Act 1996. This, in Part VI (Allocation), prohibited allocation of any social housing to a person not 'qualified', defined as a 'person subject to immigration control': and part VII (Homelessness) excluded 'persons from abroad' as claiming homelessness assistance, and continued the AIAA 1993 exclusion from homelessness assistance of asylum-seekers who had recourse to accommodation 'however temporary'.

The impact was immediate. Single in-country asylum-seekers were overnight reduced to sleeping on the street and rooting for food in dustbins. Applications were made to local authority social services departments for support. Refusals by Westminster City Council were challenged by four applicants *M, P, A and X*, brought by a West London solicitor, Jerry Clore. He argued that s21 National Assistance Act (NAA) 1948, under which local authorities owed a duty to 'those requiring accommodation and subsistence' because of their need for 'care and attention', could apply to destitute single asylum-seekers. Mr Justice Collins held at first instance that s21 was 'available as a safety-net' and was 'a provision of last resort', Local authorities continued to refuse, and injunctions continued to be granted, until the judgment was upheld in the Court of Appeal.[56] The decision 'caused consternation'.[57] Local authorities faced intense pressure on temporary accommodation and on social services budgets, and received only ad-hoc payments from central government for the extra responsibility. By the end of 1999, local authorities were supporting around 57,000 single asylum-seekers under this provision.[58]

The curtailing of access to housing and benefits was a clear change not just in public policy at a practical level but in the underlying philosophy—no longer offering *protection for* those seeking asylum, but offering the host society *protection from* the new, stigmatised, social category—'bogus asylum-seekers'.[59] Once government sees its role as *protecting the public from* that harm, success can only be demonstrated by achieving control: and in the face of rising numbers of arrivals and growing delays and backlogs, relegislating appears to be the only way of demonstrating control.[60] Minister of State Charles Wardle's suggestion of an increased budget to deal with the backlogs had gained no traction. Neither had there been any wider consideration about the definition of asylum or whether the UK's international law duties might include people outside the UN Convention definition.

* * *

All this had taken place against a background of the rise and fall of Thatcherite conservatism. Thatcher was challenged for leadership in November 1989 in a party vote which, though she won, showed her unpopularity within the party. The unpopularity of the Poll Tax, introduced in 1989 in Scotland and 1990 in England and Wales, was met with significant protests and passive resistance of non-payment, and, facing a challenge for leadership of the Conservative party later that year, Thatcher resigned. She was replaced by John Major. That government then presided over Black Wednesday, 16 September 1992, on which Britain was forced out of the European Exchange Rate Mechanism. Major subsequently managed to force Parliament to ratify the EU Maastricht Treaty (which formed the European Union) by making the vote a vote of confidence. But an air of squalor and exhaustion was slowly damaging the Conservative party. By 1997 Major's government had lost its majority, and an election was called. Labour won a shattering victory in the 1997 election with a majority of 179.

8 Labour's Approach to Asylum: Relegislating, Destitution and Litigation

The new government began with reforming zeal, introducing the Human Rights Act 1998, legislating on data protection, freedom of information and a new government for London, a national minimum wage, tax credits and increased spending on education. Directly relevant to this study, an early promise soon broken was the ill-fated 'ethical foreign policy'.[61] Following 9/11, the UK supported the USA's invasions of Afghanistan and then Iraq. Apart from the destructive impact on political trust, those invasions resulted in the long-term destabilisation of both those States. The UNHCR reported in 2002: '*An additional 511,000 people were displaced in Afghanistan in 2001, bringing the total displaced population of concern to UNHCR there to 1.2 million*'.[62] By the end of 2004, '*2.1 million Afghan refugees were reported by 78 asylum countries, constituting 23 per cent of the global refugee population*'.[63] During that period, over 300,000 people fled from Iraq. Away from the wars in the Middle East, civil wars in Somalia and Sudan continued to produce similar numbers of 'refugees of concern' to the UNHCR.[64]

Within a few months the 1998 White Paper *Fairer, Firmer, Faster—a modern approach to immigration and asylum*[65] announced a thorough examination of the Home Office immigration and asylum operation. Also proposed were the legal regulation of immigration advice, and a complete parallel system of housing and social assistance for asylum-seekers. Support and accommodation for asylum-seekers would be provided in 'dispersal areas' on a 'no-choice' basis, with subsistence payments by vouchers rather than cash. Access to mainstream housing and social security would be ended. The declared objectives were to avoid destitution while encouraging asylum-seekers to have recourse to their own communities, and to minimise the pull factors for economic migration by removing access to mainstream benefits or cash.

8.1 The Immigration and Asylum Act 1999: 'Workhouse-Style' Asylum Support

Home Secretary Jack Straw introduced the Bill in Parliament on 22 February 1999.[66] It was broadly presented and accepted as a bipartisan measure, to be scrutinised by a standing committee of the whole House. A few MPs noted that the asylum support provisions will *'create a new class of socially excluded people'* [Allan [66], Diane Abbott [91]. Criticism of previous Tory immigration policy was limited to its 'piecemeal' approach and on the 'shambles' of the Home Office as a bureaucracy, referring to *'boxes of files [kept] in an underground garage, that staff cannot enter because of health hazards* [Keith Vaz [80], the 1997 introduction of a paperless system 'using paper', staff cuts in the face of lengthening queues, and staff having to deal with applications from countries they know nothing about.

Macdonald[67] says of this Act:

> It ... virtually completes the project, started in the late 1970's, of tying access to social and welfare benefits firmly to immigration status, finally burying the welfare-state notion of provision based on need, and introduces a workhouse-type system of support for asylum-seekers.

The National Asylum Support Service (NASS) started on 3 April 2000. In its first year the scheme cost around £750 m, rising in the next year to over £1bn. The scheme set subsistence payments at 70% of income support, and less for 'failed asylum-seekers', catered for separately under s4 of the 1999 Act.[68] The standards of 'adequate' accommodation were lower than for mainstream housing. Provided through outsourcing companies, the accommodation was often poor and official complaints procedures did not work. The legal consequences of outsourcing for migrants are discussed in Chapter 6.

NASS worked poorly from the start. In the April 2002 debate on the Nationality, Immigration and Asylum Bill,[69] Gregory Barker (Bexhill and Battle) said this:

> Arrangements for dispersing asylum seekers are in chaos and the National Asylum Support Service bureaucracy has become something of a legend. ... Such inept handling of the number of asylum seekers entering Britain has impacted badly on all concerned.

In October of that same year, those working with asylum-seekers said this:

> NASS has pushed them deeper into poverty and marginalised them further ... a couple without children receive £59.26 a week. A young single adult has to live on under £30 a week. Accommodation in the dispersal areas is often far from shops, schools and the GP: to pay for bus fares can mean missing out a meal.[70,71]

Pull factor allegations were examined in a 2000 Audit Commission report.[72] It found no evidence of any relation between level of benefits and numbers seeking asylum. In 1999 around 60% of asylum claims had been made after arrival despite the consequent lack of access to benefits. Evidence presented later to the courts[73] showed little difference in asylum success rates between those who claimed on arrival and those who claimed in-country. Macdonald[74] cites government reports showing that *'the level of asylum seekers depends on the level of human rights abuse in other countries rather than the nature of welfare provision in host countries'*. Over 20 years later, the Home Office is currently facing demands to publish recent government research reaching the same conclusion.[75]

Meanwhile, House of Commons Home Affairs Committee (HAC) evidence-gathering sessions in 2000 relentlessly pressed Jack Straw on the rate of asylum decision-making (10,000 each month instead of the target of 30,000); removals (12,000 per year instead of the target of 30,000) and the number of failed asylum-seekers in the UK—predicted in 1998 to reach 115,000—Straw was unable to give the current figures.[76] In relation to *'countries where there is unquestionably major civil turbulence and violence'*, Straw asked the Committee to accept that, in places with no or no effective government, removals would be *'very difficult'*.[77]

Backlogs of unresolved applications had already begun to build under the previous administration. Once the number of applicants increased, they could not be detained at the airport, and had to be granted 'temporary admission' under the Immigration Act 1971 (permission to physically enter the UK without being granted 'leave to enter') with instructions to return for interviews. The Home Affairs Committee (HAC) Second Report of session 2003–2004,[78] shows how the backlogs in undecided claims rapidly built up.

The Home Affairs Select Committee's report '*Border Controls*'[79] warns of *'the danger of dismissing all claims of asylum as bogus'* [para 20]. Kerry Moore (2010) describes the crescendo of tabloid demands for control in the face of the asylum crisis and even '*the threat to national security*' of the Sangatte camp near Calais, from which groups of young men sallied forth each night to board lorries and trains heading for the UK.[80]

Faced with the growing cost of asylum support, Home Secretary David Blunkett announced the White Paper *Secure Borders, Safe Haven*,[81] brought to Parliament on 7 February 2002.[82] This promised a 'seamless asylum process', including the physical separation of asylum-seekers into reception centres, accommodation centres and removal centres to facilitate removals of rejected applicants.

These and other significant measures were introduced by the Nationality, Immigration and Asylum Act 2002, which also relegislated by re-amending rights of appeal and descriptions of immigration offences. Away from asylum, the White Paper proposed lengthening the probationary period for spouses before they could apply for settlement, increasing the insecurity of settled families.

8.2 The Nationality, Asylum and Immigration Act 2002, Section 55 and the High Point of Human Rights Legal Activism

The Nationality, Immigration and Asylum Bill was also treated as a bipartisan measure.[83] Criticisms were limited to MPs' fears that accommodation centres would be placed in their constituency, that asylum-seekers' children would be segregated from mainstream education, and that nothing was being done to improve the quality or efficiency of Home Office decision-making.

The accommodation centres were never built, and total removals have never risen much above 15,000 annually.[84] However, a last-minute clause receiving only 15 minutes' debate was Section 55. Those who claimed asylum only after passing immigration control were to be denied support through not having claimed asylum *'as soon as reasonably practicable'*. Immediately on commencement on 8 January 2003, destitute asylum-seekers faced having to survive on the street. The ensuing litigation virtually overwhelmed the High Court, and court judgments in favour of the asylum-seekers led to tabloid-style outbursts from Home Secretary David Blunkett. This episode arguably marked the high point of human rights-based litigation as a strategy to assist migrants. On 14 March, Sue Willman, housing and community care lawyer, reported to her Law Centre management committee:

> 6 test cases were issued … On 31st January [the law centre] applied for 6 injunctions for people who were homeless that day and had been sleeping rough and had no money for food. The judge granted the injunction at 11.30pm…. we have since applied for another 9 injunctions… (author present)

On 19 February Mr Justice Collins quashed the Home Office decisions as procedurally unfair. He said: '*Parliament can surely not have intended that genuine refugees should be faced with the bleak alternatives of returning to persecution or of destitution*'.[85] David Blunkett is quoted by Bradley (2003)[86]: '*Frankly I'm personally fed up with having to deal with a situation where parliament debates issues and the judges overturn them. … I don't want any mixed messages going out so I am making it absolutely clear today that we don't accept what Justice Collins has said*'.[87] Bradley refers to newspaper reports:

> Unaccountable and unelected judges are openly and with increasing arrogance and perversity, are usurping the role of Parliament, setting the wishes of the people at nought and pursuing a liberal, politically correct agenda of their own, in their zeal to interpret European legislation.[88]

It was precisely before and during the s55 litigation that tabloid newspaper stories emerged of asylum-seekers 'eating our swans' and 'eating our donkeys'.[89]

Blunkett's complaints were straightforwardly unfounded, since Parliament had included section 55(5), by which support may be given *'for the purpose of avoiding a breach of a person's Convention rights'.* On 18 March, in *Q & Ors,*[90] the Court of Appeal dismissed the Secretary of State's appeal. The court recast the *'as soon as reasonably practicable'* test. In public Blunkett welcomed the *Q* judgment as upholding the government's right to operate s55,[91] but he was forced to limit its operation, accepting that art 3 ECHR *as included in the legislation* precluded reducing asylum-seekers to *'a life so destitute that ... no civilised nation can tolerate it'.*[92]

Refusals and injunctions continued. By October several hundred injunctions had been lodged. On 15 October Maurice Kay J, Head of the Administrative Court, issued a statement.[93] He noted that *'About a quarter of all cases lodged in the Court this year have been asylum support cases'.* On the facts most applications were arguable; where applications had been adjourned for a hearing the Secretary of State did not defend them, and rarely were the applicant's facts challenged. On 18 December 2003 Blunkett announced that a 'credible explanation' of arrival within three days before applying for asylum would generally be accepted.[94] Meanwhile hundreds of applications remained stayed in the Administrative Court. The Court of Appeal heard a further test case, *Limbuela,*[95] in May 2004. Laws LJ's dissenting judgment [58] represented that the issue was a political one, which judges should not be deciding. However, the very granting of so many injunctions had effectively transferred the decision to provide support from the executive to the courts. Pending a Home Office petition to the House of Lords, NASS produced 'interim guidance' accepting that it 'must' provide support unless there is positive evidence that the individual has alternative support.

In the appeal, the House of Lords noted the clear words of s55(5) that support may be given *'...for the purpose of avoiding a breach of a person's Convention rights...'* Baroness Hale said:

> If a woman of Mr Adam's age had been expected to live indefinitely in a London car park, ...would we have been in any doubt that her suffering would very soon reach the minimum degree of severity required under article 3? I think not.[96]

This was a landmark judgment in more than one way. The s55 litigation operated almost like an emergency public inquiry. The Administrative Court, Court of Appeal and eventually the House of Lords permitted the applicants and the NGOs intervening in the cases (and the respondent Home Office) to present general evidence on the availability of charitable support for destitute asylum-seekers, and, at every level, the courts accepted the evidence as applying in general terms to the individuals before them. The applicants' individual facts were rarely challenged. And the Home Office 'interim guidance' effectively reversed the burden of proof in applications for support.[97] However, the courts have shown no sign of wishing to repeat this type of exercise. Chapter 5 notes how the Administrative Court subsequently and summarily dealt with another potentially enormous number of judicial review applications from migrants—the Legacy cases.

8.3 Further Relegislating: The Asylum and Immigration (Treatment of Claimants) Act 2004; the Immigration, Asylum and Nationality Act 2006

Backlogs in the asylum system continued to grow. Barbara Roche, appointed in July 1999 as Minister of State, later said: '*I was told that there were only 50 officials who were able to make decisions on asylum cases. Because of this and the inadequate processes then in place, the backlog only increased...*'[98] In the same publication Don Flynn later commented that '*under Jack Straw, [the Home Office] remained a bastion of slow-witted conservatism*'.[99] Beverley Hughes, giving evidence to the HAC committee on Asylum Applications in 2003, said:

> ... it is very difficult, when you have got rid of 1,000 experienced caseworkers, suddenly to bring people on who make those kinds of decisions,

> at the same time as very, very large increases in numbers of applications ... we have to reduce the backlog: as I see it, it is an albatross round the organisation's neck...

For the government the answer was more legislation. The Asylum and Immigration (Treatment of Claimants) Bill was described in the Commons by David Blunkett as *'part of a jigsaw' ...we all accept that many changes are still required, both in legislation and to improve administration.*[100] He concentrated on the need for further criminal measures and the need for faster removals, which face *'legal challenges and problems of documentation'*. Section 8 of the Act gave statutory force to the presumption of disbelief: courts and tribunals 'shall' have regard to certain factors, such as destruction of documents, failing to claim in a previous safe country, etc. This, Blunkett said, would lead to a *'better, faster and more sensible method of dealing with the initial decision'.* On quality of decision-making, Blunkett announced that UNHCR would provide better training for decision-makers.

To limit appeals to the Court of Appeal, relegislation reduced the appellate structure to a single tier with a paper review application to the High Court. This and other measures were described by Richard Rawlings as the Home Office's '*revenge package*' for too many allowed appeals.[101] Legal aid was curtailed, and only strong Law Lords' opposition prevented the ousting of judicial review altogether, described as '*unprecedented in peacetime*'. [102] The resulting burden of immigration appeals to the Court of Appeal led in 2010 to the restoration of a two-tier structure in line with the other statutory tribunals.[103]

In February 2005 the Home Office published *Controlling our borders: making immigration work for Britain.*[104] This five-year plan for immigration and asylum would bring asylum under control by 'rigorously examining each case', listing more countries as 'safe' and more transit countries as 'safe third countries'. Processing times would be 'speeded up'; the government would 'restrict the abuse of the legal aid system'. To 'tackle claimants without documents', arriving without documents was relegislated again as a criminal offence. Refugees would have to wait 5 years to apply for indefinite leave to remain, and for family migrants the probationary period was increased to 2 years. Removals of failed asylum-seekers and other illegal migrants would be speeded up. 'Asylum-producing' countries were warned:

> … accepting return of their nationals is a duty and failure to do so will have implications for our wider relationship. …[105]

Almost all these proposals are currently (December 2021) being relegislated by the Nationality and Borders Bill.

8.4 The 2006 Collapse of the Immigration and Nationality Directorate: The Legacy and Fresh Claims for Asylum

On Tuesday 25 April 2006 it was reported that over 1000 foreign prisoners had been freed at the end of their prison sentences before being considered for deportation, of whom over 40 had committed 'very serious crimes', and who could not be found. Home Secretary Charles Clarke resigned and Dr John Reid took over. On 23 May, speaking to the Home Affairs Committee, he said:

> Our system is not fit for purpose. It is inadequate in terms of its scope, it is inadequate in terms of its information technology, leadership, management systems and processes.

Three reports were published quickly after that announcement: a comprehensive Home Affairs Committee report on every aspect of immigration control,[106] a 'customer facing' short report *Rebuilding confidence in our immigration system,*[107] and, in September, the Government Reply to the HAC report.[108] The public administration implications of these events are discussed in Chapter 5. Here I look at the impact on applicants.

A new Case Resolution Directorate (the Legacy) was set up to process the estimated 450,000 unresolved asylum claims. Many applicants had been waiting several years, even for a first decision. The Legacy process chose cases at random to work on, leaving applicants in 'limbo'. Just to get their case worked on, many applicants made fresh claims for asylum.

By then the basis for a fresh claim was set out in para 353 of the Immigration Rules.[109]

> ... The submissions will amount to a fresh claim if ...
> 2) Taken together with the previously considered material created a realistic prospect of success, notwithstanding its rejection.

Credibility again became central. Any new evidence faced forensic consideration of why it had not been previously produced, whether it could have been manufactured, and whether, even if genuine, it would sufficiently displace any previous negative credibility findings. Not until the 2005 case of *Rahimi,*[110] upheld in 2006 by the Court of Appeal,[111] was it made it clear that the decision on 'realistic prospect of success' was to be taken by an adjudicator and not by the Secretary of State. The Home Office had merely to decide whether the claim was 'arguable', a low legal threshold, and either grant asylum or make a refusal which attracted a fresh right of appeal. And not for a further four years did the Home Office, under pressure from applications to NASS for asylum support, introduce a 'further submissions' procedure.

From 14 October 2009, a 'failed asylum-seeker' who had first claimed before March 2007 had to make their fresh claim in person in Liverpool, taking all their family members, with no funding for the fares or for any accommodation, having first of all telephoned to make an appointment. Every aspect of this arrangement caused great hardship and confusion. Meanwhile the concomitant applications to NASS for asylum support developed their own queues and backlogs, as the Home Office was unwilling to grant support until they had assessed the fresh claim, which they could not do without access to the file, which was in the Legacy. In 2004, Mr Justice Collins had decided in *Nigatu*[112] that delay in providing asylum support until the fresh claim has been examined *'may put an altogether illegitimate pressure on the individual, who may have a genuine fresh claim to give up if the alternative is destitution'.* Eventually the Supreme Court in *ZO (Somalia)*[113] suggested a screening process to identify briskly those claims devoid of merit. The Home Office said that would be *'unworkable'*—a response which astonished the court—but true, as poor record-keeping meant that weeks were needed to find an applicant's file. The Asylum Support Appeals Project (ASAP) in their 2013 report *One year on—still 'no credibility'*[114] said:

> ... 55% waited between two and eight weeks [for support] and there were 15% who had to wait between nine and 21 weeks.

These delays concerned people who were destitute and street homeless.

In *ZO (Somalia)* the Supreme Court decided that a subsequent application for asylum amounted to 'a claim for asylum' within the EU Reception Directive,[115] and the applicants therefore should be granted the right to work after 12 months if no decision has been made on the claim. Judgment was handed down on 28 July 2010. Some 45,000 fresh claim applicants who had waited over 1 year for *any* consideration of their claim, stood to benefit.[116] A quick change to the Immigration Rules[117] restricted those applicants to jobs on the 'shortage occupations' list, such as *'qualified maths teachers, chemical engineers, high-integrity pipe-welders or even experienced orchestral musicians or ballet dancers'.*[118]

From January 2015 all further submissions had to be submitted in person in Liverpool. Submissions by email were permitted briefly during Covid, but currently (December 2021), making an appointment is still fraught with difficulty, and obtaining asylum support continues to be just as slow.

9 Asylum Under the Coalition and Conservative Governments: From 2010 to the 2021 *New Plan for Immigration*

The number of 'spontaneous' migrant arrivals continued to fall during the later years of the Labour government, and, in terms of public controversy on immigration, asylum-seekers had ceased to be the main target.

Then 2015 saw a big increase in the number of people reaching Europe to claim asylum.[119] The majority of them were from Syria, where a multifaceted civil war with multiple foreign interventions has destroyed one major town and city after another. Adding to the large numbers of people still fleeing from Afghanistan, Eritrea, Sudan and other parts of sub-Saharan Africa, thousands of Syrians began to flee. Two main routes to Europe were developed. Some had begun making the journey across north Africa to cross the Mediterranean from Libya, and Europe has watched as boats sank and large numbers of people drowned. At the same time, increasing numbers of refugees crossed from Turkey and made their way across several European borders despite the attempts of some EU Member States to close borders and block their travel. In August 2015 a refrigerated lorry found near the border between Austria and Hungary was found to contain the bodies of 71 migrants.

The EU rejected demands especially from the southern border Member States Greece, Italy and Spain to amend or abandon the Dublin Regulation.[120] Schengen countries began to impose border controls against other EU Member States. Then Germany spectacularly opened its borders with a series of announcements[121] from Chancellor Angela Merkel during August 2015, accepting over 800,000 migrants, and other countries began to accept transfers of refugees. Later in 2016 the EU struck a deal with Turkey in which Turkey would prevent migrants from crossing to Greece in exchange for funds to support the refugees being hosted by Turkey—which reduced arrivals by 90% in the month of April 2016.[122] Until Russia's invasion of Ukraine in February 2022, Turkey was hosting the largest contingent of refugees in the world—over three million, mainly from Syria. In relation to Africa, the Khartoum Process, agreed in 2014 by 37 EU and African states, was set up to limit the exodus of refugees from East Africa and curb their movements to the Mediterranean seaboard, by funding and supporting African countries to support refugees on that continent.[123] The EU subsequently concluded controversial arrangements with the Libyan coastguard, other Libyan authorities, International Organisation for Migration (IOM) and sub-Saharan countries to dissuade or prevent migrants from crossing the Sahara to get to Europe.[124]

The UK, in the north-west corner of Europe and defended by a further sea, was relatively little affected by these events. The UK received among the smallest proportions of asylum-seekers of all EU Member

States in that period.[125] The UK government, who along with Ireland and Denmark had opted out from the 2013 updating of the European Common Asylum Policy Directives,[126] refused to participate in EU burden-sharing discussions though there was some public support in the UK for accepting more refugees.[127] Instead, assistance was to be provided to those still close to the conflict zones, to avoid the pressure on those refugees to make desperate journeys to Europe.

The government's wider response to the crisis, away from UK territory, was not negligible,[128] but, under public pressure, measures were introduced to bring vulnerable children from Europe. The Dubs Amendments, eventually s67 Immigration Act 2016, was *'limited to [children in] Greece, Italy and France who were registered in the EU before 20 March will be eligible for resettlement, when it is in their best interest to come to the UK'*.[129] The Government waited until 8 February 2017 to announce the 'specified number' of children it intended to relocate (initially 350); and by June 2017 *'only approximately 200 children had so far been relocated to the UK under the Dubs Amendment, all from the Calais Camp'*.[130] In September 2018 the Court of Appeal determined that it was unlawful for the Home Office not to provide 'reasons' for refusing a 'Dubs Amendment' child, but would not fault the consultation process, and the number of children to benefit was to be capped at 480.[131] The government ordered the rejection of a Lords amendment seeking to continue the Dubs scheme after Brexit.[132]

In October 2016 a further scheme was agreed to take asylum-seeking children from the clearing of the Calais 'Jungle', including those who had family in the UK, and some 769 children arrived. They did not all qualify for asylum, so a new status, 'Calais Leave', was created for those who were united with family in the UK.[133] This status may lead to settlement after 10 years.[134]

From 2019 a resurgence of 'fear of migrants' has developed in the UK in response to migrants arriving on beaches in Kent and East Sussex, having crossed by small boat from France or Belgium. Official figures reported 1829 migrants having arrived on beaches during 2019. The BBC reported on 22 November 2021 that over 27,500 had so arrived so far in that year.[135] At first, Home Secretary Priti Patel accepted that arrivals on beaches were a traffickers' response to increased lorry inspections following the deaths discovered in Purfleet in 2019. She accepted that returning such migrants to France would require new formal arrangements after Brexit. But with increasing numbers, demands to 'control' and even 'stop' the boats have intensified, and formal measures have multiplied. Since 2020 various quasi-military operations have been proposed, and, to reduce the so-called pull factor, on 10 December 2020 new Immigration Rules[136] provided that a claim made by a person who had travelled through a 'safe third country' could be declared 'inadmissible'. On this, a recent ICIBI report[137] said:

> By 18 May 2021, the Home Office had issued notices to 3,379 claimants to inform them that their case was being considered for inadmissibility action. However, few bilateral or multilateral return agreements were in place, including with France (accounting for 2,022 of the 3,379 claims), Germany (307), Belgium (213), Spain (191) and Italy (176). Consequently, none of the 3,379 claimants had been returned. Without returns agreements, the inadmissibility process is simply deferring consideration of claims.

And just as in 2002, offshore processing and purpose-built reception centres are being proposed. The government's *New Plan for Immigration* (April 2021)[138] provides a diagnosis and prescriptions which propose relegislating previously tried and failed policies: more enforcement, more detention, faster legal procedures, more criminal offences, stigmatising lawyers and less access to appeal rights or judicial review. While providing no details of future 'legal routes' to asylum, its proposed attempt to refuse asylum to any arrivals from continental Europe amounts to a breach of the Refugee Convention, without the political courage to put withdrawal from the Convention to a full public debate. Its proposals to criminalise those who steer small boats across the Channel, and criminalise hauliers who carry migrants even where the haulier took all required security precautions, show a lack of understanding of criminal liability.[139] Misrepresenting the origins of the problems being addressed, its legal reforms propose to impose duties (of 'good faith', to provide 'all reasons' for wishing to stay in the UK) on only one side, in an adversarial system in which the Home Office already holds great advantage. It blames the systemic delays and backlogs in the asylum system on applicants, rather than on the decades-long lack of sufficient resources. More than any other official document, the Plan exposes the degradation of standards of public administration and legal probity in the Home Office. It will be interesting to see the extent to which the many critiques of the Plan, now lodged in the Parliamentary library, will influence the debate on the Bill.

Notes

1. see for example Goose, Nigel and Liuu, Lien, ed. 2005 *Immigrants in Tudor and Early Stuart England* Eastbourne: Sussex Academic Press.
2. UN Convention on Refugees 1951 art 1(2).
3. *Adan v SSHD* [1998] UKHL15, overturned by *Horvath* v SSHD [2000] UKHL 37.
4. *Islam v. SSHD Immigration Appeal Tribunal and Another, Ex Parte Shah, R v.* [1999] UKHL 20.
5. *STARRED EG (Non-state actors: Acero-Garces disapproved) (Colombia)* [2000] UKIAT 00007 (24 November 2000).
6. *HJ (Iran)* [2010] UKSC 31 holds that homosexuals cannot be expected to be 'discreet' to avoid persecution. *RT(Zimbabwe)* [2012] UKSC 38 extends that principle to silent political opponents, who cannot be expected to conform to avoid persecution.
7. For example *LQ (Age: immutable characteristic) Afghanistan* [2008] UKIAT *00005*; *AA (unattended children) Afghanistan CG* [2012] UKUT 16 (IAC).
8. HC Deb 23 July 1985 vol 83 cc965-89 David Waddington 23/5/85 col 985, 9.
9. UNHCR *Handbook on procedures and criteria for determining refugee status and guidelines on international protection under the 1951 Convention and the 1967 Protocol relating to the status of refugees* reissued Geneva, February 2019 [para 195].
10. Macdonald, Ian A, Webber, Frances. 2001. *Immigration Law and Practice* 5th Ed. London: Butterworths [468].

11. Jackson, Ivor. 1991. *The 1951 Convention relating to the Status of Refugees: A Universal Basis for Protection* International Journal of Refugee Law vol 3 edition 3, 1991.
12. Council Directive 2004/83/EC of 29 April 2004.
13. Refugees and Human Rights Statement by Mr Thorvald Stoltenberg, United Nations High Commissioner for Refugees, to the 46th Session of the United Nations Commission on Human Rights 22 February 1990, *International Journal of Refugee Law, Volume* 2, Issue 2, April 1990, Pages 274–278.
14. Macdonald (3) *Immigration Law and Practice 2nd edition* 1987 Butterworths: preface [vi].
15. Webber, Frances *The new Europe: immigration and asylum,* in *Statewatching the New Europe,* ed Tony Bunyan 1993, Statewatch. [144]. See also Mayblin n32.
16. *Convention determining the State responsible for examining applications for asylum lodged in one of the Member States of the European Communities—Dublin Convention* (97/C 254/01).
17. Frances Webber n14 *Statewatching Europe.*
18. UNHCR Handbook n9 paras [62–64].
19. *HL Deb 12 April 1988 vol 495 cc979-1042.*
20. Goodwin-Gill, Guy, editorial, International Journal of Refugee Law, first edition 1989.
21. *Bugdaycay v. SSHD; Nelidow Santis v. SSHD; Norman v. SSHD; In re Musisi, [1987]* 1 AC 514, [1987] 1 All ER 940, [1987] 2 WLR 606, [1987] Imm AR 250.
22. HC Deb vol 112 col 711 16/3/87, col 728.
23. Ibid col 713.
24. Select Committee on Home Affairs Written Evidence 18. Memorandum submitted by the Information Centre about Asylum and Refugees in the UK (ICAR) https://publications.parliament.uk/pa/cm200304/cmselect/cmhaff/218/218we22.htm accessed 29/11/21.
25. The ICAR memorandum set out for the House of Commons the particulars of the asylum process obtaining at different times.

26. Statement of Changes to the Immigration Rules HC251 In Macdonald, Ian A, Blake, Nicholas. 1991. *Immigration Law and Practice in the United Kingdom* Third edition.
27. Macdonald, Ian A, Blake, Nicholas. 1991. *Immigration Law and Practice in the United Kingdom* Third edition [306].
28. Macdonald, Ian A, Blake, Nicholas. 1995. *Immigration Law and Practice* 4th ed [406].
29. HL Deb 10 February 1992 vol 535 cc457-530 [458].
30. http://www.conservativemanifesto.com/1992/1992-conservative-manifesto.shtml accessed 29/11/21.
31. HC Deb 02 November 1992 vol 213 cc21-120) col 21.
32. Mayblin, Lucy. 2019. *Imagining asylum, governing asylum seekers: Complexity reduction and policy making in the UK Home Office* Migration Studies, vol 7 no 1.
33. Asylum and Immigration Appeals Act 1993 section 4.
34. Statement of Changes in the Immigration Rules HC 395 23 May 1994, fully replacing the 1990 Rules HC 251.
35. Mayor of London. 2004. *Destitution by Design* [out of print].
37. HC Deb 11 December 1995 vol 268 cc699-808 col 699.
38. *Onibiyo* [1996] 2 All ER 901, [1996] 2 WLR 490, [1996] Imm AR 370.
39. *Sivakumuran, R (on the application of) v SSHD* [1987] UKHL. See also *Bugdaycay*, cited n 21 above.
40. UNHCR Handbook n9.
41. *Chiver (Asylum; Discrimination; Employment; Persecution) (Romania)* [1994] UKIAT 10,758; (10,758) IAT 24/3/1994 cited in Macdonald 4th ed [384], 5th ed [486].
42. Alasdair Mackenzie, 1995. *No Reason at All* London: Asylum Aid (Out of print. Author holds PDF).
43. 1994 Immigration Appeal Reports [45] *(an old set of case reports cited as [year] Imm AR xxxx SY).*
44. Mackenzie n42 [33].
45. Ibid [37].
46. Ibid [38].
47. https://www.youtube.com/watch?v=FOx8q3eGq3g accessed 3/7/20—no longer available 22/11/21.

48. Patterson, Terry. 2002. *From safety net to exclusion: ending social security in the UK for 'persons from abroad'.* In *From immigration controls to welfare controls* eds Steve Cohen, Beth Humphries and Ed Mynott, Abingdon: Routledge [162].
49. Until changes made in 1988, rates for asylum-seekers had been even lower. (Ibid p 171).
50. *Swaddling v Adjudication Officer (Free movement of persons) [1999] EUECJ C-90/97 (25 February 1999).*
51. Social Security (Persons from Abroad) Miscellaneous Amendment Regulations 1996 (SI 1996 30).
52. Hansard, 15 July 1996: Column 843, quoted in Fletcher, Emily, 2008. *Changing support for asylum-seekers—an analysis of legislation and parliamentary debates*—working paper no 49, University of Sussex.
53. Report by the Social Security Advisory Committee under s 174(1) Social Security Administration Act 1992 cmnd 3062 (1995–6) at para 10, 63–66.
54. *Joint Council for the Welfare of Immigrants & Anor, (R. on the Application of) v Secretary of State for Social Security* [1996] EWCA Civ 1293.
55. Asylum and Immigration Act 1996 ss 9-11.
56. *R (A) v Westminster City Council* [1997] EWCA Civ 1032, often referred to as *MPAX.*
57. Lord Hoffman, in *Westminster v NASS* [2002[UKHL 38.
58. Zetter, Roger, and Pearl, Martyn. 2000. *The minority within the minority: refugee community-based organisations in the UK and the impact of restrictionism on asylum-seekers.* Journal of Ethnic and Migration Studies, 26:4, 675–697.
59. Fletcher, Emily. 2008. *Changing support for asylum-seekers—an analysis of legislation and parliamentary debates*—working paper no 49. University of Sussex.
60. Ramsay, Peter. 2012 *The insecurity state: vulnerable autonomy and the right to security in the criminal law.* Oxford: Oxford University Press.

61. See Robin Cook's speech 12 May 1997 https://www.theguardian.com/world/1997/may/12/indonesia.ethicalforeignpolicy accessed 29/11/21.
62. UNHCR report 2002 https://www.unhcr.org/uk/news/latest/2002/6/3d0f6dcb5/2001-global-refugee-statistics.html accessed 29/11/21.
63. UNHCR report 2004 https://www.unhcr.org/uk/statistics/unhcrstats/42b283744/2004-global-refugee-trends-overview-refugee-populations-new-arrivals-durable.html accessed 29/11/21.
64. ibid.
65. *Fairer, Firmer, Faster* Cm 4018, July 1998.
66. HC Deb 22 February 1999 vol 326 cc37-129.
67. Macdonald 2001 n10 [vi].
68. That was shocking at the time. All the more shocking that the rates have barely increased in 20 years.
69. HC DEB 24/4/2002 vol 384, col 391.
70. Asylum Support Appeals Project steering group report, October 2002.
71. Sales, Rosemary. 2002. *The deserving and the undeserving? Refugees, asylum-seekers and welfare in Britain* Critical Social Policy.
72. *Another Country* Audit Commission 2000, pp 9, 10. Referred to in Macdonald 5th ed [598].
73. In *R (S, D & T) v SSHD [2003] EWHC 1941 (Admin)* especially para [9], *Limbuela (Adam, Limbuela & Tesema v SSHD,* [2005] UKHL 66.
74. Macdonald fn 10 5th ed. [599].
75. Townsend, Mark. https://www.theguardian.com/uk-news/2021/nov/20/home-office-covering-up-its-own-study-of-why-refugees-come-to-the-uk accessed 22/11/21.
76. HAC Session 1999–2000 *Minutes of Evidence taken before the Home Affairs Committee Tuesday 21 November 2000.*
77. Ibid q 73.
78. House of Commons Home Affairs Committee Second Report of session 2003–2004.
79. House of Common Select Committee on Home Affairs First Report: Border Controls 31/1/01 [9].

80. Moore, Kerry. 2010. *Cultural Study of Asylum under New Labour January 2010 PhD thesis* Cardiff University School of Journalism, Media and Cultural Studies [149].
81. *Secure Borders, Safe Haven: Integration with Diversity in Modern Britain* Home Office 2002 CM 5387.
82. HC Deb 07 February 2002 vol 379 cc1027-40.
83. HC Deb 24 April 2002 vol 384 cc341-432.
84. Home Office statistics show total enforced removals per year falling from 15,252 in 2009 down to 12,460 in 2014, and down further to 10,969 in 2017. *Immigration Statistics, October to December 2014* (2015) and *Jan-March 2017 (2017).* More recent figures show a continuing downward trend—Walsh, Peter William. 2021 *Deportation and voluntary departure from the UK* Migration Observatory, University of Oxford.
85. *Q, R (on the application of) v SSHD [2003] EWHC 195* (Admin) [74].
86. Bradley, Anthony *Judicial independence under attack* Public Law 2003.
87. Ibid, also BBC news channel http://news.bbc.co.uk/1/hi/uk/2779343.stm accessed 22/11/21.
88. Phillips, Melanie, 2003 (quoted in Bradley, n85) https://www.dailymail.co.uk/columnists/article-230002/DICTATORS-IN-WIGS.html accessed 29/11/21.
89. Cited by Kerry Moore n79 [149–51].
90. *R(Q & Ors) v SSHD [2003] EWCA Civ 346.*
91. For example, in his speech to the Commons on the 2nd reading of the next asylum bill 17 /12/2003 [1594].
92. See Blunkett's 18/12/2003 change of policy (set out in Refugee Council announcement n94 below).
93. Maurice Kay J Statement [2003] All ER (D) 236 (15 October 2003).
94. Refugee Council press release accessed 29/11/21: https://www.refugeecouncil.org.uk/latest/news/1031_home_secretary_announces_policy_change_regarding_section_55
95. *Limbuela (Adam, Limbuela & Tesema v SSHD,* [2004] EWCA Civ 540.

96. *Adam, (Adam, Tesema and Limbuela) v. SSHD* [2005] UKHL 66 [78] (usually referred to as *Limbuela*).
97. I give a detailed evaluation of this litigation in York, Sheona (2017) *The Law of Common Humanity: revisiting Limbuela in the 'Hostile Environment'.* Journal of Immigration, Asylum and Nationality Law, 31 (4). pp. 308–329.
98. Roche, Barbara. 2010. *Making the best of immense challenges* IPPR report 2010 ed Tim Finch and David Goodhart.
99. IPPR report n98 [27].
100. HC Deb 17 December 2003 vol 415 cc1587-620 [1587].
101. Rawlings, Richard *Review, Revenge and Retreat* Modern Law Review, (2005) 68(3) MLR 378–410.
102. ibid.
103. Tribunals, Courts and Enforcement Act 2007.
104. *Controlling our borders: making immigration work for Britain* Home Office February 2005 Cm 6472.
105. ibid, [30].
106. Home Affairs Committee *Immigration Control* Fifth Report of Session 2005–6, 23/7/2006.
107. Home Office Immigration and Nationality Directorate *Fair, efficient, Transparent and Trusted: Rebuilding confidence in our immigration system* July 2006 Home Office 9.
108. *Immigration Control* Government reply to the fifth report from the Home Affairs Committee session 2005–6 Cm 6910.
109. Introduced in HC 1112 on 18/10/2004.
110. *R (Rahimi) v SSHD* [2005] EWHC 2838.
111. *WM (DRC) & AR (Afghanistan)* [2006] EWCA Civ 1495.
112. *R (Nigatu) v SSHD [2004] EWHC 1806 Admin.*
113. *ZO (Somalia) v SSHD* [2010] UKSC 36.
114. *UKBA decision-making audit: one year on- still 'no credibility'* https://www.asaproject.org/uploads/ASAP-Audit-on-decision-making-2013.pdf accessed 29/11/21.
115. EU Council Directive 2003/9/EC of 27 January 2003 laying down minimum standards for the reception of asylum seekers (the UK did not opt in to the 2013 version).

116. Doyle, Jack 2010 https://www.dailymail.co.uk/news/article-1298431/Up-45-000-failed-asylum-seekers-given-right-work-Britain.html Daily Mail 29/7/2010 accessed 29/11/21.
117. Statement of Changes in Immigration Rules CM 7929 August 2010.
118. Travis, Alan 2010 http://www.theguardian.com/uk/2010/jul/29/restrictions-sought-asylum-seekers-jobs accessed 29/11/21.
119. https://www.unhcr.org/uk/news/stories/2015/12/56ec1ebde/2015-year-europes-refugee-crisis.html accessed 29/4/20.
120. The Dublin Regulation replaced the Dublin Convention in 2003.
121. https://www.politico.eu/article/german-identity-threat-refugees-migration-merkel/ accessed 29/11/21.
122. House of Commons Home Affairs Committee *Migration Crisis* 7th report 2016–17 HC 24.
123. Oette, Dr Lutz. 2017. *Tackling the root causes of human trafficking and smuggling from Eritrea: the need for an empirically grounded EU policy on mixed migration in the Horn of Africa*. London: SOAS, University of London.
124. Human Rights Watch. 2019. *No escape from hell—EU policies contribute to abuse of migrants in Libya* https://www.hrw.org/report/2019/01/21/no-escape-hell/eu-policies-contribute-abuse-migrants-libya accessed 13/12/21.
125. House of Commons Home Affairs Committee *Migration Crisis* 7th report 2016–17 HC 24, *Migration to Europe explained in seven charts.*
126. EU Reception Directive, Procedures Directive and Qualification Directive, all updated in 2013.
127. Withnall, Adam 2015. https://www.independent.co.uk/news/world/europe/aylan-kurdi-s-story-how-a-small-syrian-child-came-to-be-washed-up-on-a-beach-in-turkey-10484588.html Independent 3/9/2015.
128. ibid.
129. HC Deb 9 May 2016 column 488 James Brokenshire.
130. Home Office. 2020. *Factsheet: section 67 of the Immigration Act 2016 ('Dubs amendment').*

131. *Help Refugees Ltd, R (on the application of) v SSHD & Anor* [2018] EWCA Civ 2098.
132. Walker, Peter 2020 https://www.theguardian.com/politics/2020/jan/22/government-condemned-for-rejecting-lords-child-refugee-dubs-amendment accessed 29/11/21.
133. https://www.gov.uk/government/news/new-form-of-leave-for-children-transferred-during-calais-clearance-to-join-family

    Creating a new status inevitably added to legal complexity concerning those children's onward rights.
134. Immigration Rules part 11 para 352M-P (at 1/11/21).
135. BBC news online https://www.bbc.co.uk/news/uk-59375590 accessed 22/11/21.
136. HC 1043 10 December 2020.
137. ICIBI 2021 *An inspection of asylum casework (August 2020–May 2021).*
138. *New Plan for Immigration* Home Office March 2021.
139. The Crown Prosecution Service (CPS) has already indicated that it will not prosecute such offences: https://www.cps.gov.uk/cps/news/cps-publishes-updated-guidance-handling-illegal-entry-cases-small-boats accessed 22/11/21.

4

Labour Migration: A Challenge to Social Solidarity?

1 Introduction

The Second World War had left millions of displaced persons on the mainland of Europe. In Britain, facing acute labour shortages, they were perceived as an opportunity but also a threat: not just to British workers' jobs and wages, but potentially to the stability of British society. The European workers' resettlement schemes faced mixed, even racist, responses. Separately, immigration controls transformed newly-arriving British subjects from the Colonies and Commonwealth into guest workers, who nevertheless inevitably tended to settle. The resulting transformation of society speeded up with Labour's 2008 points-based system and EU enlargement in 2004. After the 2008 financial crash and subsequent recession, the new Coalition government proposed 'reducing net migration to the tens of thousands'. Growing demands for the UK to leave the EU led to attempts to renegotiate the free movement aspects of membership, then to the Brexit vote. Since leaving the EU, and exacerbated by the Covid pandemic, the fundamental social challenges posed by labour migration are re-presented, this time via acute labour shortages in essential sectors. We will surely see that the basic conflict between

S. York, *The Impact of UK Immigration Law*,
https://doi.org/10.1007/978-3-030-98721-3_4

low wages, low productivity and presumed hostility to migrants cannot be resolved by relegislating a *new Australian-style points-based system*, but requires comprehensive interlocking discussions about living standards, workers' rights, wage levels, education and social solidarity.

2 Post-War Labour Shortages—Resettlement of Refugees and Displaced Persons

Around ninety million people were either killed or displaced in Europe between the years 1938 and 1948. The unimaginable level of loss of life and the extraordinary movements of peoples that followed the end of the war are unprecedented in human history. Also unprecedented was the extent to which the nineteenth-century ideals of self-determination, which had metamorphosed into ideas of the nation based on shared language, culture and history, were deployed in cynical and often brutal ways by both the Western victorious powers, the Soviet Union and the newly-independent Eastern European countries which rapidly fell under Soviet control. Around 17 million people were moved from their historical homelands and forcibly transferred into neighbouring states.[1] These policies were justified by a desire to reduce the political inflammation of irredentism (which led to a yearning from inside a country to *include* others within it, or a yearning from a particular group *to be included* in another polity) but also a more general acceptance that '*countries are built on national lines and not on multinational ones*'[2]—a demand to *exclude* people.

Those forced migrations gave rise to thousands of refugees. Many of those ordered to move joined the many thousands of displaced persons who had been deported and enslaved by the Nazis, those who had survived concentration camps and prison camps, and those fleeing as the Eastern Front drove westwards and the Iron Curtain descended. The scale of the relief operation was enormous even compared to today's refugee problems, at a time when mainland Europe's industry and infrastructure were largely destroyed, and the whole of Europe faced significant shortages of food. In September 1945, the United Nations[3] Relief and Rehabilitation Administration (UNRRA) was caring for or arranging the repatriation of 6,795,000 liberated United Nations civilians (i.e., not including citizens of former Axis countries). A new organisation, the International Refugee Organisation, replacing UNRRA, was tasked with evaluating the displaced persons, who had to prove that they were genuine refugees and not war criminals.

A resettlement programme was developed for those who could not be returned to their own countries. Gatrell (2019) describes a rough and ready selection process based on physical health and strength and also on an 'unspoken ethnic hierarchy'. A Quaker relief worker had described the selection process as a 'slave market'.[4]

In an early example of 'burden-sharing', Britain agreed to take a share of refugees and displaced persons to be resettled in the UK. Neither for Britain nor for any of the other receiving countries was this an entirely humanitarian programme. A large proportion of the displaced persons were under 45, and most of the men were skilled or semi-skilled. Britain was suffering a desperate shortage of labour power as well as a falling population.

Contemporary government discussions of British population issues showed some of the same views as those on which the development of the Empire was based, i.e. that the general population amounts to a source of labour power (with or without attendant family members) and explicit population policies might be necessary to ensure an adequate supply of workers. Official reports published in 1942 and 1948 looked at British population trends and concluded that the birth rate was too low to avert population decline and that a rate of immigration of between 50,000 and 100,000 per year might be needed, and, given the very large numbers who wished or planned to emigrate to the Dominions, an annual immigration rate of 170,000 per year might be needed.[5] That there would be opposition to this was accepted. The PEP report of 1948[6] noted that Britain had not yet adopted a coherent population policy. The report (explicitly resting on racial thinking and eugenics) proposes consideration of a population policy in which 'good' parents should be persuaded or induced to have more children.[7] The report recommends 'careful selection' of permanent immigrants, which would '*eliminate mental defectives, people with mental disorders or heritable defects, and social misfits*' but would also avoid segregation.[8] The report considers the ethical issues of labour migration, and notes that '*provided the contract is freely entered into, there is no injustice*'. However, the report recognises that '*insofar as immigrants are permanently satisfied with lower standards... they constitute a threat to the interests of the British working class...*'.[9]

Using foreign labour was a controversial matter. In a 1946 parliamentary debate on the labour shortage, Peter Thorneycroft[10] noted that the coal industry had said that they could solve their problems by employing 100,000 Poles in the mines.[11] Some feared that the Poles might have fought for the Nazis or alternatively be supporters of the Soviet Union. Other speakers were wary of offering work to foreigners when over a million men remained to be demobilised and reintegrated into civilian work. The national Trades Union Congress (TUC), in a 1947 conference debate on a motion concerning foreign labour, argued that there were other sources of labour besides foreigners, but they did accept, as the government did, that '*there was no danger for years to come that foreign labour will rob British workers of their jobs...*'.[12]

Nevertheless, with memories of the Depression, organised labour responses were often hostile, not to the individuals but to the principle of employing foreign workers. Edgerton (2018)[13] notes that workers in heavy industries such as coal mining were desperate for unemployment not to return, and wanted labour conditions to be improved '*to attract the voluntary labour of British boys in British mines*'. Only 8,500 resettled workers were given jobs in the mines, against a target of 30,000.

To deal with the over 100,000 Polish troops stationed in Britain at the end of the war the Government proposed a Polish Resettlement Corps, in which Polish veterans would enrol and be resettled through being directed to work in essential industries including agriculture, construction and mining. A bill was presented in February 1947. The Communist Party of Great Britain (CPGB), which at that time was strongly represented in the unions and had two Members of Parliament, were strongly critical of this scheme, referring to the Poles as 'fascists', claiming that at least a third of Poles in Britain had fought for Hitler; and spread other rumours typical of any racist propaganda, such as accusations of foreign individuals sexually molesting young girls.[14] More broadly the CPGB announced its opposition to all the schemes for employing foreign labour, including Poles, Italians and Irish, as being schemes to prevent British people from achieving decent conditions of work.[15] This CPGB opposition to post-war foreign workers contrasted with its opposition to racism against Commonwealth and colonial subjects throughout the Empire, and could not solely be explained by the party's subjection to official Soviet policy requiring displaced citizens of Eastern Europe to be returned there. R Palme Dutt, a leading CPGB member and prominent Stalinist, argued that the shortage of workers arose from Britain's maintenance of its colonies, its membership of NATO and its Cold War military expenditure, and the party expressed solidarity with colonial peoples demanding self-determination. But these arguments could not account for the specific racist invective against the Poles.

Britain eventually accepted around 300,000 displaced people, of whom 86,000 were accepted into European Voluntary Worker schemes such as 'Operation Westward Ho', including 30,000 Ukrainians, 14,000 Poles, 12,000 Latvians and 10,000 Yugoslavs. These came in addition to 115,000 Polish Resettlement Corps members, and 8,000 former members of the 14th Waffen SS Ukrainian Halychyna Division, resettled from Italy '*despite the officially acknowledged inadequacy of their screening for war crimes*'.[16] The criteria explicitly required those who could work, and '*assimilable racial types*'. Conditions included short-term contracts, no guarantee of permanent resettlement, and signed undertakings not to change jobs without permission. If found unsatisfactory, a person could be returned to the DP camps. In the UK, these conditions were negotiated with the trade unions, who did at least stick out for equal pay so as not to undercut British workers. The UK recruited men to work in heavy industry, and women to work in hospitals, favouring women from the Baltic states. Jews had been routinely excluded, only around 3000 gaining entry, and, extraordinarily in the circumstances, had been regarded as economic migrants.[17] Under the Polish Resettlement Act 1947, for the first six months of the scheme dependants could be brought in, though families were often split and sent to work in different parts of the UK. After January 1948, no relatives could be brought in, and people had to sign to say that they were 'single and unattached'. Under the rules operating in the Ukrainian scheme, a young lad who lost his sight in an industrial accident and who could therefore no longer work had to be deported.[18] At the Fourth Session of the United Nations, the UK was accused of making those workers '*victims of an official policy of discrimination*'.

Those Polish workers were entitled to unemployment benefit, and several government departments were made responsible for providing health services, pension entitlement and education. Following Foreign Secretary Ernest Bevin's 1946 comment that '*we cannot launch all these people, not even knowing our language, onto the labour market and leave the whole thing in chaos*',[19] significant resources were provided for teaching English, providing lengthy health and safety training for miners and providing basic accommodation despite the severe housing shortage.

For Foot, it was the post-war promise of full employment along with the terrible fear of not being able to attain it which led to the post-war Labour government's continued support for restrictive policies towards aliens—even despite the desperate shortages of labour in almost every branch of the economy.[20] Tory MP Peter Thorneycroft again: '*What about the foreign workers? … I find something a little contemptible about a party which preaches internationalism abroad and yet takes every step to prevent free men coming here to work.*[21]

Future Prime Minister James Callaghan, an ex-union official and then a back-bench MP, agreed. He supported a motion demanding that Britain '*become a country where immigrants are welcomed. We should break away from this artificial segregation of nation from nation … who is going to pay for the old age pensions and social services unless we have an addition to our population, which only immigration can provide for years to come?*'.[22]

3 Turning Commonwealth Citizens into Guest Workers: The Commonwealth Immigrants Act 1962, the Immigration Act 1971

However, racial thinking intervened. Chapter 2 recounted how the Commonwealth Immigrants Act provided for restrictions on entry both of citizens of independent Commonwealth countries ('Commonwealth citizens') and certain Citizens of the UK and Colonies (CUKCs). Government discussions had considered restrictions based on the availability of accommodation, but settled on controlling entry via controlling access to the labour market. Work vouchers were to be prioritised for skilled workers and those who had job offers, explicitly to ensure that most applicants from the white dominions would be successful, while black and Asian applicants, more often unskilled and without job offers, would fail. The Bill also required five years' residence before a Commonwealth citizen could acquire British nationality, and introduced measures allowing for Commonwealth citizens to be deported.

Chapter 2 showed how neither that Act nor the 1968 Act quelled the demands for more restrictions, and how eventually both main political parties supported comprehensive immigration control. The Immigration Act 1971 reduced Commonwealth and Colonial citizens seeking entry to the same status as 'aliens'—only able to enter if meeting the Immigration Rules' requirements for visitors, students, family members or labour migrants.

It was noted in debates that the 1971 Immigration Bill's labour migration measures were bound to weaken workplace solidarity. The Bill provided for Commonwealth citizens to enter on 12-months work visas tied to specific workplaces. Callaghan, an ex-trade union official, described the problems facing all labour migrants on limited visas and conditions—the risk of discrimination and of being subject to employers' 'petty tyranny'. Macdonald, in the first immigration law textbook following the Act,[23] notes however that while the Tories' Industrial Relations Act 1971, passing through Parliament at the same time as the Immigration Act, faced significant opposition, the Immigration Act met almost none, despite its proposing '*a far more rigid system of control and discipline over one section of the work-force than anything contained in the Industrial Relations Act ... to discipline, with the threat of deportation, the kind of action which the immigrant population has been taking at work and in their communities, and to make sure that any new immigrants are under such tight discipline from the moment they land in Britain that they are incapable of initiating struggle*'.[24]

Paul Gordon argues that the 1971 measures rendered Commonwealth immigrants into guest workers as in West Germany, showing the UK's increasing reluctance '*to bear the social cost of providing housing, education, health and social security for the worker's dependants, while benefiting from the profits of his or her labour*'.[25] He notes that it remained a criminal offence for an 'alien' to promote industrial unrest unless he or she had been employed for over 2 years.[26] It is not known whether this measure was ever used, either against isolated individuals or against groups of strikers during a major industrial dispute. But those measures must have helped to perpetrate the racial discrimination and workplace segregation present in Britain at that time: and may well have contributed to the lack of support from the trade union movement and Labour politicians for black and Asian workers in major workplace disputes such as at Grunwicks.

4 Open Doors? Expansion of Work Permits; the Points-Based System

The 2002 White Paper *Secure Borders, Safe Haven*[27] set out the Labour government's more open policy on labour migration:

> We have taken steps to ensure that people with the skills and talents we need are able to come into the UK on a sensible and managed basis.

Some of the changes were technical, including simplifying the eligibility criteria and introducing an electronic application system, which had improved processing times from 70% in one week by January 2001 to

90% within one week at the time of the White Paper. A new Innovator Scheme was introduced:

> We estimate that each individual entering through this Scheme will create an additional 10 jobs for UK workers.

The White Paper did not ignore the potential impact on the host community of increasing labour immigration:

> It is, however, in those communities least likely to have benefited from added value economic activity and entrepreneurship where the biggest challenge lies. For even at a time of high levels of economic activity and buoyant employment, the low skill or no skill groupings are likely to be most fearful of the low skill, no skill entrant into the local economy. But research suggests that migrants do not compete for jobs with existing workers. The idea that there are only a fixed number of jobs in the economy has been discredited.

The White Paper provides a table giving numbers of work permits and first permissions to work from 1946 to 1998, which shows that yearly work permit numbers expanded steadily from around 10,000 in 1946 to around 70,000 in 1974, the year of the UK's accession to the European Common Market, upon which work permit grants fell to around 30,000. From then until the mid-1980s grants fell further to around 15,000, not reaching around 30,000 again till around 1992. This may be explained by mirroring the White Paper table with a table[28] showing UK unemployment rates from 1970 to 2015. This shows unemployment rising from around 4% in 1975 to 6% in the late 1970s, then spectacularly to 12% in 1985, falling from then back to around 5% in the early 2000s until rising again in the late 2000s after the 2008 financial crash. The unemployment figures suggest that in 2002, after a long and steep fall in the unemployment rate, an increase in labour migration could have been thought less likely to affect job-seeking in the host community and may even have been necessary to fill skill shortages. A 2009 Home Affairs Committee report noted that '*from 1992 to 2007 the UK experienced a continuous period of sustained economic growth, averaging real growth of 2.8 per cent per annum. However, in 2008 growth fell to 0.7 per cent, and in the third quarter of 2008 it was negative*'.[29]

The White Paper gives figures for 2000 for all the labour migration routes into the UK. This shows that work permits were the largest category at 67,100 or 35.1%, working holidaymakers a surprisingly large category at 38,500 or 20.1%, larger even than EU nationals at 35,700 or 18.7%. The remaining categories were domestic employees of foreign residents, au pairs, those of UK ancestry, seasonal agricultural workers, ministers of religion and 50 investors, totalling 190,830 for that year.[30] The Home Affairs Committee report contrasts work permits given in 1995 and 2007, just before the points-based system was introduced: '*In 1995 a total of 24,161 permits were issued, and in 2007 a total of 83,968: over three times as many. In 1995 the greatest proportion of permits was issued for administration, business and management services, whereas in 2007 it was for computer services*'.[31]

As well as deciding to charge for the issue of work permits, the White Paper confirmed the introduction of a new Highly Skilled Migrant Programme:

> [3.18] ... This represents a further step in developing our immigration system to maximise the benefits to the UK of high human capital individuals, who have the qualifications and skills required by UK businesses to compete in the global marketplace.

The White Paper also proposed to allow students to remain for work after graduating, to enable the UK to remain competitive in the market for international students, who would be more attracted to studying in a country that permitted postgraduate work experience:

> [3.23] we will make explicit provision in the Immigration Rules for graduating degree level students, student nurses, and postgraduate doctors and dentists to transfer into the work permit employment category...

It was suggested that this measure was also intended to help pay for the expansion of higher education.[32]

On 13 November 2003, David Blunkett announced on Newsnight that he wanted '*more skilled workers to come legally…especially in the catering, hospitality and construction industries*'. He saw '*no obvious limit*' to the number of skilled migrants who could arrive.[33] A later Migration Watch report[34] notes, however, that a significant proportion of post-study work students were employed in semi-skilled or unskilled roles, implying that their presence in the UK was unnecessary as they were not bringing the benefits said to accrue from postgraduate migration.

By 1 May 2004, the date of EU enlargement, there were over 80 different routes of entry to the UK for non-EU nationals for the purpose of work.[35]

In 2006 the government published *A Points-Based System: Making Migration Work for Britain*.[36] In the introduction Home Secretary Charles Clarke stated:

> The UK needs a world class migration system to attract the brightest and the best from across the world, while at the same time being more robust against abuse. … By simplifying the current complex system in this way we can ensure that only those who legitimately apply and have the necessary skills can come to this country.

The aim was to eliminate the two-stage process in which an employer, satisfying a labour market test, may be granted a work permit, but the particular migrant applicant could still be refused leave to enter in a decision taken by different officials according to different criteria. The new system required employers as sponsors to obtain a licence to employ foreign workers, and the prospective workers to apply via a simplified and more objective system based on their current qualifications, salary and experience. Points were to be awarded for attributes (intended to predict a migrant's success in the labour market) and control factors (which relate to whether someone is likely to comply with the conditions of their leave),[37] with prescribed evidence required for each attribute, enabling a 'more structured approach' to decision-making. There would be no discretion in considering the application, and no right of appeal except on human rights grounds, though there would be limited administrative review. Additionally, educational establishments would have a continuing responsibility for seeing that their students complied with the terms of their visa, by checking on their attendance on courses and that they do not exceed the hours of employment permitted to them. As well as administrative review, oversight of the new system was to be achieved by augmenting the role of the Independent Monitor of entry clearance applications:

> 54. ... [giving] a remit to report on a six-monthly rather than annual basis. This will enable UKvisas to respond more quickly to any lapses in quality that might be identified in the reports.

The points-based system was launched on 28 February 2008 with the implementation of Tier 1. Tiers 2 and 5 were implemented on 27 November 2008; Tier 4 on 31 March 2009. Tier 2 required satisfaction of a labour market test.

Launching the new system in February 2008, the then Home Secretary Jacqui Smith MP stated:

> 'The introduction of our Australian-style points-based system will ensure that only those with skills the country needs can come. Migrants benefit this country economically, contributing an estimated £6bn to our national output, as well as socially and culturally, and it is right that we have a system which is fair but firm, accessible but controlled'. (my emphasis)

In February 2009, tightening up the Tier 1 and Tier 2 criteria, the Home Office said: '*it is right in a downturn to be more selective about the skill levels of those migrants, and to do more to put British workers first*'. CBI Chair John Cridland was reported by the HAC as saying '*whilst he was sympathetic to the concerns of British workers facing possible job losses, "it is important that people understand that all workers in the European Union, unless there are transitional arrangements as with some East European states, have the right to work here if there are jobs to be done"*'.[38]

Although Tier 3 had been set up for unskilled or 'low-skilled' labour, the intention was to phase out non-EU unskilled labour. Tier 3 was never opened, despite pressure from the hospitality, agriculture and social care sectors. However, the TUC, responding to consultation, had said: '*In some cases, for instance, the labour shortages which exist are due to the low levels of pay and conditions on offer'*.[39] The HAC report noted at [115] that in 2004, the Seasonal Agricultural Workers Scheme (SAWS) and Sectors Based Scheme (SBS) together provided approximately 32,000 migrants to the UK, compared to the 329,000 EU A8 workers who registered to work in the UK in the 2 years since enlargement, the 294,000 students who are free to work (20 hours/week in term-time and 40 hours/week in holidays) plus working holidaymakers and migrants on family visas with permission to work. The evidence was that the hospitality and agricultural sectors were increasingly recruiting EU national workers and there was no need for non-EU unskilled labour. Nevertheless, altogether the expansion of the work permit system and the operation of the subsequent points-based system led to the arrival of around one million new non-EU labour migrants.

In 2009 the Home Affairs Committee published a report on the new system.[40] The predictable criticisms included its lack of ability to reflect work experience in the 'attributes', for example, preferring a masters' degree to 25 years' proven international management experience, or being unable properly to reflect what ballet dancers, sportspeople or musicians actually do. John Cridland, Chair of the CBI, urged that UKBA telephone enquiry lines be answered by people '*who are able to use their discretion in giving advice rather than a tendency to read out the literal wording of regulations, which is not always helpful to someone who has bothered to phone them*'. The biggest criticisms concerned delays in issuing visas, especially for those seeking to enter for a short but prestigious occasion such as to conduct an opera performance, and the lack of legal redress, in particular that the administrative review procedure did not admit further evidence such as a payslip inadvertently left out of the application. This system predictably led to major litigation.

In her short essay in a 2010 IPPR report,[41] Barbara Roche recounts how, on being appointed Minister of State in the Home Office in 1999, she had asked 'what our policy was' on immigration other than asylum and was told that there was no policy. She stated that 'Britain was a country of immigrants', and that her time at the Department of Trade and Industry and at the Treasury had convinced her that, in an age of globalisation, legal migration was an economic as well as a social and cultural good. That lay behind her 2000 speech to the IPPR which emphasised the benefits of immigration. Britain wanted to attract '*the entrepreneurs, the scientists, the high-technology specialists who make the world economy tick*'. However, in her 2010 essay she accepted that '*Labour struggled to convince the public that it had a grip on the issue and failed to articulate how managed migration could be a source of competitive advantage ... the failure to do so left us vulnerable to the anti-immigration message of our political opponents and groups such as Migration Watch*'.[42]

Sarah Spencer, in the same IPPR report, says that IPPR had been arguing since 1994 that Britain needed to be more open to labour migration if it was to remain competitive. She referred to Tony Blair's '*campaign to secure 25% of the English-speaking international student market*'. However, she notes that '*there is less agreement now on the benefits of large-scale migration. A much-cited House of Lords inquiry in 2008 was notably sceptical, and, emerging from recession, it is easier to see that the benefits to an employer do not necessarily translate into benefits for all*'.[43] She sets that against the extra 9,500 doctors and 20,000 nurses brought in to work in the NHS.

More interesting are her broader comments on the issue of labour migration. She notes that Labour did invest in training places for doctors and nurses, to reduce reliance on labour migration, but found it difficult in a climate of public expenditure cuts to tackle the low pay and poor working conditions in sectors such as social care, and '*in sectors where employers and agencies are determined to exploit irregular migrants. The Gangmasters' Licensing Authority and the Minimum Wage were important steps, but ultimately inadequate to curtail the spaces in which vulnerable workers can be exploited...High tech border controls are no substitute for tackling demand*'.[44] The Gangmasters Licensing Authority, now the Gangmasters and Labour Abuse Authority, was set up in 2006 after the horrific deaths in Morecambe Bay of 23 Chinese cockle-pickers who, working at night, drowned in the incoming tide. A 'gangmaster' was convicted of manslaughter, facilitating illegal immigration and perverting the course of justice.[45] It is clear that, from an employer's point of view, the pressures in construction, social care and food production to keep prices low and still make a profit clearly favour non-unionised workforces on low wages in poor working conditions, often leaving migrant workers as the only ones prepared, or able, to accept such conditions.[46]

5 Unlimited Free Movement Following EU Enlargement in 2004

On 1 May 2004 ten new Member States joined the EU, made up of eight countries from Eastern Europe referred to as the A8 countries, plus Cyprus and Malta. Along with Ireland and Sweden, the UK did not set any limits on free movement of workers from the A8 countries. Those coming for employment were required to obtain a Workers Registration Scheme (WRS) certificate showing where they were working, and remain with that employer for 12 months, after which they entered free movement proper. The WRS was not intended to limit the number of applicants, but rather to enable the numbers to be monitored.

Free movement status also automatically included the estimated 100,000 A8 nationals already in the UK, including holders of sector-based permits, seasonal agricultural workers (SAWS) permits, the self-employed, au pairs, students, dependants, asylum-seekers and others unlawfully present or undefined. Especially for those who were 'failed asylum-seekers' or people with outstanding asylum claims, such as Polish Roma, accession had the effect of an amnesty. The Joseph Rowntree 2006 report *Fair enough?*[47] researched the background and experiences of those A8 nationals who were already in the UK on accession day. Of those who were working, most were working in *agriculture and food processing*, in which seasonal demands for labour are typically filled through agents or 'gangmasters'; *construction*, in which workers generally present as self-employed under the long-standing tax-avoiding 'labour-only subcontractor' arrangement; *hospitality*, often employing students, working holidaymakers and other young people; and in the *au pair sector*, in which the work often informally expanded into the provision of home care. Generally their pay was lower than the national average and at or around the minimum wage for the occupation. Very few received non-wage benefits such as paid sick leave or holiday pay. Many interviewees explained that they had been prepared to take hard low-paid work below their level of education or intellectual ability, simply to earn far more money than they ever could in their own country.

The *Fair Enough?* report notes the different stratagems some A8 workers and Ukrainians had used before enlargement to get into the UK to work and notes that some A8 nationals had tolerated the disadvantages and risks of working illegally in the knowledge that they would soon be entitled to free movement. But even those who were working legally faced problems typical of the sectors they were working in—no written contract, not paying tax or national insurance, no job security, especially for those working through agencies. The *Fair Enough?* project re-interviewed their sample workers a few months after enlargement and found that some of those existing labour migrants were complaining about newly-arrived Polish workers offering and agreeing to work for lower wages.[48] This highlights the inevitable problems of using labour migrants in low-paid non-unionised sectors such as hospitality, catering and social care.

Formally, both government and business had completely accepted the premise and the effect of permitting free movement to A8 citizens, even accepting the premise of a 'citizenship of the EU' at least for workers. The 2006 paper proposing the points-based system had said this:

> [migration] can leave settled populations, including many in the UK, concerned about the impact on jobs, public services and their way of life. The system should therefore be focused primarily on bringing in migrants who are highly skilled or to do key jobs that cannot be filled from the domestic labour force or from the EU ...[49]

It has been estimated that from 2004 to 2010 over 600,000 EU nationals arrived, mainly from the A8 countries. Migration Watch later described this as '*one of the largest peacetime movements of people in European history*'.[50] It is accepted now that the predictions of quite small numbers of prospective arrivals relied on the other EU Member States' not imposing restrictions on free movement from the newly-acceded countries—which they did not do until the last minute. It was also argued that those assumptions were also based on past experience of previous

EEC accessions where the wages and living standards of the new Member States were not so far below those of the existing EEC members—though that was disputed.[51] Migration Watch asserts: '*There was no public discussion or consultation and David Goodhart later claimed that this decision was taken by a small group of officials and Special Advisers prior to a European Council meeting in Brussels*'.[52]

In the 2010 IPPR report referred to above, John Denham, Minister of State at the Home Office until 2003, offers a critique of the decision on unrestricted free movement for the newly-acceded EU nationals in 2004, based on his experience as MP for Southampton Itchen during that period. He notes the lack of coordination within government:

> Much of the government machine … worked against the Home Office ministers struggling valiantly to get the system in order. Treasury growth forecasts relied on the wage-depressing effects of continued migration. Business departments reflected the economic need to bring in skilled labour … and were wary of onerous enforcement of employers' use of illegal or exploited labour. Successive education departments resisted attempts to close bogus colleges. Social security disowned problems with national insurance numbers and did not want to tackle anomalies in the EU benefits agreements. And when [EU migration] exceeded all predictions, the entire government system proved unable to provide … timely and reliable analyses of what had actually happened.[53]

He emphasises Labour's failure to pay attention to the 'corrosive' local effects:

> I tracked A8 migration in my constituency, but was confronted with official data which underestimated the number of migrants by 90% and did not reflect the impact on wage rates in the construction industry …

The Guardian reports how he pressed those concerns after he had resigned from the government over the Iraq war:

> In February 2006, [John Denham] wrote a prophetic memo to Tony Blair, chancellor Gordon Brown and home secretary Charles Clarke, warning that … roughly 14,000 eastern European immigrants had arrived

> in Southampton within the previous 18 months. This was placing immense pressure on maternity services and leading employers to lower wages …
>
> Outlining the impact on the everyday lives of his constituents, Denham argued at the time that resentment of immigration would grow. '*One of the problems was that people were supposed to register if they were employed but many came as self-employed*', Denham says. '*The biggest impacts were in self-employed trades like construction, where you didn't have to register.*' … the daily rate for a builder in the city had fallen by 50% since 2004. He also noted that hospital accident and emergency services were under strain because migrants tended not to use GPs as a first port of call. It also turned out that the local further education college had to close its doors after 1,000 migrants attempted to sign up for an English-as-a-second-language course on just one day. Whitehall, Denham argued, was wholly out of touch with the concerns of his constituents.[54]

The percentage of UK residents born abroad (non-UK-born nor UK national) is now 14%, of which those born in the European Union are the largest group, at 5% of the UK resident population.[55]

6 The 2008 Financial Crash and Aftermath: Brexit and Beyond

Towards the end of 2007 it became evident that a major financial crisis was about to hit the world. Arising from a combination of deregulation of banking and financial services especially in the US and UK, and a world recession leading to unemployment and mortgage defaults, major banks around the world faced failure, and the world's leading capitalist economies were forced to prop up the banking system and take further measures to prevent economic collapse. Those measures were accidentally described in public by then Labour Prime Minister Gordon Brown as '*we not only saved the world…*'[56] and by the Conservative Party in their 2010 election manifesto as '*Labour's debt crisis … the terrible legacy that Gordon Brown is bequeathing to our country*'.[57] The crisis and its aftermath led to a government debt still, ten years later, twice as high as before the crisis, despite severe spending cuts, and a fall of 6% in economic growth in the year following the crash, leaving GDP at around 16% less than if the crisis had not happened.[58] UK unemployment, at around 5% in 2008, rose to almost 8% in 2009 and remained there for some time. (All that is predicted to be dwarfed by the recession caused by the impact of Covid, the outcome of which is not clear at the time of writing.)

The 2008 crash may have contributed to a slowdown in the number of migrants entering the UK, and seemed to have also reduced rates of emigration—entirely understandable, as the crisis affected most of the world.[59] The impact on immigration appears to have been that while some EU migrants returned home (for example, to Poland, where the economy continued to grow), more migrants came to the UK from EU countries more severely affected by the crash, such as Greece and Spain, as well as more people from France and Germany.[60] The numbers of working-age people from outside the UK slowed slightly in 2008 before continuing to rise as before.[61]

It is not clear to what extent the crash and ensuing recession influenced the salience of immigration in the 2010 election. That seems to owe more to a widespread feeling that control over immigration had been lost in every way, whether shown by the continued presence of 'illegals', the 'human rights barriers' to deporting foreign criminals, the alleged proliferation of 'dodgy colleges' with 'dodgy foreign students', with the vastly increased labour migration and unlimited free movement of EU workers being the last straws. The 2010 election results were unconvincing, leading to a Liberal Democrat-Conservative coalition, but it was the Conservatives' immigration control agenda which has dominated since then. Priority—to reduce labour migration to a controllable element, as it arguably had been before EU enlargement so significantly increased those arriving through free movement.

In relation to non-EU labour migrants, the principal restrictions have been to limit the categories able to move to settlement and to increase the salary levels for jobs allowed to be filled by foreign workers. The first led to the *HSMP* litigation,[62] discussed in Chapter 6, in which it was accepted that migrants on that programme did indeed have a legitimate expectation of being allowed to settle. After losing in court, the Home Office was careful not to make any more such promises. The second predictably led to problematic shortages in the health and social care sectors, requiring the introduction of ad-hoc programmes and increased access to shortage occupation measures.

Once the UK had voted for Brexit, the Conservative government immediately made proposals for an *Australian-style points-based system.* There appear to be no legal or conceptual differences between it and the system introduced by Labour in 2007 apart from that it will apply to EU nationals. This type of labour migration policy, consciously aimed at recruiting the 'brightest and the best', treats the rest of the world as a *reserve*, in which workers already trained, educated and experienced at the expense of their own country will be permitted to enter and work, but on worse terms than UK workers. Two well-known problems arise from such a system. As in West Germany's post-war guest worker system, and the similar 'rotation' system imposed in Switzerland, businesses and public entities face extra costs of recruitment, training and wasted on-the-job experience from having constantly to replace workers on time-limited visas. For the migrants themselves, this means no putting down roots, no falling in love, no accidental pregnancies and no protection in case of changed circumstances. The difference between such migrants and, for example, Filipina domestic workers in Singapore and Hong Kong on yearly contracts with compulsory pregnancy tests and deportation if found pregnant, and the well-known oppressive conditions facing Bangladeshi construction workers in the Gulf states,[63] is only a matter of degree. Even our coronavirus hero overseas doctors and nurses are legally 'precarious'.[64]

To work quickly, such schemes must resort to contrivances, such as assessing skill by salary levels. This never works. Low public sector salaries, reduced further by austerity, meant that the scheme excluded most nurses, requiring the introduction of a special scheme, and the post-Brexit scheme excludes care workers, even lower paid because of cuts to local authority funding for social care, and classed as low skilled. Even before the Immigration Bill 2020[65] received its second reading, the government announced a special 'fast track NHS visa'.[66]

In 2018 the Conservatives said of their proposals: '*This will be a system where it is workers' skills that matter, not which country they come from*',[67] and in the 2019 election campaign they defined '*fairness*' as '*blind to ethnic origin*'. But preference may be given as part of future trade deals, and those from 'low risk countries' would be able to apply for visas from inside the UK '*or have different evidential requirements*'—policies which have previously led to complaints of discrimination from affronted foreign officials, industry bodies and commentators.[68] Countries of emigration do not all have the same provision of high-quality education and experience—nearly half the skilled work visas issued during 2019 were to people from India.[69]

In contrast, legal and academic commentators have criticised as 'unfair' any policies which seek to limit numbers of labour migrants, whether from a particular country or to fill particular roles such as unskilled or seasonal. Even the 2020 Home Office policy statement[70] suggests that current policy is '*failing the highly-skilled migrants from around the world who want to come to the UK and make a contribution to our economy and society*'. But to speak of '*failing... the people who want to come...*' implies that 'wanting to come' has created a reciprocal obligation. It is unlikely the Conservative government, or the voting population generally, intends that.

The 'new' system was declared 'open' on 1 December 2020. In a press release,[71] Home Secretary Priti Patel said:

> Applications for the new skilled worker visa open today (1 December), meaning the brightest and the best from around the world can now apply to work in the UK from 1 January 2021.
>
> ...
>
> It will also encourage employers to focus on training and investing in the UK workforce, driving productivity and improving opportunities for individuals, especially those impacted by coronavirus.

A lengthy 'further details' statement[72] sets out among other things the salary amounts and qualifications required for the different 'routes'; whether dependants may accompany the applicant; whether 'switching' (applying to remain in the UK on a different basis, such as marriage) is permitted, and whether settlement is possible. Already, between the announcement of the scheme in February 2020 and its introduction, low-paid sectors stigmatised as low skilled, including social care workers and fruit pickers, have argued that the new scheme's salary requirements will make it impossible to recruit, and already the vaunted simplicity of the scheme has had to be muddied, either by the introduction of special rules for certain sectors, or simply adding the category to the shortage occupation list—a rough and ready way of disapplying the scheme, arguably also having the political benefit of distancing the decision to an independent body—the Migration Advisory Committee.

The plethora of different categories makes the scheme look more like the pre-2007 work permit system, and the lack of family reunion and settlement for many 'routes' make those routes look like a true guest worker programme. Neither is it clear how the scheme '*will encourage employers to focus on training and investing in the UK workforce*', since that clearly requires resources, whether from increased wages and benefits enabling higher prices to be paid for those employers' outputs, or from government subsidies. It is more likely that sectors such as social care will become more 'broken' as recruitment becomes even more difficult: and British fruit growing will become uncompetitive. Neither is it clear how the scheme will '*[drive] productivity and improving opportunities for individuals, especially those impacted by coronavirus*'. While there are robots which can accurately pick fruit, nobody has yet shown how individual social care can be robotised. What we see instead is a brutal system involving care workers travelling between clients' homes in their own vehicles and on their own time, to microwave a meal, wipe the client down and do rudimentary washing up in the 15 minutes allowed before moving to the next client, all paid for by local authorities starved of funds. The 'new Australian-style points-based system' is already worsening the enormous problem of social care, a major sector highly dependent on low-paid migrant labour. During the summer of 2021 Britain endured significant fuel shortages exacerbated by a shortage of HGV drivers.[73] This led to a quick announcement offering 3-month visas. By 5 October, only 27 had applied, and the length of visa had to be extended.[74]

Altogether the discussions about the 'new' scheme ignore a tension between the urgent needs for workers which can only be filled by recruitment from abroad, and existing residents' fears of competition in the labour market—and, as economic conditions worsen in the receiving country, these fears grow. Social and workplace solidarity demand that migrants should work and live on the same basis as existing residents. On the other hand, giving newly-arrived migrants equal rights, especially to social benefits, may itself be socially corroding. Arguments about 'benefits scroungers' were used to support demands for curtailing EU nationals' access to social benefits, and eventually for curtailing free movement altogether. And it is accepted that there may be local impacts especially in sectors paying low wages. Labour MP John Cruddas:

> Immigration has been used as an informal reserve army of cheap labour. People see this at their workplace, feel it in their pocket and see it in their community, and therefore see it as a critical component of their own relative impoverishment. Objectively, the social wage of many of my constituents is in decline … at work, their conditions, in real terms, are in decline through the unregulated use of cheap immigrant labour. [Cruddas, Lab, Dag, 2005][75]

On the other hand, there are other cohorts of migrants already in the UK who may have the relevant qualifications and experience, who are desperate to work and make a contribution, and who, realistically, are unlikely to be removed. However, residence and permission to work is refused to asylum-seekers and others in the 'migration refusal pool', even if possessing the same qualifications as a person to be recruited from the global South, 'to maintain the integrity of immigration control'.[76]

In conclusion, inviting a cohort of migrants into the UK to work, on time-limited visas and conditions, and with no or limited access to social benefits, family reunion or settlement, raises a multiplicity of contested political issues which are not capable of being resolved by importing an imprecise notion of 'fairness' into the discussion, nor by airy assertions that other large economic problems will thereby be solved, but needs a wide democratic discussion of all the issues.

Notes

1. Gatrell, Peter. 2019. *The unsettling of Europe—The great migration 1945 to the present* London: Allen Lane.

2. Wladyslaw Gomulka, a communist who subsequently led Poland—quoted in Gattrell, ibid. [23] fn [8].
3. At that time still just the wartime Allies, as not yet formally constituted as a supranational body.
4. Gatrell n1 [47].
5. Stadulis, Elizabeth. 1962. *the resettlement of displaced persons in the United Kingdom* Population Studies vol 5 no 3 pp 207–237.
6. PEP *Population policy in Great Britain—A report by PEP* April 1948.
7. Ibid. [95].
8. Ibid. [9].
9. Ibid. [110–112].
10. Conservative MP for Monmouth who under the 1951 Tory government became President of the Board of Trade, and who became a strong opponent of immigration.
11. HC Deb 27 February 1946 vol 419 cc1938-2043 (*Thorneycroft at 1941–2*).
12. Stadulis, n5 [211 fn5].
13. Edgerton, David. 2018. *The rise and fall of the British Nation* London: Allen Lane [97].
14. Smith, Evan. 2015 *Polish migration to post-war Britain* Hatful of History blogpost 5/5/2015, Communist Attitudes towards Polish migration to post-war Britain; https://hatfulofhistory.wordpress.com/2015/05/05/communist-attitudes-towards-polish-migration-to-post-war-britain/ accessed 24/11/21.
15. Ibid., see also Smith, Evan. 2018. *British communism and the politics of race* Chicago: Brill Historical Materialism series, Haymarket.
16. Key, Diana. 1995. *Resettlement of displaced persons in Europe, 1946–65* In *Cambridge Survey of World Migration* ed Robin Cohen, 51–56, Cambridge: Cambridge University Press.
17. Ibid.
18. Foot, Paul. 1965. *Immigration and race in British politics* London: Penguin Special [119].
19. Ibid. [118].
20. Ibid. [116].
21. Ibid. [116] This was a second debate on the issue, on 21/11/1946.
22. Ibid. [117].

23. Macdonald, Ian. 1972. *The new immigration law* London: Butterworths.
24. Ibid. [17].
25. Gordon, Paul. 1981. *Passport raids and checks* Runnymede Trust pamphlet, later reproduced as *Policing Immigration: Britain's internal controls* 1985 Pluto Press.
26. Ibid. [2].
27. *Secure Borders, Safe Haven: Integration with diversity in modern Britain* Home Office 2002 CM 5387.
28. *Secure Borders, Safe Haven:* Source: Department of Employment (1977, 1981); Department for Education and Employment (unpublished); UK SOPEMI Reports (annual); Work Permits (UK). The unemployment figures are from FullFact.org https://fullfact.org/economy/unemployment-under-Labour/ accessed 24/11/21.
29. House of Commons Home Affairs Committee *Managing migration: The points based system* Thirteenth Report of Session 2008–09 HC 217-1 15 July 2009.
30. *Secure Borders, Safe Haven* Source: Home Office admissions data, International Passenger Service (IPS). The citation notes that the table describes the number of entrants to the UK with work permits, a different figure to the number of work permits issued in 2000 (80,000).
31. House of Commons Home Affairs Committee *Managing migration: The points based system* Thirteenth Report of Session 2008–09 HC 217-1 15 July 2009.
32. Finch, Tim and Goodhart, Goodhart. 2010 *Introduction* to *immigration under Labour* London: Institute of Public Policy Research (IPPR).
33. BBC Newsnight 13/11/2003 http://news.bbc.co.uk/1/hi/uk_politics/3265219.stm accessed 24/11/21.
34. Migration Watch. 2015. *Immigration under labour* briefing paper no 355 https://www.migrationwatchuk.org/briefing-paper/355 accessed 24/11/21.
35. Anderson, Bridget et al. 2006. *Fair enough? Central and East European migrants in low-wage employment in the UK* Joseph Rowntree Foundation [3].

36. *A Points-based system: Making migration work for Britain* CM 6741.
37. Ibid. [42].
38. House of Commons Home Affairs Committee *Managing migration: The points based system* Thirteenth Report of Session 2008–09 HC 217-1 15 July 2009.
39. TUC 2006 *Making a rights-based migration system work* para 3.2 https://www.tuc.org.uk/research-analysis/reports/making-rights-based-migration-system-work accessed 24/11/21.
40. HAC report 2009 n38.
41. Owen, Ed. 2010. *Reactive, defensive and weak,* in *Immigration under Labour* ed Finch, Tim and Goodhart, David Goodhart, IPPR.
42. Roche, Barbara. 2010. *Making the best of immense challenges* in *Immigration under Labour.* IPPR [16].
43. Spencer, Sarah. 2010 *Economic gain, political cost* In *Immigration under Labour* IPPR.
44. Ibid. [19].
45. *Morecambe Bay cockling disaster's lasting impact* 3/2/14 (10 years after the event) BBC https://www.bbc.co.uk/news/uk-england-lancashire-25986388 accessed 24/11/21.
46. Anderson 2006 n35.
47. Ibid.
48. Ibid. [59].
49. CM 6741 n36. para 7.
50. Migration Watch. 2015. *Immigration under Labour* 18.21 https://www.migrationwatchuk.org/briefing-paper/355 accessed 24/11/21.
51. Moore, Kerry. 2010 *A cultural study of asylum under new labour* PhD thesis 2010 University of Cardiff School of Journalism, Media and Cultural Studies.
52. Migration Watch. 2015 n50 citing David Goodhart, *Accidental immigration;* Prospect February 2010.
53. Denham, John. 2010. *Fairness, entitlement and common obligation* in *Immigration under Labour* IPPR.
54. Watt, Nicholas and Wintour, Patrick *How immigration came to haunt Labour: the inside story* Guardian 24 March 2015 https://www.theguardian.com/news/2015/mar/24/how-immigration-came-to-haunt-labour-inside-story accessed 24/11/21.

55. Population of the UK by country of birth and nationality: 2020 Office of National Statistics https://www.ons.gov.uk/peoplepopulationandcommunity/populationandmigration/internationalmigration/bulletins/ukpopulationbycountryofbirthandnationality/2020#non-uk-populations-analysis accessed 24/11/21.
56. Gordon Brown, Prime Minister's Questions 10-12-08 cited in the Guardian *Financial crisis- timeline* 7/8/2012, referring to his work persuading the G20 nations to pump money into the world economy. See Kingsley, Patrick https://www.theguardian.com/business/2012/aug/07/credit-crunch-boom-bust-timeline accessed 24/11/21, and Aditya Chakrabortty https://www.theguardian.com/commentisfree/2012/feb/06/gordon-brown-save-world-uk accessed 24/11/21.
57. Conservative Manifesto 2010, Foreword file:///C:\Users\sfy\Downloads\Manifesto2010%20(1).pdf.
58. Cribb, Jonathan and Johnson, Paul, 2018 *10 years on—Have we recovered from the financial crisis?* Institute for Fiscal Studies https://www.ifs.org.uk/publications/13302 accessed 24/11/21.
59. Clark, Ken et al. 2014. *Migration, economic crisis and adjustment in the UK* Bonn: Institute for the Study of Labour (IZA) August 2014 http://ftp.iza.org/dp8410.pdf, accessed 24/11/21, looking at National Insurance registrations.
60. Ibid. [9].
61. Ibid. [10] referring to the 'stock' of migrants.
62. *HSMP Forum UK Limited v SSHD* [2008] EWHC 664.
63. Karasapan, Omer. 2020. *Pandemic highlights the vulnerability of migrant workers in the Middle East* Brookings Institute provides a good summery of the issues. https://www.brookings.edu/blog/future-development/2020/09/17/pandemic-highlights-the-vulnerability-of-migrant-workers-in-the-middle-east/ accessed 24/11/21.
64. *Rhuppiah* [2018] UKSC 58.
65. The resulting Immigration Act 2020 was the legislation which formally ended free movement for EU citizens and introduced the revised points-based system.

66. Stewart, Heather. 2020. https://www.theguardian.com/uk-news/2020/may/18/tories-accused-of-hypocrisy-over-key-workers-with-immigration-bill accessed 24/11/21.
67. HM Government *The UK's future skills-based immigration system* December 2018 Cm 9722.
68. House of Commons Home Affairs Committee *The work of the UK Border Agency (January–March 2013)* Eighth Report of Session 2013–14 HC 616 8/11/13 [40–41]—India, Pakistan, Nigeria, Ghana, Sri Lanka and Bangladesh were the countries to be targeted.
69. ONS Migration Statistics Quarterly Report February 2020.
70. Home Office *The UK's points-based immigration system: Policy statement* https://www.gov.uk/government/publications/the-uks-points-based-immigration-system-policy-statement/the-uks-points-based-immigration-system-policy-statement accessed 24/11/21.
71. Home Office press release https://www.gov.uk/government/news/points-based-immigration-system-opens accessed 24/11/21.
72. Home Office policy paper: *UK points-based immigration system: Further details statement* https://www.gov.uk/government/publications/uk-points-based-immigration-system-further-details-statement/uk-points-based-immigration-system-further-details-statement accessed 24/11/21.
73. Kingsley, Thomas. 2021. https://www.independent.co.uk/news/uk/home-news/fuel-shortages-hgv-drivers-b1928309.html accessed 29/11/21.
74. Duncan, Conrad, Independent 5/10/21. https://www.independent.co.uk/news/uk/home-news/fuel-crisis-eu-drivers-visa-b1932336.html accessed 24/11/21.
75. Cruddas, John. 2005. https://www.theguardian.com/politics/2005/may/20/labour.immigration accessed 29/11/21.
76. Note the case of Ms Oludoyi, a trained nurse with no leave to remain: *Oludoyi & Ors, R (oao) v SSHD (Article 8—MM (Lebanon) and Nagre) (IJR)* [2014] UKUT 539 (IAC).

5

UK Immigration and Asylum Administration—A Public Administration Failure?

1 Introduction

Chapters 2 and 3 demonstrated how successive governments' choices of immigration control measures have led to the bureaucracy's inability to cope. This chapter first shows how the efforts to 'reduce net migration to the tens of thousands' by restrictive Immigration Rules and 'a really hostile environment' have not worked. They have merely exposed the incompetence and casual cruelty of current UK immigration control. It should be astonishing that a UK department of state, responsible for administering the rights and entitlements of millions of people, should fall so short of accepted standards of administration. Surely such poor public administration of immigration control for so long must amount to a *policy*. To discuss this, a simple definition of good public administration is used to evaluate the Home Office's long-standing poor administration and waste of resources on performative and ineffective policies. The evaluation reveals implications both for those who must encounter the system, and for the legal systems by which applicants must manage access to their rights and entitlements. A brief account of the EU Settlement Scheme shows in contrast how simplified requirements,

S. York, *The Impact of UK Immigration Law*,
https://doi.org/10.1007/978-3-030-98721-3_5

a shared burden of proof and adequate administrative resources, have ensured a UK-based legal status for over five million people in just over two years.

2 The Catalysing Effects of Coalition and Conservative Policies

2.1 The 2012 'New Rules'

In 2010 the new government announced important changes to immigration policy: to reduce net migration to the 'tens of thousands'; to reduce labour migrants' and overseas students' access to settlement; to further cut migrants' access to public funds; to cut down reliance on human rights claims especially by foreign criminals and 'illegals'; to restrict the impact of European court judgments giving rights to non-EEA nationals. For family migrants, a pre-arrival English language test, a £18,600 minimum income requirement and a further lengthening of the pre-settlement probationary period were intended '*to test the genuineness of the relationship before permanent residence is granted on the basis of it*'. A further guiding principle was that '*a person who remains unlawfully should not be able to gain advantage by only informing us of their family or private life when they face removal …*'. Applicants meeting all the requirements now enter a '5-year route', requiring three applications to reach settlement. 'Exceptional' provisions allow entry into a '10-year route'. This entails five applications, over 10 years, during which an applicant must continue to satisfy the compulsory criteria and their circumstances must remain broadly the same. Access to public funds is prohibited unless by explicit request showing exceptional circumstances. Application fees for a parent and two children from arrival to settlement have increased from around £1500 in 2009 to over £27,000 by 2021 for the 10-year route plus Immigration Health Surcharge (IHS).[1] The increased administrative burden of repeat applications with more complex requirements was not met by increased resources. Neither was it understood how dragging out routes to settlement would increase insecurity and illegality.

2.2 The 'Hostile Environment' and the Windrush Debacle

By June 2013, the public viewed immigration as the UK's second most important problem behind unemployment and jobs.[2] In October Theresa May announced her plan to create 'a really hostile environment' for illegal immigrants. '*What we don't want is a situation where people think that they can come here and overstay because they're able to access everything they need, ... Most people will say it can't be fair for people who have no right to be here in the UK to continue to exist as everybody else does with bank accounts, with driving licences and with access to rented accommodation*'.[3]

Building on internal controls introduced during the 1980s and 1990s, the formal hostile environment was implemented through the Immigration Acts 2014 and 2016. Outside bodies including private individuals were charged with operating immigration control measures, aiming to prevent 'illegals' from sheltering among the general population.

By those Acts, unlawfully-present migrants were prohibited from working, renting property, holding a bank account, keeping any money earned or held in a bank account, holding a driving licence, or 'driving a car while unlawfully present'. Criminal sanctions were imposed on employers and landlords for employing or letting property to unlawfully-present migrants. There was little formal opposition. It was a Conservative who recommended 'compassion' in relation to '*people who in 2010 had been in this country for five, six, seven years ... and children who had grown up in our schools when their parents had no right to be here ... what is compassionate about sending a child who turns 18 back to a country they have never really understood? ...*'.[4] The measures would lead to '*families split apart; valuable jobs and support will be lost*' ... '*destitution is once more the immigration policy of choice ...*'.[5]

Then in April 2018, seemingly out of the blue, the plight of the so-called Windrush generation exposed the consequences of hostile environment-style policies. The publicity led to the resignation of a Home Secretary and the rapid introduction of a 'regularisation' process, with a compensation scheme to be consulted on.[6] Brought to public notice largely by Guardian journalist Amelia Gentleman (2019),[7] the

Windrush scandal concerned the fate of those who had arrived as or were born to British subjects, Commonwealth citizens and CUKCs and who had or gained a status equivalent to citizenship or settlement by operation of law. Never required to hold or keep documentation, and not affected by the 1980s checks on entitlement to benefits, housing and employment, as it was generally accepted that they belonged here. However, the new regime required presentation of specified immigration documents. People found themselves jobless, homeless, denied State pensions and health care. Some were detained and removed or deported from the UK, and some died before their status could be reinstated. A few more have died before compensation could be paid to them.[8]

On 26 April 2018, after the Windrush debacle broke, Theresa May, by then Prime Minister, said[9]: '*it is right to clamp down on illegal immigration. "Up and down the country people want to ensure [we] are taking action against those people who are here in this country illegally … [but the Windrush people] were not documented with that right, and that is what we are now putting right"*'. She appeared not to understand that many others with lives just as rooted in the UK *appear illegal and even become illegal* precisely because of those policies. This will be discussed in Chapter 6.

3 The Origins and Development of Poor Public Administration in Immigration Control

3.1 'Large Backlogs and Waiting Times'

Questions about the *administration* of control and specifically of delay, bias and racism, first arose in the 1970s in relation to spouse applications from India, Pakistan and Bangladesh.[10] In any other public application process, such lengthy delays would have been a public scandal. House of Commons Home Affairs Committee (HAC) Chair Keith Vaz MP said 40 years later, questioning Sarah Rapson, the new Interim Director General, UK Visas and Immigration Section, '*if you have a case that takes 45 minutes to sort out, …there is no excuse for spending 10 months or even years [on it]*'.[11] The failure to provide enough resources for spouse applications was never justified. It was argued at the time that the lack of resources was itself a method of control—and amounted to racial discrimination. In 1989 the HAC noted '*The most vivid illustration of failings in the IND [Immigration and Nationality Division] lies in large backlogs and waiting times...*'.[12] Backlogs grew of naturalisation applicants and for those acquiring the right of abode by operation of law, but who by the Immigration Act 1988 had to obtain a certificate before travelling to the UK.

In a 1992 debate[13] Lord Meston had said that '*The delays are clearly excessive and beyond anything that would be expected or tolerated in any other bureaucratic exercise*'. The Home Office response in that debate has provided a model for subsequent Home Office responses, precisely followed by the March 2021 *New Plan for Immigration*. The model consists of regretting some element of error without acknowledging the true extent of the problem; making minor improvements and announcing some relegislating such as an ostensibly new law, policy or practice which generally reduces entitlements and access to redress. For example, the 1992 backlog of 23,000 appeals against refusals of visitors' visas was dealt with by abolishing the right of appeal.[14] But only after Prime Minister John Reid declared the IND to be 'not fit for purpose' in 2006 were the HAC able to insist on quarterly reports on the working of the new UK Border Agency (UKBA). And not until 2013 did the HAC force the Home Office to face up to the immigration and asylum 'shambles' as it was still being described in 2012.

Speaking about asylum applications in 1995, David Alton MP gave these figures:

> ... 3,333 people have waited for five years or more for their applications to be processed—more than 13,000 since 1991, 23,000 since 1993 and 49,000 for more than 11 months. At 31 October this year, 66,000 applications were still awaiting an initial decision.[15]

Chapter 3 noted a minister accepting the scale of the Home Office 'shambles', as early as 1995. Charles Wardle, Minister of State at the Home Office, said:

> … to process the queue of 75,000 asylum applicants will take additional resources, manpower and facilities—within the asylum division and the appellate section of the Lord Chancellor's Department… it will probably take £150 million a year for two years, … to reduce the queue to a manageable work-in-progress level of three months.[16]

No Home Office minister since then has made such a comprehensive proposal.

The 1998 White Paper *Fairer, Firmer, Faster* comprehensively set out the extent of delays and backlogs in the system, but made only piecemeal proposals to deal with them. In January 1999, in the face of a nearly 30% increase in asylum applications in one year, a 'backlog clearance exercise'[17] had allowed for grants of exceptional leave to remain to be made quickly. Then, in response to the introduction of the new administrative removal procedures in Section 10 of the Immigration and Asylum Act (IAA) 1999, a 'regularisation of overstayers' programme[18] had allowed any overstayer who had no criminal convictions to apply for indefinite leave to remain. Then a 'one-off exercise'[19] (the 'family amnesty') provided for the grant of leave to those families who had applied before October 2000. A few of these cases were still unresolved in 2006 when the Legacy programme was introduced.[20,21]

3.2 'Not Fit for Purpose'—The Collapse of the Immigration and Nationality Department

With hindsight, not entertaining a wholesale amnesty looks like a mistake, if only because the regularisation schemes were of the same order, but the process took longer while failing to eliminate the backlogs.[22,23]

Summarising the failures of the immigration bureaucracy, Humphrey Malins, (Woking) said[24]:

> … What of the quality of those decisions? They are made largely by inexperienced Home Office officials who are on a starting salary of £15,500 per year—two thirds of the national average. With only 27 days of

> training, those officials have to make decisions that can literally mean life or death to the applicant.
>
> ... considerably more than 20 per cent. of appeals against their decisions are successful. The percentage used to be 4 per cent.

After the 2006 'foreign national prisoners' debacle Home Secretary Charles Clarke resigned and Dr John Reid took over. He said:

> Our system is not fit for purpose. It is inadequate in terms of its scope, it is inadequate in terms of its information technology, leadership, management systems and processes.

After that announcement, three reports were quickly published: a comprehensive HAC report on every aspect of immigration control,[25] a 'customer facing' report *Rebuilding confidence in our immigration system*,[26] and, in September, the Government Reply to the HAC report.[27] Acknowledgement of 'success' in having reduced asylum applications below the rate of removals of failed asylum-seekers—Tony Blair's 'tipping point'[28]—read strangely in documents noting '*the legacy of undecided asylum cases*'.

The reports are highly critical. The criticisms range from the technocratic and managerial (poor choice of targets, failures of accountability and divided management structures) to the legal (complexity of legislation, unclear and contradictory aims and poor quality of decision-making), and included failures of policy coordination across government. An independent Migration Advisory Committee was to be set up, to look at migration in the light of wider government policies and objectives, and in the context of changing economic conditions. To deal with continued problems of inefficiency and poor quality decision-making, an independent inspectorate would be set up—the Independent Chief Inspector of Immigration and Borders (ICIBI). A quick law would provide for a presumption of deportation for foreign national prisoners. The Home Office promised a simplification programme, including a points-based system for students and labour migrants.

The HAC demanded that the Chief Executive of the then IND, Lin Homer, write to that committee every three months, providing an update. The fourth letter, on 19 February 2007, '*also discussed the IND's efforts to tackle a backlog of between 400,000 and 450,000 unresolved asylum cases, some dating back more than a decade, which became known as the Legacy Casework Programme*'.[29] The HAC reported:

> On 19 July 2006, the then Home Secretary, the Rt Hon John Reid MP, informed Parliament that he intended the backlog of 400,000-450,000 electronic and paper records relating to asylum cases to be tackled and cleared in five years or less. He described the records as "riddled with duplication and errors, and including cases of individuals who have since died or left the country, or are now EU citizens …".

On 1 April 2007 the IND was replaced by the Borders and Immigration Agency (BIA), a shadow agency replaced on 1 April 2008 by the UK Border Agency (UKBA), an arm's length agency including the BIA, UKVisas (a joint unit of the Foreign and Commonwealth Office (FCO) and the Home Office which had previously taken over visa-issuing functions from the Foreign Office)[30] and the border detection functions of HM Customs and Excise. Since then, the ICIBI has published regular critical inspection reports.

Giving evidence to the HAC on asylum applications in 2003, immigration minister Beverley Hughes blamed the 1996 decision to introduce a new IT system and the decision to dismiss '1,000 staff' before that system was working properly, combined with the continued increase in asylum applications.[31] But the policy imperatives should have been obvious: recruit more staff or simplify application processes and requirements. Neither was done.

To improve quality of decision-making, a New Asylum Model (NAM) aimed to complete an entire asylum determination in six months, including any appeal and subsequent removal of failed applicants. The legal impact of these and other targets will be discussed in Chapter 6. But the NAM process was to be handled throughout by the same 'caseowner', to provide continuity. Included in the NAM was the Solihull Early Legal Advice Pilot, in which 'caseowners' were encouraged to adopt more of a shared burden of proof, working with applicants' legal representatives to obtain full evidence before making a decision. However, the

NAM, under-resourced along with the Legacy programme, itself soon began to fail as new backlogs grew. The 2013 final report on the Solihull Early Legal Advice Pilot noted that the whole asylum system suffered from a lack of resources and so some of the hoped-for improvements such as continuity of case owner had not been possible.[32] The grade of caseworker required to make asylum decisions was lowered.[33]

Yet, despite both the Legacy and the NAM targets looking unattainable, the principal responses consisted of relegislating. More complex and restrictive requirements were imposed on applicants both in asylum and immigration, including increasing the numbers of applications an individual had to make to achieve settlement and citizenship. Legal aid was curtailed and the appellate system was reduced to one tier. Responding to delays and poor decision-making, more applicants lodged fresh claims for asylum, judicial reviews and applications to the Court of Appeal. Meanwhile their continued presence in the UK without leave to remain increased the costs of asylum support. All this left large numbers of migrants in the UK on 'temporary admission', able neither to contribute to British life nor integrate into it, but against whom it became increasingly difficult to encourage or even enforce departure.

The Legacy programme had been intended to conclude in July 2011. The new government decided that the over 100,000 remaining applicants should be subject to the then-current Immigration Rules and asylum policies. Since Legacy files had been worked on at random, applicants with identical claims were treated differently. Some unresolved cases entered the subsequent backlog categories discussed below. Some were then caught by the 2012 changes in the Immigration Rules requiring 20 rather than 14 years' residence for a 'private life' claim. Some fetched up as 'illegals' targeted by the 2014 and 2016 Acts' hostile environment measures.

Having decided to return to decision-making based on the Immigration Rules, good public administration surely required the provision of the means. The Institute for Government later recommended that the government should be '*clear about the inevitable trade-offs in immigration policy and start making choices*'.[34] As it was, the lack of a full and efficient amnesty coupled with increasing numbers of more complex application processes and fewer staff resources led straight to the 2013 collapse of the UK Border Agency.

In his 2011 examination of the asylum appellate system as an example of administrative justice,[35] Robert Thomas says of the UKBA: '*The agency has sometimes been castigated as the UK's most opaque and unhelpful bureaucracy subjecting claimants to an almost Kafkaesque bureaucratic nightmare*'. He refers to the 2006 description of the Immigration and Asylum Directorate by its own Minister as 'not fit for purpose' as '*unprecedented*'. He describes various attempts to manage the system as '*dysfunctional*' and '*dire*', as operational problems led the Home Office to '*focus on process and politically driven organisational imperatives rather than on decisional quality*'. A 2019 Institute of Government report describes the 50% appeals success rate as:

> Approximately 50% of a tribunal's time is spent correcting the decision of caseworkers from another department. Or … of the £110m annual budget for tribunals, a huge proportion is spent reversing poor decisions made elsewhere …[36]

The HAC repeatedly begged for more resources to be spent on improving administration, rather than more legislation. They opposed an amnesty, believing that without strengthening enforcement, an amnesty would just act as a pull factor. However, enforcement—attempts to increase the numbers of removals, deportations and voluntary departures—not only failed to increase departures. The desperation to pick the 'low-hanging fruit'[37] eventually led to precipitous, unlawful removals and deportations of British and settled people who could not prove their status under the hostile environment—the Windrush generation.

The Legacy programme originally defined 'concluding' cases as a grant of leave or the removal of the applicant from the UK. Growing backlogs led the UKBA to redefine 'conclusion' to mean that a case had been reviewed and faced 'barriers to removal'.[38] Incomprehensibly, existing guidance on difficulties of removal was not relied on to grant leave to those applicants.[39] Though many were from countries still facing civil war and insurgency, they were not dealt with as people 'of concern' to the UNHCR, but left to survive as 'failed asylum-seekers' with half-hearted or no attempts to remove them. The UKBA were forced to reveal new non-asylum backlogs, and in 2013 were accused of deceiving Parliament.[40]

3.3 'Not Good Enough'—The Collapse of the UK Border Agency and Aftermath

Following the 2006 collapse of the IND, delays and other administrative problems persisted, and new backlogs developed, partly because of cuts in staff resources. As early as 2009, a HAC report looking into Legacy work[41] noted 88,500 'errors'—people who may have been given leave to remain, or have left the country, or who could not be traced. The report also noted a new pile of 40,000 immigration cases where nothing was known about the people to whom the files related. That HAC report again begged for more resources devoted to administration rather than further legislation. By 2011 the 'errors' category had risen to 112,500,[42] and a backlog was growing in new asylum cases. In 2012 yet more categories were discovered of unlawfully-present migrants who had not been removed.[43]

On 18 September 2012 the UKBA announced a programme to deal with the 174,000 migrants listed in their 'migrant refusal pool', presumed to consist of students and workers who had overstayed their visas. Tracing these migrants and ensuring their removal was to be outsourced to Capita, to be paid by results, under a contract worth £40m if all the listed migrants were removed. By the end of December ILPA members were reporting that clients had received texts and calls stating that they were in the UK illegally, and requiring them to email a copy of their departure ticket by 1/1/2013 '*or the UKBA would be informed of their refusal to leave the UK*'. In January 2013 ILPA reported formally that some hundreds of those so contacted either had valid leave to remain or outstanding representations. Some were British citizens.[44]

In January 2013 the ICIBI described UKBA backlogs in handling marriage applications as '*completely unacceptable*'.[45] In the Introduction he says:

> Once again, I was concerned to find that the Agency had a backlog of cases amounting to 14,000 requests from applicants to reconsider decisions to refuse them further leave to remain. This had been growing by approximately 700 cases a month. In addition, there were a further 2,100 cases where people were awaiting an initial decision on their application for further leave to remain. Some dated back nearly a decade. This is completely unacceptable and I expect the Agency to deal with both types of case as a matter of urgency'.

In March 2013 the ICIBI inspected progress in Legacy asylum and migration cases.[46] This discovered that cases put away in a 'controlled archive' had not, as promised, been subject to the full range of checks against police and other national databases—and found some files where the applicants could be easily contacted. Straight away the Home Affairs Committee gathered comprehensive evidence about those backlogs along with those in every other area of the UKBA's work, summoning the present and two previous Chief Executives for questioning. Their report is savage[47]:

> 16. We are astonished that the Agency provided this Committee, and its predecessors, with information that turned out to be patently wrong on so many occasions over the last six years. If it was not attempting to mislead the Committee then it must be a sign that senior officials had no idea as to what was actually going on in their organisation. We find it very hard to believe that no one within the Agency had any idea that checks were not being carried out as they should have been and we expect the Agency to share the findings of its disciplinary investigation with us as soon as it is completed. (my emphasis)

Further backlogs were disclosed, including 33,000 asylum cases, mainly refugee applications for indefinite leave, for whom an Active Review process had been introduced; and 'leave in line' applications for children born in the UK, '*where the original asylum application fell before March 2007*' (and for whom there is still no formal application procedure).[48] These cases were said to be '*only 30–40%*' of the work of a particular team, the Case Assurance and Audit Unit (CAAU), which had not been previously mentioned, and the previous Chief Executive, Lin Homer, was stated to have misled the Committee on several previous occasions about this. The HAC said:

> It is shocking that after five years under Lin Homer's leadership an organisation that was described at the beginning of the period as being 'not fit for purpose' should have improved its performance so little.[49]

The Committee was then concerned to find that a further new team, the Complex Casework Directorate, was being set up to solve the '*more difficult cases which still remain outstanding*', of which a further group of 11,000 cases were to *form a part.* There were further revelations that 59,000 new applications remained not logged into the Agency's computer system. In summary, the Committee concluded (Recommendation 40):

> Despite the closure of the controlled archives, 96,000 cases since last quarter, the total backlog has only reduced by 1%. New backlogs are continuing to emerge. The Agency's work affects thousands of people's lives, public safety, public services and the economy, but it continues to be an Agency playing catch up. Until we are able to publish a Report on the Agency both without the discovery of a new backlog and with a decrease in the present backlogs we will not be able to declare it fit for purpose. (my emphasis)

A week later Theresa May announced that the UK Border Agency was to be abolished, calling it '*closed, secretive and defensive*'.[50] She described the UKBA as '*often caught up in a vicious cycle of complex law and poor enforcement of its own policies*'.[51] In that summer, some performative action was taken—the 'go home' vans—a project involving driving around London in vans with '*Illegal Immigrants—Go Home or be arrested*' posters on the sides—was launched in July and ran for one month.[52] The Home Office claimed that there had been 60 voluntary departures '*we believe can be directly attributed to*' that operation. It was not continued.

On 26 March Home Secretary Theresa May declared the UKBA '*not good enough*'. The whole operation was brought back into the Home Office. The work was divided into a 'customer-focused' UK Visas and Immigration and an immigration enforcement operation. Notably, the trigger for abolishing the UKBA, as with the 2006 abolition of the IND, was the narrow issue of mishandling files such that particular categories of migrant could not be traced; and in 2013 that Parliament had been misled by officials. The pervading issues of lengthy delays, poor decision-making and failure to follow the law, and the effect of those on migrants and on wider society, were not formally part of UKBA's downfall.

By 2016, instead of 'backlogs' of 'older cases' there were 'straightforward' cases decided within published service standards, while the 'non-straightforward' cases face long and uncontrolled delays. These include applications relying on art 8 ECHR, cases involving foreign criminals, and asylum applications. The HAC demanded performance measures which do not permit the Home Office to state that it meets '99%' of service standards while those standards cover only 60% of its work.[53] In 2017 the ICIBI reported that one-third of 'non-straightforward' cases had been incorrectly marked as such, to avoid missing performance targets. The Institute for Government reported that by the 3rd quarter of 2018, around a half of asylum cases had been waiting more than a year for a decision.[54]

The National Audit Office (NAO), in its 2014 report *Reforming the UK border and immigration system*,[55] criticises the reorganised bureaucracy for persistent backlogs, high levels of error, poor workforce planning, lack of clarity between performance targets and policy objectives, poor management of IT reform. It then set a goal of improving all those things while further reducing its budget.

In November 2021 an ICIBI inspection of asylum casework noted growing backlogs, decision-makers focusing on targets rather than the applicants, openly disbelieving applicants and not having time to read evidence. It noted that without agreements with EU countries to take back migrants, the new rules on 'inadmissibility' simply defers casework. Finally, '*whatever changes [the New Plan for Immigration] brings, there will still be a need to ensure that the Home Office is properly resourced, equipped and organised to make timely and good quality asylum decisions*'.[56]

4 Pervading Problems of Public Administration in Immigration Control

4.1 Delay

Avoidance of delay must be an important component of good public administration. However, for over four decades, a wait of six months for an immigration or asylum decision has been considered acceptable, and far longer delays have become entrenched in staff and workflow planning. In the 1970s it may have taken a few weeks for an entry clearance officer in Dhaka or Mumbai to receive confirmation of the immigration status of the British or settled husband of a spouse applicant. But even then, the decision itself would have taken comparatively little time. Recent performance targets, accepted to be 'stretching', were noted to have often been exceeded, with staff taking '*just over 3 minutes for a decision*',[57] leaving little excuse for a 6 months wait. As HAC chair Keith Vaz MP asked Sarah Rapson, new director of UK Visas and Immigration: '*If you have a case that takes 45 minutes to sort out... there is no excuse for spending 10 months or even years ...*'.[58] The only conclusion to be drawn is that, over four decades, inadequate and inappropriate resources have been provided.

On the quality of decision-making, the 2019 Institute of Government report notes that '*outside of government, it would be up to qualified lawyers to make the judgements that, inside the Home Office, are left to junior, relatively poorly-paid officials with little formal training*'.[59]

In 2007 a challenge to the Legacy process was brought. In *FH & others*,[60] Collins J considered the requirements of good public administration:

> 8. ...No doubt, delays of 12 months or more in dealing with an initial claim to asylum may well need an explanation, but, provided the approach of the defendant was based on a policy which was fair and applied consistently, such delays could not be regarded as unlawful.

Collins J accepted as *Wednesbury* reasonable[61] the Home Office Legacy protocols:

> We will prioritise those who may pose a risk to the public, and then focus on those who can more easily be removed, those receiving support, and those who may be granted leave. All cases will be dealt with on their individual merits.

He also accepted the Secretary of State's witness evidence that '*This has been put into effect*'. However, the Home Office filing system did not allow for case selection by category[62] except for those receiving support, for which there were separate files. The Legacy programme worked by selecting files at random, surely *Wednesbury* unreasonable.

In *Hamzeh*,[63] finally decided in 2014, some applicants still left at the end of the Legacy argued that they should not be subject to the '*more restrictive approach to the consideration of what constituted exceptional circumstances justifying non-removal*'. Underhill LJ said:

> … it is an important principle underpinning the immigration system that cases 'should, wherever possible, be decided on the basis of the law and policy in place at the date of decision'.

Perhaps lacking sympathy because the applicants were 'failed asylum-seekers', the court decided that those applicants' cases were not '*in the territory mapped out, albeit uncertainly*' in the '*abuse of process*' cases of *Rashid* and *R(S)*, discussed in Chapter 6. In 2013 the Court of Appeal decided that '*it is not the Courts' function to impose sanctions on a government department for inefficiency*'.[64]

In short, though good public administration requires timely decision-making, and a more than 12 months' wait for a first asylum decision '*may well need an explanation*', the courts' position is that, regardless of whether the catastrophic backlogs were caused by exogenous factors or departmental administrative incompetence, applicants had no remedy unless the scheme of 'repair' was *Wednesbury* unreasonable. And those making fresh claims for asylum, and those who simply had not left the UK following the rejection of their claim, had no legitimate expectation in law. The legal consequences of delay, for applicants and for the whole system, are discussed in Chapter 6.

4.2 'Harm'

In June 2020 the NAO produced a new report on immigration enforcement.[65] It notes that 'illegal' migrants are targeted for enforcement on the grounds of the 'harm' they cause. But not only is there no common Home Office definition of 'harm'—one official is reported as saying '*we know it when we see it*'.[66] Worse, their view of 'harm' completely ignores the wider harm to society—the harm done to families and communities by immigration enforcement measures, including hostile environment measures, described in this report as '*reducing incentives*'[67]—and so fails to provide any basis for a wider policy evaluation of immigration enforcement. The Home Office, even by 2020, had not '*considered whether some of the transformational changes it has introduced may inadvertently have led to new problems elsewhere in the system*'. The report confirms that the problems identified by the NAO in its two 2014 reports, of lack of management coordination, inefficiency, failures and mistakes, have not been resolved.

From 2016 the HAC ceased producing its three-monthly reports but has produced critical reports on the Windrush debacle, on preparedness for Brexit and on the introduction and operation of a completely new immigration application scheme—the EU Settlement Scheme. The prospect of Brexit with its requirement for a fundamentally changed immigration system led to a HAC review of whether the current system could cope, and the answer was 'No'.[68] The HAC report on the 'Windrush generation'[69] noted six salient features of the Home Office's conduct of immigration control over the previous decade. These include the removal of Home Office caseworker discretion; the use of targets (both the high-level 'reduce net migrant to the tens of thousands' and specific targets such as for removals)[70]; restrictions on independent checks and appeals[71]; and the formal hostile environment measures introduced in the 2014 and 2016 Immigration Acts. Two further features referred to by the HAC[72] are also noted in reports from the Independent Chief Inspector of Borders and Immigration (ICIBI): Home Office administrative incompetence, and Home Office reluctance to monitor and evaluate the recent hostile environment measures, whether for effectiveness or for unintended consequences. All of these were noted in the Institute for Government report.[73] That report also criticised the involvement of Ministers in individual cases, poor information technology and top-level ignorance about front line operational processes.

The wooden-headedness of pursuing more restrictive measures with insufficient and reduced resources is particularly shown by **Home Office policy towards foreign offenders**. A 2014 National Audit Office report[74] assessed the spending of £850m on 'managing' the presence of 12,250 foreign offenders present in the UK—a sum of nearly £70,000 per prisoner, exclusive of their accommodation and subsistence costs—asking '*whether the bodies involved are achieving value for money for the taxpayer*'. The report describes failures of file-keeping, poor information management, poor coordination with other government departments and lost documents, all familiar from HAC and ICIBI reports. Highlighting how many foreign offenders are 'living in the community' until deported, the report nowhere asks whether they have committed any offences during that time, or what other harm they cause, other than the fact of their presence in the face of Home Office obduracy. The NAO noted that '*the Department and the Ministry [of Justice] do not use cost data to manage FNOs, and do not have a good understanding of the costs involved*'. Despite policy having changed from giving '*considerable weight to those with family ties in the UK' to, by 2013, seeking to deport any FNO serving 12 months or more …*' [1.5] and '*despite … toughening powers, by 2013 the number of FNOs in prison and those deported from the UK remained broadly unchanged from 2008*' [1.6].

> 3.15 Another systemic problem is the lack of prioritisation of casework. Cases are only prioritised on the basis of release, not removability or cost–benefit. This means that some of the most non-compliant cases, which consume large resources and have little chance of success, are pursued at the expense of cases … more likely to result in removal and greater savings overall.

The NAO *did not ask why* 'the taxpayer' is spending £850m a year trying to deport a few thousand people for whom, if British, their convictions may well have by now been 'spent'. Introduced by s19 Immigration Act

2014, Section 117C NIAA 2002 does indeed say that '*the deportation of a foreign criminal is in the public interest*', but presumably not at any cost.

4.3 Accuracy

For an organisation whose legal function is administering fundamental rights and entitlements which remain crucial throughout a person's entire life and beyond,[75] good public administration surely requires *good knowledge management*—accuracy, comprehensiveness and care in keeping and maintaining paper and electronic records and efficient access to them. Unlike delay, where an underlying lack of allocation of resources may conceivably enjoy a political justification, there can be no good public administration argument that would excuse the kind of administrative incompetence complained of.

The effect of institutional mistakes is clearly graver in a world where the burden of proof falls on the applicant. This has been exposed recently by two linked issues—the impact of the hostile environment measures and the Windrush debacle. The hostile environment measures required checks on immigration status which, for people not in possession of a biometric residence permit, were to be carried out by contacting Home Office employment or landlord checking services, while banks and the DVLA were provided with lists of those to be denied banking facilities or have their driving licence revoked. An ICIBI report confirmed that these lists showed unacceptably high numbers of errors, resulting in loss of jobs, housing and access to bank accounts and driving licences for people lawfully present in the UK.[76] The Home Office rejected the Chief Inspector's request for the data to be checked. The Windrush scandal showed the consequences of a combination of an error-ridden record-keeping and filing system and '*institutional amnesia*' about previous laws and policies on people who were then required to prove their status.

5 *'This Is Not a Way to Run an Immigration System'*: Official Criticisms

In February 2018 the Home Affairs Committee's report on the delivery of Brexit[77] set out major criticisms of Home Office immigration operations, including the hostile environment policies. As background, the report notes (para 9) that UK Visas and Immigration (UKVI, the successor to UKBA) deals with 3 million visa applications a year and was proposing to register 3 million EU citizens resident in the UK—a huge undertaking. The HAC was not confident: *'The UKVI has a poor accuracy record'... in asylum one-third of cases are wrongly marked as non-straightforward in order to meet targets (para 27); 'the sheer complexity of the immigration rules and pressure on staff resources were leading to concerns about decision-making processes... both in terms of accuracy... and procedures' (para 54); 'over a third of refusal notices included factual inaccuracy, inappropriate grounds of refusal and unclear refusal reasons'* (para 59). The section on litigation notes the reduction in rights and grounds of appeal and loss of legal aid, the numbers of appeals being upheld as an indication of poor accuracy, and the lack of feedback from allowed appeals (para 67). The HAC concludes that '*this is not a way to run an immigration system*' [69]. Significantly, the report recommends simplifying rules and guidance, reducing bureaucracy, including eliminating repeat applications for settlement [75], and an end to rejecting applications for small technical faults [79].

Those conclusions are followed by an equally critical section on immigration enforcement, noting cuts in enforcement staff, and the government's decision to '*outsource much of its enforcement function*' which is '*changing behaviour towards people who are lawfully resident*'. This report again criticises the government for not monitoring the effectiveness of the hostile environment policies; and quotes David Bolt, Independent Chief Inspector of Borders and Immigration (ICIBI):

> *Of the 40 reports I have produced ... the one that has caused me the most irritation was the report into the hostile environment and the response I got from the Department, where I believe they need to do more to understand the*

> *effectiveness of [these provisions] ... and to be able to give an account of the effectiveness of those measures, or not.*[78]

The HAC demanded a dedicated helpline for people wrongly declared to be unlawfully present. Against these criticisms, the Home Office response merely referred to applicants' rights to bring an administrative review, statutory appeal or judicial review.[79] The March 2021 *New Plan for Immigration*[80] has made it clear that migrants' access to judicial review is now under threat.

During this period the Home Affairs Committee demanded a review of the 'right to rent' policy, reporting the ICIBI evidence that '*the Home Office does not have in place measurements to evaluate the effectiveness' of the hostile environment measures*'.[81] This was echoed in a House of Lords briefing paper on the hostile environment[82] issued on 14 June 2018, which reviewed the three ICIBI inspection reports covering 'sham marriage' investigations, the driving licence and bank account provisions, and the 'right to rent' measures.[83] As well as there being no monitoring or evaluation of the measures, the inspection reports noted that Home Office errors in record-keeping and caseworking are a significant issue.

The Home Affairs Committee, in their report *Immigration policy: basis for building consensus*,[84] published in January 2018, had said:

> **57.** The Government should not rely on its 'hostile environment' policy as a panacea for enforcement and building confidence, especially given the current concerns about accuracy and error. We are concerned that the policy is unclear and, in some instances, too open to interpretation and inadvertent error. Not only can these errors be deeply damaging and distressing to those involved—as with letters being sent to EU nationals about their right to live in the UK—they also undermine the credibility of the system. Recent high-profile reports of the Home Office threatening to deport individuals based on inaccurate and untested information, and before an independent appeal process, risk undermining the credibility of the whole system. This is particularly worrying in advance of the need to register EU nationals in preparation for Brexit.

In early March 2020 the *Windrush Lessons Learned Review* was published.[85] That concluded that the Home Office held no 'institutional memory' of those people's rights, and thus was incapable *as an organisation* of recognising or dealing with any risks to them, even when warning signs appeared. It also concludes that the introduction and administration of increasingly restrictive internal immigration controls from the 1980s, through the Thatcher, Blair and Coalition governments to the present Conservative administration, showed several elements of institutional racism as identified by the Macpherson report following the murder of Stephen Lawrence.

The report refers to the 'politically contentious' nature of immigration, forcing the Home Office under great ministerial pressure to introduce new legislation at speed, and implement policy '*relentlessly without proper consideration of the impact of the proposals*'. The report quotes Amber Rudd, Home Secretary at the time the scandal broke: '*she could not understand why people would make a decision to treat people the way they had, knowing they'd been here 30 or 40 years*'.

Despite publicly accepting the recommendations of the *Windrush Lessons Learned Review*, Home Secretary Priti Patel appears to have taken little or no notice of the welter of official criticisms of the administration of immigration control. In the *New Plan for Immigration*,[86] the Home Office justifies its tired repetition of previous failed policies with a demonstration of ignorance.[87] In chapter 4 of the Plan, in relation to the 'broken' asylum system, it complains: '*The rapid intake has outstripped any ability to make asylum decisions quickly*'; the asylum backlog now stands at 109,000 applications, and maintaining the applicants is costing '*over £1bn*'. However, for reasons both of international law and common humanity, the answer cannot be to try to prevent new entrants, as the Plan proposes. The Home Office needs to commit sufficient resources to the system to ensure timely right-first-time decision-making, reducing the need for unnecessary appeals and lengthy periods of asylum support.

6 The EU Settlement Scheme [EUSS]—A Better Way?

This chapter concludes by reviewing the EU Settlement Scheme, showing what the Home Office can achieve with three fundamental but conceptually simple reforms—simplified legal requirements, sufficient resources to make consistently accurate decisions and a shared burden of proof.

After the 2016 vote to leave the European Union the government decided to protect the EU law rights of the estimated three million UK-based EU citizens, by giving them a new legal status within UK immigration law. Those who by 30 June 2021, the end of the Brexit transition period, would have been entitled to permanent residence under EU law would obtain 'settled status', equivalent to indefinite leave under UK law. Those EU nationals and family members here less than five years would be granted 'pre-settled status', with the right to progress to 'settled status' after five years of the equivalent of exercising Treaty rights. The government aimed to ensure that every EU national present in the UK by the deadline had applied. Applicants would enter biometric details through a mobile phone app. The Home Office would obtain tax, national insurance, benefits, pension and other official information to check the person's residence and economic activity in the UK, and the person would be informed of their status by email within a few days. Two large-scale trials of the scheme took place, one involving NHS and university staff in Liverpool, then broadened to include similar groups around the UK. The full scheme began in March 2019. At first the application cost £65 but then became free of charge, with fees refunded to those who had paid.

The EU Settlement Scheme Statement of Intent, as quoted in the ICIBI report *An inspection of the EU Settlement Scheme Nov 2018-Jan 2019*,[88] celebrated the opportunity for the Home Office to develop a fresh culture in this 'new business area', one that reflected the aim of 'looking to grant, not for reasons to refuse'. Those and further reports[89] noted that the success of the two trials of the new scheme and of the full scheme so far was largely due to good levels of staff resources, with high morale. *'Everyone said that they were committed to providing a world class customer service' ... to ensure that the decision the applicant received was 'right first time'.*[90] Home Office caseworkers were permitted (i.e., afforded the time) to contact applicants to assist them to find additional information.[91] The Home Office provided 'up to £9m' for voluntary organisations to assist vulnerable applicants.[92] The Home

Office appeared to adopt a shared responsibility for the stability and security of status of EU nationals and their families, into the future, and adopted a shared burden of proof of entitlement under the scheme.

Critics of the scheme noted that there were groups of vulnerable and marginalised EU nationals and their families who may fail to apply in time, despite the increasing public information and growing numbers of organisations offering to help identify and assist them. One difficulty often mentioned is that the government has never known how many people would be eligible to apply under the scheme. But, unusually, that is hardly a fault of the Home Office, since free movement rights provided that EU nationals were not subject to immigration control and did not need to hold or apply for residence permits (though their non-EU family members had to obtain a biometric card). Only a rough estimate could be made, based on information such as applications for national insurance numbers and Census data.

A Migration Observatory report from September 2020[93] provides a comprehensive analysis of the different categories of people who may fail to apply. The report includes vulnerable people such as people with mental and physical health problems, children in care and adults in care homes, but also people who may not realise they need to apply, such as very long residents, people who already have EU permanent residence, people who were refused permanent residence but who will succeed under the more generous EUSS criteria; those who do not know that their children need to apply separately.

Both before and immediately after the 30 June 2021 deadline, the Home Office introduced extra application processes and has announced guidance about how it will treat late applications. But the probability of missed applicants, and the current fact of a large backlog of outstanding applications, should not detract from an evaluation of the scheme as startlingly successful. The most recent ICIBI report on the scheme[94] discussed the period April to August 2019, and a measure of its satisfaction is shown in recommendations which almost entirely deal with special cases, hard-to-reach applicants, and cases taking 'longer than the 4 days advertised'. The number of concluded applications up to 30 September 2021 was 5.91m. Of these, 52% (3.07m) were granted settled status and 42% (2.46m) were granted pre-settled status.[95]

The contrast with the rest of the immigration and asylum operation is unavoidable. The EUSS was launched on 30 March 2019, and within one year nearly 3 million applications have been processed, with fewer than 1% of applications found invalid for want of information, and an even smaller proportion refused. Technical progress has speeded up processing, but more significant must be the Home Office sharing responsibility for evidence gathering, and the simplification of legal requirements. In contrast, applications for permanent residence under the EEA Regulations required completion of an 80-page form and a complete set of original evidence covering 5 years, showing comprehensive private health insurance for periods not covered by employee or self-employed national insurance contributions, and proof of receiving wages higher than a Home Office-specified minimum. Both those requirements were strongly contested as being in breach of EU law.

Looking at the current statistics, it is likely that the numbers failing to apply in time will be relatively low—which, so far, appears to be making it politically easier for the administration to be generous about accepting late applications. *With political will*, a similar scheme could be applied to any or all of Britain's three groups of insecure migrants, at once providing a chance for integration for millions, and reducing the burden of future administration of their status to a manageable level.

Notes

1. https://www.gov.uk/government/publications/visa-regulations-revised-table/home-office-immigration-and-nationality-fees-6-april-2021, accessed 24/11/21, https://www.gov.uk/healthcare-immigration-application/how-much-pay accessed 24/11/21.
2. Duffy, Bobby and Frere-Smith, Tom. 2014. *Perceptions and reality—Public attitudes to immigration* Ipsos Mori Social Research Institute [11].
3. Kirkup, J. and Winnett, R., interview with Home Secretary Theresa May, 25 May 2012, *Daily Telegraph.*
4. HC Deb 13 Oct 2015 col 253, Richard Fuller (Con, Bedford).

5. Stuart McDonald, SNP, Cumbernauld, Kilsyth and Kirkintilloch East, HC Deb 13 October 2015 col 221.
6. Few have received compensation. On 24/11/21 the Home Affairs Committee published a critical report *The Windrush Compensation Scheme* Fifth Report of Session 2021–22 HC 204.
7. Gentleman, Amelia. 2019 *The Windrush Betrayal: Exposing the hostile environment* Guardian Faber 2019L.
8. HAC 2021 n6.
9. Crerar, Pippa and Walker, Peter. 2018. *MPs accuse Home Secretary of protecting the PM* Guardian 26/4/18 https://www.theguardian.com/uk-news/2018/apr/25/amber-rudd-deeply-regrets-failure-to-spot-scale-of-windrush-issue
10. Hansen, Randall. 2000. *Citizenship and immigration in post-war Britain* Oxford: Oxford University Press [229].
11. House of Commons Home Affairs Committee *The work of the UK Border Agency (January–March 2013)* Eighth Report of Session 2013–14 HC 616 witness evidence q14.
12. Home Affairs Committee 6th report *Form and content of the Home Office annual report* HC 464 session 1989–90.
13. *HL Deb 07 December 1992 vol 541 cc75-84*.
14. HC Deb 02 November 1992 vol 213 cc21-120—debate on the Asylum and Immigration Appeals Bill, discussed in Chapter 2.
15. HC Deb 11 December 1995 vol 268 cc699-808 699.
16. Ibid., col 747.
17. Immigration Service Union Evidence to Home Affairs Committee July 1999.
18. Immigration (Regularisation Period for Overstayers) Regulations 2000 SI 2000 no 265.
19. APU Notice 4/2003, set out in *Zekaj* [2007] NIQB 13 https://www.refworld.org/pdfid/492aceac2.pdf accessed 25/11/21.
20. ICIBI 2012 *An inspection of the UK border agency's handling of legacy asylum and migration cases: March–July 2012*, paras 4.1, 4.4.
21. Chief Inspector of Borders and Immigration,—Immigration System Unfit—Reid, *BBC News* (2006) http://news.bbc.co.uk/1/hi/uk_politics/5007148.stm accessed 25/11/21.
22. ICIBI 2012 n 20.

23. *Immigration System Unfit* n21.
24. HC Deb 17 December 2003 vol 415 cc1587-620 [1609].
25. Home Affairs Committee *Immigration control* Fifth Report of Session 2005–6, 23/7/2006.
26. Home Office Immigration and Nationality Directorate 2006 *Fair, efficient, transparent and trusted: Rebuilding confidence in our immigration system* Home Office.
27. Government reply 2006 to *Immigration control,* the fifth report from the Home Affairs Committee Session 2005–6 Cm 6910.
28. Maughan, Bethany. 2010 *Tony Blair's asylum policies: The narratives and conceptualisations at the heart of New Labour's restrictionism.* Working Paper Series No. 69. Refugee Studies Centre, University of Oxford [8].
29. Home Affairs Committee *The work of the UK Border Agency* October 2009 9.
30. HAC 2005–6 *Immigration control* n25.
31. Home Affairs Committee Minutes of Evidence 8/5/2003 [q37] https://publications.parliament.uk/pa/cm200304/cmselect/cmhaff/218/3050801.htm accessed 25/11/21.
32. Home Office *Evaluation of the early legal advice project final report* Research Report 70 May 2013.
33. Reported at the *Roundtable on due process considerations relating to the use of country of origin information in refugee status determination procedures 22 May 2012,* author present.
34. The Institute of Government *Managing migration after Brexit* 2019 [24].
35. Thomas, Robert. 2011. *Administrative justice and asylum appeals—A study of tribunal adjudication* Oxford: Hart Publishing [53].
36. Institute of Government 2019 n34 [32].
37. As a Home Office official had described those affected in the Windrush debacle - https://www.independent.co.uk/voices/letters/windrush-amber-rudd-theresa-may-immigration-a8325841.html accessed 25/11/21.
38. House of Commons Home Affairs Committee *The Border Agency—Follow-up on Asylum Cases and E-borders programme* Twelfth Report of Session 2009–10.

39. The archived Enforcement Instructions and Guidance (EIG) ch 53.1.1 provided: (iii) *Any other case where the length of delay by the Home Office in deciding the application, or where there were factors preventing departure, may be considered exceptionally on grounds of delay where the person has lived in the UK for more than six years.* https://assets.publishing.service.gov.uk/government/uploads/system/uploads/attachment_data/file/653020/Chapter53_v16.pdf accessed 25/11/21.
40. House of Commons Home Affairs Committee *The Work of the UK Border Agency (July–September 2012)* Fourteenth Report of Session 2012–13, 19/3/2013 [36].
41. House of Commons Home Affairs Committee *The work of the UK Border Agency* 2nd Report of Session 2009–10.
42. House of Commons Home Affairs Committee *The work of the UK Border Agency* Fourth Report of Session 2010–11.
43. House of Commons Home Affairs Committee: *The work of the UK Border Agency (April–June 2012)* 31 October 2012.
44. Webber, Frances. 2013. *Capita wrongly telling people to leave the UK* London: Institute of Race Relations https://irr.org.uk/article/capita-wrongly-telling-people-to-leave-the-uk/ accessed 25/11/21.
45. ICIBI. 2013. *An inspection of applications to enter, remain and settle in the UK on the basis of marriage and civil partnerships:* foreword para 2.
46. ICIBI 2013. *An inspection into the progress made on legacy asylum and migration cases January to March 2013.*
47. House of Commons Home Affairs Committee 2012 n40.
48. Even many officials such as social workers assume such children are British.
49. House of Commons Home Affairs Committee 2012 n40 [36].
50. Hansard 26 March 2013 Vol 560 col 1501, *BBC News* 26 March 2013, https://www.bbc.co.uk/news/uk-politics-21941395 accessed 26/11/21.
51. Hansard 26 March 2013 Vol 560 col 1502.
52. Hattenstone, Simon. 2013. https://www.theguardian.com/commentisfree/2018/apr/26/theresa-may-go-home-vans-operation-vaken-ukip accessed 26/11/21.

53. House of Commons Home Affairs Committee *The work of the Immigration Directorates Q2 2015* HC 512 30/5/15.
54. Institute for Government report 2019, House of Commons HAC *The work of the Immigration Directorates Jan–June 2014* HC 712.
55. National Audit Office. 2014. *Reforming the UK border and immigration system* HC 445 Session 2014–15 22 July 2014.
56. ICIBI. 2021. *An inspection of asylum casework* (August 2020–May 2021).
57. ICIBI 2017 *An inspection of entry clearance processing operations in Croydon and Istanbul November 2016–March 2017.*
58. House of Commons Home Affairs Committee *The work of the UK Border Agency (January–March 2013)* Eighth Report of Session 2013–14 HC 616 witness evidence q14.
59. Institute of Government *Managing migration after Brexit* 2019 n34.
60. *FH and others* [2007] EWHC 1571.
61. *Associated Provincial Picture Houses Ltd. v Wednesbury Corporation* [1948] 1 KB 223, setting the standard legal test for an unlawful decision—so unreasonable that no reasonable public official could so decide.
62. Information to author provided at a National Asylum Support Forum conference 2007.
63. *Hamzeh* [2014] EWCA Civ 956, para 16.
64. *EU (Afghanistan)* [2013] EWCA 32.
65. National Audit Office 2020 *Immigration enforcement.* HC 110 Session 2019–2021, 17 June 2020.
66. Ibid., 1.19–1.20.
67. Ibid., 2.8 onwards.
68. House of Commons Home Affairs Committee, *Home Office delivery of Brexit: Immigration*, Third Report of Session 2017–19, HC 421 [32].
69. House of Commons Home Affairs Committee *The Windrush generation* Sixth Report of Session 2017–19, HC 990, 3 July 2018.
70. Ibid., paras 46, 54 onwards.
71. House of Commons Home Affairs Committee *delivery of Brexit: Immigration*, n68.
72. Ibid.

73. Institute for Government 2019 n34.
74. National Audit Office *Managing and removing foreign national offenders* NAO Oct 2014 HC 441.
75. Since a person's status many years ago often impacts on the status of children and grandchildren.
76. ICIBI 2016 *An inspection of the 'hostile environment' measures relating to driving licences and bank accounts January to July 2016.*
77. House of Commons Home Affairs Committee *Home Office delivery of Brexit: immigration* Third Report of Session 2017–19.
78. Ibid., para 119.
79. *Home Office delivery of Brexit: Immigration: government's response to the Committee* Recommendation 38 published 25/5/18.
80. https://www.gov.uk/government/consultations/new-plan-for-immigration/new-plan-for-immigration-policy-statement-accessible published 24/3/21.
81. House of Commons Home Affairs Committee *Immigration policy: Basis for building consensus* HC 500 Session 2017–19.
82. House of Lords library briefing. 2018. *Impact of the Hostile Environment policy* [16].
83. The inspections can be accessed on the ICIBI website.
84. House of Commons Home Affairs Committee *Immigration policy: Basis for building consensus* HC 500 Session 2017–19.
85. *Windrush lessons learned review* Independent review by Wendy Williams Ordered by the House of Commons to be printed on 19 March 2020.
86. https://www.gov.uk/government/consultations/new-plan-for-immigration/new-plan-for-immigration-policy-statement-accessible published 24/3/21.
87. The author and colleague Dr Richard Warren made formal submissions on the New Plan - https://blogs.kent.ac.uk/kentlawclinic/kent-law-clinic-academics-respond-to-home-office-consultation-on-new-plan-for-immigration/
88. ICIBI *An inspection of the EU Settlement Scheme November 2018–January 2019* published May 2019.
89. House of Commons Home Affairs Committee EU Settlement Scheme Fifteenth Report of Session 2017–19 https://publicati

ons.parliament.uk/pa/cm201719/cmselect/cmhaff/1945/1945.pdf page 17.
90. ICIBI ibid., para 6.13.
91. ICIBI ibid., para 6.39, 6.45–48.
92. ICIBI ibid., para 6.51.
93. Sumption, Madeleine and Fernández-Reino, Mariña *Unsettled status—2020: Which EU citizens are at risk of failing to secure their rights after Brexit?* https://migrationobservatory.ox.ac.uk/resources/reports/unsettled-status-2020/ accessed 26/11/21.
94. ICIBI *An inspection of the EU Settlement Scheme* (April 2019 to August 2019).
95. Home Office. 2021. *EU Settled Status Scheme quarterly statistics, September 2021.*

6

UK Immigration and Asylum Administration and Adjudication: Home Office Indifference to Rule of Law Principles

1 Introduction

UK immigration control stands out from other UK administrative law systems as learning little from scandals, mistakes and lost cases and showing indifference to outcomes. The evidence of the last 70 years shows that this is true of every aspect of immigration control, from the preparation of legislation, the design of application processes to decision-making, enforcement and conduct of litigation. This chapter reviews the legal issues raised by each aspect of immigration control against the basic requirements of the rule of law, referring to Lord Bingham's rule of law principles[1] and to Simon Halliday's discussion of legal conscientiousness.[2]

The rule of law is essential to a democracy. Lord Bingham sets out basic requirements:

> The law must be accessible … intelligible, clear and predictable;
>
> Ministers and public officers … must exercise the powers conferred on them in good faith, fairly, for the purpose for which the powers were conferred, without exceeding such powers and not unreasonably;

S. York, *The Impact of UK Immigration Law*,
https://doi.org/10.1007/978-3-030-98721-3_6

> Adjudicative procedures provided by the state should be fair;
>
> Means must be provided for resolving... bona fide civil disputes which the parties themselves are unable to resolve ...

2 The Design and Preparation of Legislation and Rules

Already from the 1950s the contested political pressure to control immigration led to the introduction of legislation, rules and procedure which were not transparent. That lack of transparency has lessened the 'intelligibility, clarity and predictability' of such laws: and led to complexity, unintended consequences and the frequent need for panic-driven measures to plug loopholes. I revisit examples from earlier chapters.

Chapter 2 showed that the underlying political aims of the Commonwealth Immigrants Acts 1962 and 1968 and the Immigration Act 1971 were to limit non-white settlement and labour immigration. However, designing legislation explicitly in terms of race was objectionable to many, and contrasted poorly with British pressure on its colonies to implement non-discriminatory constitutions providing for black majority rule. Ostensibly non-racial legal tests were devised. The 1962 Act focused control on 'those with passports issued in the Colonies'. The 1968 'Kenyan Asians' crisis showed that that test would not work, as the Kenyan Asians' passports had been issued in London after Kenya achieved independence. The 1968 Act quickly found another ostensibly non-racial test—'having a parent or grandparent born in the UK'. That test then did not work to assuage anxieties about large 'pools' of Commonwealth citizens still holding a right of entry. The incoherence of that legal test led in turn to the proliferation of specific Immigration Rules favouring people from the white Dominions, and the ineffective 'overseas' citizenships in the British Nationality Act 1981.

The Immigration Rules show similar gaps between real aims and the ostensible target, and equally unattractive unintended consequences. Governments wished to impede Asian men's access to the UK labour market. But the 'primary purpose' test for spouses and fiancé(e)s was legally odious because not an objective test and required an applicant to prove a negative: and the 'virginity testing' scandal showed that it was difficult to find an acceptable assessment mechanism. That test entrenched the imposition of the burden of proof on the applicant, and, precisely because not objective, enlarged the terrain of operations for the 'culture of disbelief'. Though formally repealed by Labour in 1997, the primary purpose test and its consequences live on in the consideration of 'genuine' relationships and 'sham' marriages.

Similarly, as asylum claims increased and demands grew to discourage them, legislative and procedural contrivances were sought as markers of a 'bogus' claim. These showed indifference to the legal content of an asylum claim, to what people actually had to do to get to a safe country, and to the unintended consequences of the legislation. The 1980s carriers' liability laws rested on a belief that 'genuine' asylum-seekers were already in the UK. But the Asylum and Immigration Act 1996 refusal of benefits to those did not claim on arrival, and the Nationality, Immigration and Asylum Act 2002's refusal of support to those who did not claim 'as soon as reasonably practicable', both precisely targeted those already in the UK. The markers of 'credibility' introduced in the Immigration Rules and then in the Asylum and Immigration (Treatment of Claimants) Act 2004, such as 'having travelled through other European countries' or 'having destroyed their identity documents', or 'not having provided full details straight away' were shown (and continue to be shown[3]) by NGO research and appeal statistics not to be useful indicators of 'genuine' claims. The 2021 proposals for a two-tier asylum system once more rely on specious arguments to offer more rights to those arriving on resettlement schemes than to those arriving 'spontaneously'.[4]

Important aspects of immigration legislation and rules have retrospective effects, violating the requirement of predictability. For example, the legislation stating that *the deportation of foreign criminals is in the public interest* is leading to what most people can only understand as retrospective punishments. Predictability was also violated in the Legacy programme, discussed in Chapter 5. Files were selected at random, leading inevitably to different treatment for people from the same country, with the same claim of persecution—and even for those who had escaped together or who were members of the same family. Retrospectivity, delay and legitimate expectation are discussed in Sect. 8 below.

Ensuring clarity and consistency in legislation and rules has been made difficult by the sheer frequency of legislative and rule changes. Chapters 2–5 have shown that many changes amount simply to relegislating, or to restrictions of rights with retrospective effect. The higher courts have criticised immigration law *as an architecture*.[5,6] The *Windrush Lessons Learned Review*[7] criticised the Home Office for its 'institutional amnesia' about the rights of Windrush people, and said:

> The ... sponsoring department ... ought to know its area of law in detail, from a contemporary and historical perspective. The public expect it to retain a full knowledge of its area of law, for the very reason that the public cannot be expected to understand the immigration process, especially as the complexity grows.

The *Windrush* review ascribes the complexity of immigration law and the 'institutional amnesia' of the Home Office to the climate of political pressure under which they work. This echoes the 2019 Institute for Government report:

> [the Home Office] operates under pressure to deliver high volumes of decisions and it operates in the face of societal and political pressures. This does not just affect the department's culture through the political will and intent coming from ministers; it also influences the work of staff whose experiences and views shape their actions.[8]

Simplification of laws, rules and procedural requirements would assist. Clearly, however, even this would require significant political determination. In 2020 the Home Office responded positively[9] to the Law Commission's proposals on simplifying the content and structure of the Immigration Rules. This will not make the rules less restrictive, but, *if sufficiently publicised*, may lead to fewer applications rejected for mistakes.

Lack of clarity of purpose and effect of changes in the Immigration Rules and policy, and lack of predictability, is facilitated by the *lack of democratic accountability*. The broader question of democratic accountability in immigration control is addressed more fully in Chapter 7. Here I simply note how big, controversial changes, whose undesirable effects could have been foreseen and may well have been widely objected to, have been introduced with little or parliamentary scrutiny. Some big changes have been introduced pursuant to previous subordinate legislation,[10] or even in redrafts of guidance to caseworkers,[11] with no scrutiny or publicity until the first applicants fell foul of them.

3 The Rule of Law and Operational Procedures: Legal Changes by Stealth[12]

Achieving clear linkage between legislative aims and measures implementing them, including clarity and accessibility of legislation and rules, would not be enough. The same must apply to operational procedures. It is difficult to navigate most immigration application procedures, as essential information is effectively hidden from the applicant. The Home Office separates its customer-facing communication from the applicable law and rules. The web page '*Family visa, apply, extend or switch*' contains a short summary. There is no link to the Immigration Rules—no reference even to the existence of 'immigration rules'; no reference to what is required for a valid application, what are the general grounds for refusal, or where to find the precise requirements of 'specified evidence'. On a separate UK Visas and Immigration website the Rules are hidden in the 'operational guidance' section. Nevertheless, applications are routinely refused for presenting evidence in the wrong format, and a wrong answer to an obscure question can be classified as 'deception', resulting in a mandatory refusal and a re-entry ban. And because the Home Office does not promptly or correctly reflect higher court decisions in its rules, regulations or policies, it is difficult for migrants to establish the caselaw which affects them.

The 2008 points-based system aimed to simplify applications and decision-making for students and workers. However, almost immediately, decisions were seen which were shocking to an ordinary, common-sense view of administrative decision-making. Applicants were refused for not providing a piece of evidence which they did not know they had to provide. Eventually, in the 2012 case of *Alvi*, the Supreme Court decided that if failure to comply with a requirement could lead to a refusal then that requirement had to be part of the Rules. Now the Immigration Rules consist of several hundred pages—itself an indigestible, incomprehensible barrier for many applicants.

Legal changes by stealth: The Home Office has gradually moved to online applications. The structure and methodology of the online forms *legally distance* applicants from accessing their rights and entitlements. The forms cannot be viewed without completing them. Without paying the fee, an applicant cannot see when or where to present documents. Questions on the form imply legal requirements going beyond the relevant rules. For examples, refugees applying for indefinite leave are asked what connections they still have in the country they fled from, which forms no part of a refugee's 'safe return review'.

The Home Office has deliberately introduced substantial changes in rules and procedures with little warning, to prevent a rush of applicants before new restrictions or mandatory procedures are brought in. Notable examples are: the 2011 requirement for new asylum-seekers to telephone for an appointment before making a claim[13] and the new 2012 family migration rules introduced after only 4 weeks' notice. The 2018 move to online forms for in-country applicants was so little heralded that applicants only found out when the appropriate paper form disappeared from the Home Office website.

A different type of stealth was shown in the Home Office failure to publicise the availability of support for 'failed asylum-seekers' under s4 Immigration and Asylum Act 1999. In 2004 *Salih & Rahmani*[14] determined that it was unlawful for the Secretary of State not to publicise the existence of the scheme.

4 Legal Conscientiousness: The Heavy Burden and Standard of Proof

Lord Bingham's second test requires that everyone from the Minister down to the outsourced deportation escort officer '*must exercise the powers conferred on them in good faith ...*'. Simon Halliday develops the concept of *legal conscientiousness*:

> Knowing what the law requires of you as a decision-maker is not enough to ensure compliance ... Decision-makers must also care about acting lawfully. ... They must be conscientious about applying their legal knowledge to the full range of their decision-making tasks. ... '*compliance is problematic unless there is an underlying attitude of willing co-operation*' ... *This, however, is a tall order.*[15]

Halliday identifies typical traits and features of decision-making in a public service lacking legal conscientiousness. These include reliance on '*professional intuition*' or a '*gut feeling*' that the applicant is lying; a culture of suspicion which arises from a 'siege mentality' in a public office under pressure. Officials often '*lack faith that the law will produce the right decision*', particularly when their decisions are overturned by the courts—not accepted as their having made a legal mistake. Quality of decision-making depends on there being a mechanism for decision-makers to learn about why their decisions were overturned: but there is often no institutional interest in learning from litigation.

All the characteristics described by Halliday are present in the immigration and asylum system. Exacerbating all of these in the world of immigration control is **the placing of the burden of proof on the applicant**. The effects of this were explored in relation to entry clearance cases in Chapter 2 and in relation to asylum in Chapter 3. Those analyses showed that where the burden of proof falls on an applicant there is little or no legal or procedural control on an institutional defendant. Refusing a claim on the basis that the applicant has not discharged the burden of proof is acceptable if properly reasoned. But decision-makers often go further, relying on their own 'professional intuition', 'gut feeling' or collective institutional folklore about 'that kind of applicant'. Or they may throw into the decision some unproven or insufficiently grounded 'facts'—with no duty to provide evidence or reasoning in support.

In immigration and asylum these phenomena have led to (at least) three legally repugnant outcomes. First, bureaucratic failings such as mistakes in recording names and dates lead to decisions where, because of the operation of the burden of proof, no effective challenge is possible. Negative 'findings of fact', even when arising from mistakes, remain as if indelibly marked on to the applicant. A Palestinian client was 'indelibly marked' with 'having made more than one asylum application' (a mandatory ground for refusal) because different officials transliterated his Arabic name variously as Ghalib and Khalib. An unaccompanied child client wrapped in five jackets to survive crossing the Channel in a refrigerated lorry was 'indelibly marked' with 'lying about being in touch with his parents' because there was a phone number on a scrap of paper in one of the jackets. No official, in charge of a 13-year-old child, had thought of telephoning it.

Secondly, the unequal burden of proof underlies the 'culture of disbelief' in both immigration and asylum decision-making, requiring applicants to prove negatives, where failure gives credence to government descriptions of certain types of applicant as 'bogus'.

Thirdly, it has led to a parallel tightening of the *standard* of proof. In 2018 the Home Office was forced to apologise to families for stating that 'it was imperative' that they provide DNA evidence of relationship.[16] The Home Office is ever reluctant to accept that an unremovable applicant's removal is indeed 'remote'.[17] Windrush people are still having to persuade officials that they had indeed been in the UK for X decades.[18]

It is salutary to contrast this with the position in the welfare benefits jurisdiction. In the 2004 case of *Kerr*,[19] Baroness Hale described and evaluated the process of making a claim and its adjudication. The complexity of the benefits system meant that '*the general public could not be expected to understand it*' but that should not result in claimants being denied their entitlements. '*What emerges from all this is a co-operative process of investigation in which both the claimant and the department play their part …*'.

In contrast, the placing of the burden of proof on the applicant and the unlawful tightening of the standard of proof together have tended to produce a standard of proof amounting to the criminal standard of 'beyond all reasonable doubt'. This view is echoed in a Freedom from Torture report[20] and has been highlighted in the *Windrush Lessons Learned Review*[21]:

> ... there is evidence that the Home Office had set the standard [of proof] much higher—... This is akin to the standard set in the criminal justice system of proving their status 'beyond reasonable doubt'. This interpretation of the standard is wrong in law. No one in the department knew the origin of this requirement, which a senior official confirmed to the Home Affairs Committee wasn't in the department's guidance to caseworkers. The fact that such a practice was adopted in parts of the organisation, yet its origins were unknown, is also indicative of the culture of the department...

5 Home Office Lack of Legal Conscientiousness in Decision-Making

5.1 Failure to Follow Its Own Policies and Guidance

Individual refusals often fail to apply the correct immigration rule or caselaw. The most notable examples of this are in asylum decision-making, in particular where clear guidance exists, such as on gender-based asylum claims,[22] the processing of asylum claims from children[23] and the treatment of credibility issues generally.[24] The 'best interests of the child', to be applied since the passing of s55 Borders, Citizenship and Immigration Act 2009, is noted in a stock paragraph in all Home Office guidance and in every refusal letter. But this has not prevented decision-makers from ignoring issues about children—and even ignoring the actual children in the case. Similarly, decisions fail to follow general definitions in the Immigration Rules such as where 'a parent' refers to anyone exercising a parental role.

Decisions which do not follow the law or published guidance, and which therefore have to go to appeal or judicial review, are wasteful for both parties and for wider society. Current waiting times for an appeal hearing are on average 52 weeks, 126 weeks in entry clearance appeals. Worse still, the Immigration Act 2014 changes in the grounds of appeal, discussed in Sect. 6.2 below, limit the protection an appeal could provide to applicants where the Home Office has not followed the rules or their own policies.

5.2 Bad-Faith Reliance on Poor Evidence in Large Categories of Cases

In 2011, when their university's sponsor licence was withdrawn because of immigration breaches, all international students at London Metropolitan University had their leave curtailed, leaving them 60 days to find an alternative course.[25] In 2014 around 40,000 students were accused of falsifying language tests in the 'TOIEC'[26] scandal, and had their leave curtailed.[27,28] In 2015 scores of Eritrean refugees saw their asylum applications refused on the basis of a much-criticised Danish 'fact-finding' report. In 2018 the Home Office used para 322(5) of the Rules to refuse labour migrants' applications for indefinite leave relying on agreed amendments to their tax returns.

The first two sets of cases showed a ready move from undoubted evidence that *some* students' visa breaches were not being dealt with by their sponsoring university, and that *some* people who had taken the ETS English language test had cheated, to an operational conclusion that everyone was guilty. The TOIEC litigation clearly showed Home Office indifference to the quality of the evidence. In the Eritrean cases the ready reliance on the Danish report despite its poor reputation showed a similar desire to grasp at any 'evidence' justifying the refusal of a large category of applicants.

The use of Para 322(5) of the General Grounds of Refusal (in which an applicant 'represents a threat to national security') to refuse indefinite leave showed a Home Office eagerness to rely on a transformation of 'deception' from how most people would understand it, i.e. as a deliberate act to disguise a true situation, to a retrospective punishment for past, innocent, errors. The Court of Appeal has allowed some appeals and litigation continues for others.[29]

5.3 Delay and Failure to Follow Legal Precedents

Home Office decision-making does not conscientiously follow caselaw. The 2006 'Stansted Afghans' case of *S & Ors* showed the Home Office unlawfully attempting to delay granting leave following an allowed appeal, to give time to introduce a new 'restricted leave' status to apply to foreign criminals. The courts declared this to be '*conspicuous unfairness amounting to an abuse of power*' ... '*authorised if not initiated "at the highest level"*'.[30]

Also during the 2000s the Home Office resisted deciding thousands of applications which should have been decided positively in line with important UK and European legal precedents. The Home Office took three years to implement the CJEU *Metock*[31] judgment. Similar delays were seen in relation to the marriage cases *Baiai*[32] and *Quila*,[33] and the Court of Justice of the European Union cases of *Teixeira/Ibrahim*[34] and *Zambrano*.[35]

Following the introduction of the 2012 'new rules' on family migration, the Home Office issued guidance to caseworkers advising that previous caselaw on art 8 rights to family and private life should not be followed—since the 'new rules' were a 'complete code'. This attempt to change the law through guidance took over a year to correct.[36] But not until *MM (Lebanon)*,[37] some five years after the 'new rules' were introduced, did the courts deal with the apparent exclusion of discretion for out-of-country applicants. During the four years of the *MM* litigation the Home Office 'paused' considerations of entry clearance applications relying on art 8. This was legally inappropriate. The *MM* cases were applications for judicial reviews by people who had not yet made an application, but who were challenging the legality of the rules themselves. People who had submitted applications were entitled to a determination of their case under the then-applicable rules, discretion and legal precedents. Similarly, the Home Office has currently 'paused' applications for fee waivers from out-of-country family applicants until Home Office guidance is updated following a settlement of an unreported legal challenge.[38] The Home Office's immediate reaction to the fall of Kabul in August 2021 was to try to adjourn or stay Afghans' appeals against refusal of asylum, removal and deportation 'until the situation is clarified', while the legally correct position is to consider the risk of harm at the date of the hearing.[39] It is encouraging that some immigration judges have refused adjournments and promptly allowed the appeals.[40]

The Home Office delayed accepting that the two-year extension of the 2004–2009 Workers Registration Scheme for nationals of the A8 countries was unlawful,[41] wrongly delaying thousands of A8 nationals' access to permanent residence, and wrongly deeming their children born after the original five-year period not to be British citizens.

6 The Rule of Law and the Conduct of Appeals

A 2018 Justice report[42] noted the increased proportion of allowed appeals, then 37% of asylum claims and over 50% of 'managed migration' claims compared to 12% in 1977–1985, with three-quarters of Home Office appeals to the Upper Tribunal being defeated.

A complaint that applicants often provide new evidence in the appeal that was not available to the original decision-maker has been used by the Home Office to justify removing certain rights of appeal, suggesting that applicants should make a further (charged-for) application instead. However, often 'new evidence' has been presented to the Secretary of State, but lost, misfiled or ignored by decision-makers. This is shown in appeals where Home Office Presenting Officers withdraw the decision on the day as unsustainable, leaving the tribunal ready to decide an appeal but with no jurisdiction to hear it. This has been deprecated by judges, and recent Home Office guidance[43] sets out a clear position: *A decision should only be withdrawn with a view to granting leave.*

Recent Tribunal practice directions dealing with costs[44] require the Secretary of State to review an appeal within 6 weeks of its being lodged, and then again whenever there are any 'material developments' such as the receipt of further evidence or a change in the law. The Secretary of State is reminded not to persist in defending unjustifiable decisions. New Directions[45] require the Secretary of State to provide a list of agreed and contested facts. Practitioners wait for evidence that this is taking place.

The Justice report recommended a more rigorous approach to enforcement, including time limits for submission of evidence, and a greater use of wasted costs orders for non-compliance, which should be *exercised even-handedly between appellants and the Home Office.* The *New Plan for Immigration*[46] persists in ascribing delays in the appeals system to a lack of good faith on the applicants' side—but delays largely arise from the institutional respondent's own behaviour, as well as the cuts in Ministry of Justice resources discussed below.

An important aspect of legal conscientiousness is the **conduct of litigation**. There has been no specific review or inspection of the Government Legal Department's immigration casework,[47] but applicant lawyers' experience and caselaw evidence suggest that the GLD considers itself less independent from its 'client', and as owing fewer duties to the courts, than do solicitors in practice, otherwise there would surely be less inclination to 'defend unjustifiable decisions' or to countenance poor litigation standards in high-profile cases, recently demonstrated in the 2021 *Napier Barracks* case.[48] In relation to the tribunals, the ICIBI has looked at the Home Office Presenting Officer (HOPO) function,[49] but again concentrated on the 'efficiency' of the function, only briefly looking at aspects of legal conscientiousness such as permitting HOPOs to concede an appeal without consulting a senior officer.

7 Curtailing and Undermining Access to Redress—The 'Revenge Package'

Lord Bingham's third requirement is that '*adjudicative procedures provided by the state should be fair*'. Arguably this includes access to those procedures, but since 2010 access has deteriorated.

7.1 Cuts in Legal Aid[50]

As part of post-2008 austerity, in 2010 all legal aid payment rates were reduced by 10%. That precipitated the 2010 financial collapse of Refugee Migrant Justice, handling over 30% of asylum claims in England and

Wales. New legislation[51] taking virtually all non-asylum immigration cases out of scope of legal aid led to the 2011 financial collapse of the Immigration Advisory Service, responsible for 10,000 immigration and asylum cases annually. Deep cuts in local authority funding led to the closure of many law centres and advice agencies.[52]

The Justice report noted the fall in numbers of legal aid practices, and a re-emergence of very poor and even corrupt 'advice' given to appellants in the immigration and asylum tribunals. Jo Wilding (2019)[53] shows how hard it is even for asylum applicants to find good quality legal assistance. Reports from specialist agencies describe the lack of good quality advice for child asylum-seekers (even though legal aid has been reintroduced for them)[54] and for those wishing to make fresh claims.[55]

The *New Plan for Immigration* proposes to '*provide more generous access to advice, including legal advice, to support people to raise issues, provide evidence as early as possible and avoid last minute claims*'. However, the vague references to '*how advice can be improved at different points in the process*'[56] imply poorly funded 'initiatives' providing small segments of 'advice' in a detention centre or prison, rather than the full advice and representation provided before the cuts.

7.2 Reduction in Rights of Appeal, Limiting Grounds of Appeal; Limiting Access to Judicial Review

The Immigration Act 2014 was celebrated by Theresa May as *reducing 17 rights of appeal to four*, a mendacious claim, since the previous rights of appeal attached to specific 'immigration decisions', and any individual migrant might face at most two or three 'immigration decisions' in a complicated immigration history. The new appeal rights related to the 'right' being denied: a protection (asylum) claim, a human rights claim, a revocation of protection status, appeals specified under EEA regulations, and against deprivation of citizenship. The changes have led to a big rise in the number of judicial reviews and appeals to the Court of Appeal.[57]

The Act also amended the *grounds* of appeal. There is now no appeal on the simple ground that the Home Office has not followed the law, the

Immigration Rules or its own policy. A person wrongly found not to have met the Rules can only appeal on human rights grounds, and the appeal may only be allowed on human rights grounds. Home Office guidance[58] states that if the tribunal determination finds that the Rules are met, the relevant leave should be granted—but not all determinations make such clear findings, leaving the family and long residence appellants at risk of being relegated to the '10-year route'.

For visitors, students, workers and statelessness applicants, an administrative review is available. This procedure is limited to 'caseworking errors'.[59] There is no reassessment of the facts, the application of any Convention rights or the reasonableness of any decision: and certainly no opportunity to present oral evidence, arguably essential where credibility is in issue. In the TOIEC case of *Mohibullah*,[60] the Upper Tribunal described the effect on that appellant:

> this decision effectively branded the Applicant a fraudster, a person who had abused immigration laws and control; required him to leave the United Kingdom, where he had been established for several years; blighted his academic and career prospects; rendered null the substantial financial investment which he had made in his studies in the United Kingdom; and blacklisted him with regard to future immigration decisions.

In section 94B Immigration Act 2014, the government introduced a 'deport first, appeal later' procedure to limit foreign criminals' access to art 8 ECHR. The 2016 Act extended s94B to all family and private life applicants, seeking to 'remove first' even those family migrants with strong human rights claims. Following the Supreme Court case of *Kiarie & Byndloss*[61] the Home Office has not attempted to implement s94B. But the online application form requires all family and private life applicants to explain why an out-of-country appeal would not work for them, even where their applications meet the relevant Immigration Rules.[62]

The Home Office has effectively abandoned the one-stop appeals procedure, in which an appellant must raise all reasons for wishing to remain in the UK. The legal basis of this, section 120 Nationality,

Immigration and Asylum Act (NIAA) 2002, remains in force. However, current Home Office practice to refuse to consider different types of reasons for remaining in the UK in the same application has been approved in the Court of Appeal.[63] The driver of this policy appears to be to force applicants to pay the prohibitive fees for each 'reason for remaining in the UK'. The court decided that the consequences, which include applicants making what are defined as non-human rights applications necessarily becoming unlawfully present before they can make their (separate) human rights application, could not be considered without a separate public law challenge. The *New Plan for Immigration* proposes 'introducing' a one-stop process, having failed to notice its own responsibility for eroding the operation of the existing provision.[64]

Finally, fees for judicial review have significantly increased and restrictions in the legal aid regime have made it prohibitive for legal aid practices to take on immigration judicial reviews, since all work up to the grant of permission is at risk to the practitioner.

None of this is new. The 6th (2005) edition of *Macdonald's immigration law and practice*[65] noted that the '*the government's reaction [to judicial decisions] has been unprecedented and … quite disproportionate*', including '*seeking to curtail judges' decisions on credibility and the safety of particular countries*'… '*telescoping appeal rights*', introducing '*non-suspensive appeals*' and '*curtailing legal aid*'. Richard Rawlings (2005) characterised the Home Office's actions in this period as a '*revenge package*'.[66] In 2003, during the passage of the Asylum and Immigration (Treatment of Claimants) Bill, attempts were made to exclude migrants' access to judicial review altogether. By the UK Borders Act 2007 some immigration judicial reviews (fresh claims for asylum and age disputes of child asylum-seekers) were removed into the Upper Tribunal. The Crime and Courts Act 2013 removed the remainder of immigration judicial reviews into the Upper Tribunal.[67] The effect of this has been significant. Judicial review, the tactical nuclear weapon of public law, is essential in immigration and asylum precisely because the only way of ensuring an urgent and legally competent response is a formal threat of judicial review and an application for an injunction. But a simple judicial review of a Home Office mistaken treatment of a migrant can now take several months if not more than a year.[68] In 2017, of 22,610 pre-action letters, 13,855 resulted in the issue of proceedings.[69] Thus some 9,000 applicants may have obtained a remedy without going to court—inconceivable through a complaints mechanism lacking injunctive relief. But 'reforms' mean that such applicants' legal costs can only be claimed from the Home Office if the applicant 'obtained the remedy sought'—further deterring legal aid solicitors from lodging judicial review claims.

8 The Rule of Law and Delay, Mistakes, Legitimate Expectation and Retrospective Measures

The courts' view of caseworking delay in immigration and asylum has moved a long way. Early in the 2000s, asylum applicants left in backlogs by changes of policy were deemed to have suffered '*an abuse of process*'. In 2005, *Rashid*[70] found '*conspicuous unfairness*' in treating this applicant less favourably than previous applicants with identical cases. Similarly, the case of *R(S)*[71] found that S had suffered '*an abuse of process*' as a new performance target led to the neglect of older cases. Boswell (2018) focuses on those targets in her critical analysis of Home Office performance management.[72] The judicial approach to the Legacy cases in *FH* and *Hamzeh*, discussed in Chapter 5, revealed a reexamination of the *Rashid* and *R(S)* position. Those cases were criticised for introducing a 'corrective principle' into immigration and asylum law, marking an unacceptable retreat from requiring that the test of a well-founded fear of persecution had to be met at the date of decision.[73] It was subsequently decided that *Rashid* and *R(S)* should no longer be followed.[74,75] The 'corrective principle' was demolished. Asylum claims must be decided according to risk at the time of decision. The Home Office should not be 'sanctioned' for administrative incompetence or other past policy errors. Applicants left high and dry by delay, mistakes or past unlawful policies must be assessed in accordance with current Immigration Rules and guidance. Recent research[76] and litigation[77] concerning delays in children's asylum claims show the particular impact of these court rulings on those whose rights depend upon their age.

Looking at the issues in a less strictly legal way, considering wider issues including good public administration, some important features can be identified.

8.1 People 'of Concern'

Many whose cases finished up in the Legacy and those who fell victim to the rejection of the 'corrective remedy' argument arguably should straight away have been treated as 'of concern' to the UNHCR, and granted some kind of leave.[78] It is unsurprising that nationals of 'failed states', such as Somalia, Iraq, Afghanistan and Zimbabwe, have not made voluntary returns. It is unsurprising that they would have retained expectations of their being allowed to remain in the UK. Even if a grant of *asylum* must be based on a present risk of individual persecution, a high-level decision from the late 1980s to identify a separate category of people 'of concern' and promptly grant humanitarian leave to them may have largely avoided the issue of backlogs (as well as avoiding the wider effects of stigmatising so many as 'bogus'). Even a later identification of that category would have provided a more politically acceptable pathway through the Legacy and afterwards, based on international law.

8.2 Retrospective Effect

The courts have held that deciding a case in accordance with rules brought in since an application was made, and making a deportation decision in accordance with legislation not dreamed of when the crime was committed, is not 'retrospective'.[79] That may be 'the law' but, looked at in the light of Lord Bingham's demand that law should be predictable, and especially in a context of long caseworking delays, such decisions are discomfiting. Retrospective measures are generally deprecated as unfair and eroding of respect for the law.[80] Since no parliament can bind a successor, and political opinions may well change about the rights and entitlements to be offered, laws and rules may validly become more restrictive over time. But 'simple fairness' surely suggests that the effect on *individuals* should be minimised, as people cannot always adjust their lives to meet new requirements without loss. The tribulations of a public authority, in failing to meet demand for the permissions over which it keeps guard, in delaying thousands of decisions, in being deemed 'not fit for purpose' or 'not good enough', should surely have no bearing on whether that individual application met the requirements applicable at the time.

I argue that future heavier requirements for people starting a 'route to settlement' should not apply to people already embarked on that 'route'. We cannot bind a future parliament, but we should surely expect it to respect the way ordinary people plan their lives. This was central to the *HSMP Forum* case.[81] That concerned a group of 'highly-skilled migrants' offered a visa to work in the UK with a view to settling here. The court decided that the scheme was *presented* as a long-term scheme, encouraging and expecting the applicants to make significant life changes. It was found to be unfair, and a breach of *those applicants'* legitimate expectations, for amendments to be made affecting those already in the scheme. But anyone embarking on a scheme entitled 'route to settlement' may reasonably wonder why this does not apply to them. As it is, anyone on a 'route to settlement' remains legally precarious,[82,83] facing the possibility of future rule changes and fee increases impossible to meet, clearly interfering with the 'quiet enjoyment' of an immigration status labelled as a 'route to settlement'.

Changes to the good character requirements for naturalisation, introduced almost without notice in January 2015, have a clear retrospective effect. Illegal entry now precludes naturalisation for 10 years. This principally affects refugees, almost all of whom will have entered illegally, but who previously were eligible to apply for naturalisation after 5 years leave to remain and one year's indefinite leave. Though the Refugee Convention rules out punishment for illegal entry, the new guidance may still be applied to those who '*travel across several European countries to claim in the UK*'.[84] It also affects EU nationals, in respect of whom the heavy requirements to have held comprehensive private sickness insurance[85] for every part of that 10-year period not covered by national insurance contributions will deny citizenship for many years.

Two welfare benefits measures, the 'bedroom tax' (brought in by Regulations, after the Welfare Reform Act 2012), and the 'two-child policy', brought in in 2017,[86] bear the same performative style, uncertain benefits and negative unintended consequences of many Home Office measures. Both those policies apply 'now' and 'in future' to people for whom the operative decision may have been made some time ago when their personal circumstances were different: and where, certainly in the case of the two-child policy, there is no future act the person can reasonably do to avoid falling foul of the provision.

The Immigration Act 2014's introduction of 'public interest' criteria into judicial consideration, in the form of the present-tense slogans of timeless application '*the maintenance of immigration control **is** in the public interest*' and '*deportation of foreign criminals **is** in the public interest*', similarly introduced factors to be considered 'now' and 'in future' in respect of a person's past conduct, about which it has been said '*not even God can abolish historical fact*'.[87] The deportation case of *MA (Pakistan)*[88] concerned a person who had won an earlier appeal against deportation and been granted two subsequent periods of leave to remain, but on a further application for leave had been refused and served with a decision to deport. The court determined that there are just two questions to be answered: 'Is deportation of that applicant conducive to the public good?' and 'did any change in the law entitle the Secretary of State to reopen the decision?', and the court's answer to both those questions was 'yes'—the second being answered by the 2014 introduction of the public interest criteria. The Court of Appeal decided that the decision to deport him was not retrospective. However, a previous tribunal had decided that *his* continued presence in the UK was *not* 'not conducive to the public good'. That had been confirmed by the Home Office by two subsequent grants of leave. He had since done nothing to make *his* deportation conducive again. By itself, the change in the law, declaring deportation to be timelessly 'in the public interest' could not make it 'conducive' *for him.* A brave Court of Appeal should have decided that the conducive issue is *res judicata* for that applicant.[89] They did not. A subsequent case, *Abidoye*,[90] discusses and rejects the application of *res judicata*, nevertheless sympathising with the appellant, '*empathising*' with the characterising of the new decision as '*moving the goalposts*' where there had been no '*adverse factual changes in the circumstances*'. This case raises two related legal questions. In *Odelola*, decided over ten years ago, the Lords decided that since the Immigration Rules do not create a 'vested right', no transitional provisions could be inferred. But, given that the deportation cases concern primary legislation, it is not clear why transitional provisions were not inferred, limiting applicability of s117C to those convicted after a certain date, as in the 'automatic deportation' provisions of the UK Borders Act 2007.[91] Secondly, as presented in an application to the Supreme Court,[92] Mr. Abidoye asks the simple and what may in the end have to be a political question, since the labyrinthine common law arguments seem unable to confront it head on:

> ...whether [s117C NIAA 2002] is to be construed so as to deprive a successful applicant of a judgment rightly given and still subsisting in the absence of any reoffending or a material change in the factual circumstances ...

Nevertheless, on 15/12/21 the Supreme Court refused permission to appeal, '*because the application does not raise an arguable point of law of general public importance*'.

Referring back to the NAO report on foreign criminals quoted in Chapter 5,[93] the greater political question is in what way is the public interest served by deporting, at great expense, someone long since accepted by both a court and the Home Office to pose no threat of reoffending.

9 Outsourcing and the Hostile Environment: 'Legal Distancing', Criminalising, Creating and Perpetuating Illegality

Since the 1980s the Home Office has steadily increased its use of the private sector to provide asylum accommodation and carry out enforcement and application processes; and placed obligations on individuals and institutions in civil society to play the role of immigration officers, to the point of introducing criminal penalties for failure to participate in this. These developments have had two important consequences, each raising questions about the operation of the rule of law. First, the migrant is *legally distanced* from remedies for breaches in the provision of services for them or for breaches in the duty of care, for example to someone in detention or in receipt of 'no-choice' accommodation.

The second legal consequence arises from the criminalising of non-compliance by the rest of civil society. It is proposed that these measures both require and will engender a regime where society's relation to the migrant implies a prior acceptance that an irregular migrant's mere presence is not just technically unlawful, but *always anti-social and always and indubitably unacceptable.* This amounts to a profound divergence from an essential aspect of the rule of law—that the law must be clear, and that those implementing laws must stay within their bounds.

9.1 'Legal Distancing'

Discussing outsourcing of public sector functions, Peter Cane[94] concludes that the legal position is that where a public authority is charged by primary legislation with a public duty according to a legislative scheme for assessing entitlement, that authority *remains* charged with such duties despite any contracting out of any of the relevant 'functions'. However, Cane argued that such reasoning is unlikely to provide reliable protection against the '*hollowing out of the state*'. Paul Craig, writing in 2002, argued that: '*contracting out will serve to preclude any meaningful action against the public body*'.[95] This was considered by the Supreme Court,[96] which decided that a personal non-delegable duty of care may be found in limited circumstances.[97] The court's criteria include the vulnerability of the claimant, a high degree of control, custody or care, a lack of choice for the claimant on how the obligations may be performed; that the function delegated is integral to the positive duty owed by the defendant; and where the negligence is in the performance of the very function assumed by the defendant and delegated to the contracted out entity.[98] This should apply to people placed in 'no choice' accommodation—and would certainly apply to people placed in immigration detention and removal centres, or transported under custodial escort.

However, looking at the different outsourcing contracts concerning migrants, it is easy to see why there are so few legal claims despite copious evidence of poor and even negligent service.[99] There are basic questions of economics. Outsourcing must inevitably provide a worse service, since profit is being extracted from a contract awarded to the lowest bidder, by a public authority attempting to save money from providing an in-house service. The ability of an applicant to achieve an appropriate remedy in any case where a public body has failed in a duty of care, or to administer an application process correctly, depends on there being properly-kept records of transactions and proper complaints procedures correctly followed. But outsourcing to a cheap contract from which profit is extracted leads to cuts in staff time, lower morale, poor office procedures and inadequate office equipment, all reducing an applicant's ability to collect the evidence to show the mistreatment or other breach in provision of the 'service'. '*Routinely, public bodies run contracts in ways which do not adhere to the formal contractual provisions, and fail to lay the paper trail needed to translate councillors' complaints of bad practice into specific and cogent evidence, which could justify treating the service agreement as repudiated*'.[100] Thus the outsourcing process inevitably *legally distances* the migrant from any remedy for breach. For example, Bales and Mayblin (2018) examine the way immigration detainees are effectively forced to work.[101]

Legal distancing also results from the mode of operation of hostile environment policies such as the 'right to rent' and controls on employment. Before a migrant can enter into a legal contract for accommodation or a job, the prospective employer or landlord must enter a transaction *with the Home Office*, on which the migrant's 'right' to rent or work depends, but to which they are not a party. A Home Office mistake gives rise to a judicial review—which however cannot ensure either the accommodation or the job, or any compensation.

The most significant of the hostile environment measures were the draconian controls on access to private accommodation. The 'right to rent' scheme was misnamed, since the legislation gave no rights to anybody, but set out a scheme of *prohibition*. The 2014 Act prohibited an irregular migrant (as defined) from 'occupying premises under a residential tenancy agreement'.[102] The Immigration Act 2016 made it a criminal offence for an owner or landlord to let property where not only the tenant but any of the occupants do not have leave to remain.[103] The 'right to rent' scheme appears to include some discretion. Section 21 (3) says:

> (3) But P is to be treated as having a right to rent in relation to premises ... if the Secretary of State has granted P permission ...

However, it transpired following two pre-action letters sent by the author[104] that there was no intention that a migrant should be able to *apply* for permission to rent. Following that pre-action correspondence and a House of Lords debate, that guidance was amended[105] to say this:

> **How can an individual enquire upon their permission to rent?**
> A migrant without leave who is looking to take up a new tenancy and considers that they meet the criteria set out above can enquire whether they have permission to rent ...

Not '*may apply for permission to rent*'. There is still no room for representations (by someone awaiting an appeal against refusal of a meritorious application, or having been wrongly classified by the Home Office as unlawfully present). Clearly this is not 'an application procedure' under public law. The migrant is not a party *to the decision to give them permission to* rent but is expected to *accept a decision made about them* or try to make urgent representations to the 'team dealing with their case' which is unlikely to respond for several months or at all.

The JCWI litigation[106] focused on the law's discriminatory effects. It did not deal with the issue of the *legal distancing* of the migrant from the decision, nor highlight the effect on 'mixed families', where, in an existing tenancy, one or more family members may be, or have just become, unlawfully present, leaving a British or settled tenant an ugly choice between kicking their partner or grown-up child out of the house or losing their home altogether. A cross-party group of MPs urged a review of the policy, noting that there had been no proper assessment of its impact.[107]

9.2 Criminalising the Very Person of the Migrant

Making it a criminal offence for an individual to contract with another individual on the basis of irregular immigration status, far from being straightforwardly 'the right thing to do', raises profound issues of how we regard each other in society, and what duties any of us owe to the authorities in respect of other people. These measures represent an attempt to equate in the eyes of wider society the irregularity of any particular migrant's immigration status with the unassailable public unacceptability of, for example, allowing one's home to be used for sexually assaulting children or for employing trafficked children in the growing of illegal drugs. There are two kinds of difficulties here. First, the position of an insecure migrant is complex and changing. At any moment, their 'illegality' may be merely alleged, may be temporary (as in the case of a refugee applying for indefinite leave a few days after his leave expired), may be challengeable, may be subject to application, or wrong but unprovable, as in the Windrush cases. In contrast, the letting of property to or the making of other types of contracts with *convicted* criminals is not itself a crime: and only in limited circumstances is it a distinct criminal offence to use premises for other criminal activity. Secondly, criminalising citizens or institutions for entering into contracts with irregular migrants effectively requires and encourages citizens to develop the view that the mere unlawfulness of a migrant makes not just the *presence* of that migrant but *that migrant herself* antisocial, corrosive, corrupting and so on. The imposition of criminal penalties on individuals and organisations in civil society in those circumstances appears to violate basic principles of British criminal law: '*indeed the whole basis of the common law is the right of the individual to refuse to answer questions put to him by persons in authority*'.[108]

And, given the significant chance that the decision on the unlawfulness might be a bureaucratic mistake (discussed in Chapter 5), such views may be applied wrongly to lawful migrants, with limited access to effective legal challenges. A brief look at the NHS responsibility for imposing charges for access to health care shows the conflict between the principles of health care and the imposition of these measures; the lack of support for the measures; the indifference to cost-effectiveness; the public health risks and the degradation of the rule of law for affected migrants. Despite the evidence that the scheme is not cost-effective,[109] and despite the 2015 introduction of the Immigration Health Surcharge,[110] the scheme continues. This scheme forces NHS staff to *treat as illegal* all those who have the right to be in the UK but who cannot prove it in the precise way required by the NHS charging regulations. All those who are too afraid to register with a GP, or ask for the medical treatment they require, are driven to *act as if illegal*, i.e. by not seeking medical treatment they need. Such people, even if lawfully present, are thus contingently *rendered as if illegal* in their relationship to the NHS, whose role is thus not that of a neutral public authority, but an arms-length enforcement branch of the Home Office which, because no discretion is permitted, requires migrants to prove their status 'beyond reasonable doubt'.

9.3 Creating and Perpetuating Illegality

Chapter 3 described how the headline policies of 'reducing net migration to the tens of thousands', reducing access to art 8 ECHR and creating a 'really hostile environment' for unlawful-present migrants have all made it increasingly difficult not just for people wishing to regularise, but for those who must make repeat applications to remain lawfully present. It is proposed that, far from succeeding in a policy to encourage voluntary returns of those without leave to remain, Home Office policies are themselves *creating and perpetuating illegality*.[111] The combination of lengthy probationary periods of five and ten years, which must be survived on a regime of no recourse to public funds, and with every application costing significantly more than the one before, makes it difficult for irregular migrants to regularise even when their situation is provided for in the Immigration Rules. Future increases and future restrictive rule changes make it difficult for lawfully-present migrants to keep up their status, and often families fall back into the hostile environment through not being able to afford to renew their visa, without being quite poor enough to qualify for a fee waiver. The application for indefinite leave to remain is particularly expensive, and a fee waiver cannot be used, so migrants are forced to reapply for further limited leave, thereby remaining 'precarious'. The ICIBI noted that in 2016 the Home Office had decided that *for most 'non-growth routes' ('settlement, nationality and other/family leave to remain') the [fees] increase would be higher and be front-loaded: 25/18/0/0%, equivalent to a 47.5% compound increase over the 4 years.*[112] He noted that [the impact assessments] '*have not assessed the non-financial, non-economic impacts of the fees and proposed annual changes, for example how the wellbeing of vulnerable groups, families or children may be impacted, or the potential consequences for social integration*'.[113] These difficulties were brought to public attention during the Covid emergency, as people wishing to extend work visas and those hitherto on 'routes to settlement' with no recourse to public funds find that they can no longer meet all the requirements, while no government assistance is being provided to them. A November 2021 report from Citizens Advice exposes '*a comprehensive picture of hardship*' suffered by this cohort of migrants.[114]

The 2019 Institute for Government report[115] noted that the revenue from application fees is now a significant proportion of the Home Office budget, and is used to spend on projects and programmes with no cost control (such as the £780m annually on trying but failing to deport foreign criminals), or with no monitoring or evaluation for effectiveness (such as the hostile environment measures themselves), while at the same time the actual work for which the fees are paid continues to be slow, inefficient and prone to legal mistakes.

This is despite the entire stated purpose, as set out in the Rules themselves, of the 5- and 10-year routes is that they are routes *to settlement*, for family and long-resident migrants who, *at the beginning of the route*, met the rules, policies and art 8 requirements for those routes. The March 2019 ICIBI report on immigration and nationality fees[116] recommended a new (wider than 2013) public consultation on Home Office charging, in time for the 2019 Spending Review, considering in particular:

> …the negative effects on individuals and families of requiring repeated applications for leave prior to considering settlement, the option of tapering the fee for second and subsequent applications for leave where the applicant's circumstances have not changed, and setting shorter timescales for decisions to grant or refuse applications.

The current world of long-delayed case decision based on current rules and settlement schemes based on repeated, expensive applications over many years at risk of future rule changes, along with the hostile environment measures, place long-resident migrants in a world of retrospective effects and so tend to *create and perpetuate illegality.*

Notes

1. Bingham, Tom 2011. *The rule of law* London: Penguin [88].
2. Halliday, Simon. 2004. *Judicial review and compliance with administrative law* London: Bloomsbury Publishing.
3. See for example the Migration Observatory's recent Q&A on migrants arriving in small boats, https://migrationobservatory.ox.ac.uk/resources/commentaries/qa-migrants-crossing-the-english-channel-in-small-boats/ accessed 26/11/21.
4. Home Office. 2021. *New Plan for Immigration.*
5. *Alvi, R (oao) v SSHD* [2012] UKSC 33, [2012] WLR(D) 211, [2012] 1 WLR 2208.
6. *Pokhriyal v SSHD* [2013] EWCA Civ 1568.
7. Williams, Wendy. 2020. *Windrush lessons learned review* Home Office.
8. Institute for Government. 2019. *Managing migration after Brexit* [36].
9. Home Office. 2020. *Simplifying the immigration rules: A response* Policy paper March.
10. The very big increases in application fees—see Sect. 9.
11. The significant extension back in time of the reach of the good character requirement for citizenship—see Chapter 7.

12. I first discussed this and other aspects of 'legal distancing' in York, Sheona 2020. Privatisation, '*mission creep*' *and lack of Home Office legal conscientiousness in the immigration application process*. Journal of Immigration, Asylum and Nationality Law, 34 (1).
13. ILPA *Making an asylum claim* Information sheet 15/8/2011; letter from Home Office to ILPA 10/2/2012 replying to criticisms about the screening process.
14. *R (Salih & Rahmani) v SSHD* [2003] EWHC 2273 Admin.
15. Halliday, Simon. 2004. *Judicial review and compliance with administrative law* London: Hart Publishing Limited.
16. HC Deb Immigration: DNA Tests Volume 648 25 October 2018 col 468.
17. York, Sheona. 2015. *Revisiting removability in the 'hostile environment'*. Birkbeck Law Review, 3 (2). pp. 227–257.
18. House of Commons Home Affairs Committee. 2021. *The Windrush Compensation Scheme Fifth Report of Session 2021–22.*
19. *Kerr* [2004] UKHL 23.
20. Freedom from Torture. 2016. *Proving Torture—Demanding the impossible—Home Office mistreatment of expert medical evidence.*
21. *Windrush Lessons Learned Review* n7 [98].
22. Home Office. 2018. *Gender issues in the asylum claim.*
23. Home Office. 2019. *Children's asylum claims.*
24. Home Office. 2015. Asylum Policy Instruction *Assessing credibility and refugee status* Version 9.0 6.
25. Richardson, Hannah. 2013. BBC *London Met wins back foreign student licence* 9/4/2013 https://www.bbc.co.uk/news/education-22080301 accessed 26/11/21.
26. Test of English for International Communication.
27. NUSUK 2018 *The TOIEC Scandal—An ongoing injustice.*
    Dunt, Ian. 2016. http://www.politics.co.uk/blogs/2016/03/23/disaster-for-theresa-may-as-legal-ruling-brings-student-depo accessed 26/11/21.
28. *R(Mohibullah) v SSHD* [2016] UKUT *00561* (IAC); *Ahsan and others v* [2017] EWCA Civ 2009.
29. *Balajigari and others v SSHD* [2019] EWCA Civ 673.

30. *S & Ors, R (oao) v SSHD* [2006] EWHC 1111 (Admin) [102], upheld by the Court of Appeal in *S & Ors* [2006] EWCA Civ 1157.
31. *Metock and Others (Area of Freedom, Security and Justice)* [2008] EUECJ C-127/08.
32. *Baiai* [2008] *UKHL* 53; https://www.freemovement.org.uk/certificates-of-approval-abolished/ accessed 10/7/20.
33. *Quila* [2011] UKSC 45.
34. *Teixeira (European citizenship)* [2010] EUECJ C-480/08 23/2/2010, *Ibrahim (European citizenship)* [2010] EUECJ C-310/08 (23 February 2010).
35. *Ruiz Zambrano (European citizenship)* [2011] EUECJ C-34/09 8/3/2011.
36. York, Sheona. 2015. *Immigration Control and the Place of Article 8 in the UK Courts—An update.* Journal of Immigration, Asylum and Nationality Law, 29 (3). pp. 289–307.
37. *MM (Lebanon) & Ors, R (on the applications of) v SSHD and another* [2017] UKSC 10.
38. Reported on Free Movement 8/3/21.
39. *Ravichandran,* cited in Sect. 8.
40. Immigration lawyers' Google group information.
41. *The Secretary of State for Work and Pensions v Gubeladze* [2017] EWCA Civ 1751, on appeal from a 30/1/2015 judgment of the Upper Tribunal (Administrative Appeals Chamber).
42. Cranston, Sir Ross. 2018. *Immigration and asylum appeals—A fresh look* A report by JUSTICE, see also Taylor, Diane, 2018. https://www.theguardian.com/uk-news/2018/sep/03/inhumane-three-quarters-of-home-office-asylum-appeals-fail Guardian 3/9/2018 accessed 27/11/21.
43. Home Office. *Withdrawing decisions. Version 3.0 Guidance for Presenting Officers* February.
44. PRESIDENTIAL GUIDANCE NOTE No. 2 of 2018.
45. DIRECTIONS TO REPRESENTED APPELLANTS (PRESIDENTIAL PRACTICE STATEMENT No 2 of 2020), Annex 1 to Immigration and Asylum Chamber First-tier Tribunal User Guide 12/6/20.

46. *New Plan for Immigration* 2021 n4.
47. ICIBI 2018 *An inspection of the Home Office's mechanisms for learning from immigration litigation April–July 2017* said little about the role and ethos of the Government Legal Department itself.
48. *NB & Ors [Napier Barracks] [2021] EWHC 1489 (Admin).*
49. ICIBI 2021 *An inspection of the Home Office Presenting Officer function* (November 2019 – October 2020).
50. York, Sheona 2013. *The end of legal aid in immigration: A barrier to access to justice for migrants and a decline in the rule of law.* Journal of Immigration, Asylum and Nationality Law, 27 (2). pp. 97–194.
51. Legal Aid, Sentencing and Punishment of Offenders Act 2012.
52. York n50.
53. Wilding, Jo. 2019. *Droughts and deserts: A report on the Immigration legal aid market* University of Brighton.
54. The Legal Aid, Sentencing and Punishment of Offenders Act 2012 (Legal Aid for Separated Children) (Miscellaneous Amendments) Order 2019 No. 1396.
55. For example from Coram Children's Legal Centre.
56. *New Plan for Immigration* 2021 n4 [28].
57. Cranston 2018 n42.
58. Home Office 2020 *Implementing allowed appeals* [5].
59. Appendix AR of the Immigration Rules.
60. *R(Mohibullah) v SSHD* [2016] UKUT 00,561 (IAC).
61. *Kiarie and Byndloss* [2017] UKSC 42.
62. The Ministry of Justice 14/12/21 *Human Rights Act Reform: A Modern Bill Of Rights A consultation to reform the Human Rights Act 1998* proposes further limits of appeal rights for foreign offenders.
63. *MY (Pakistan) v SSHD* [2021] EWCA Civ 1500.
64. *New Plan for Immigration* 2021n4.
65. Macdonald Ian A and Webber, Frances. 2005 *Immigration law and practice in the United Kingdom* London: Butterworths. preface [vi].
66. Rawlings, Richard. 2005. *Review, revenge and retreat*. Modern Law Review, 68(3) MLR 378–410.
67. The exceptions include unlawful detention and allegations of a rule's incompatibility with the ECHR.

68. FOI request no 105464 to Robert Thomas, 16/6/2016; request no 180629004 of 29/6/2018.
69. ICIBI 2018 n45 para 3.25.
70. *R (Rashid) v SSHD* [2005] EWCA 744.
71. *R (S) v SSHD* [2007] EWCA Civ 546.
72. Boswell, Christina. 2018 discusses the background to Home Office target setting—*Manufacturing political trust: Targets and performance measurement in public policy* Cambridge: Cambridge University Press.
73. *Senathirajah Ravichandran v United Kingdom*: Court of Appeal (England and Wales), 11 October 1995, [1996] Imm AR 97, CA.
74. *TN & MA (Afghanistan) v SSHD* [2015] UKSC 40.
75. Warren, Richard and York, Sheona. 2014. *How children become failed asylum-seekers: Research report on the experiences of young unaccompanied asylum-seekers in Kent from 2006 to 2013, and how 'corrective remedies' have failed them.* Project report. Kent Law School, University of Kent.
76. Elder Rahimi solicitors. 2018. *Systemic delays in the processing of the claims for asylum made in the UK by unaccompanied asylum seeking children (UASC)* London: March 2018.
77. *MK, R (On the Application Of) v SSHD* [2019] EWHC 3573 (Admin). This case found that the Home Office could not be faulted for delay, principally because there is no clear legal benchmark even for dealing with claims made by unaccompanied children.
78. The Solihull Early Legal Advice Pilot led to a larger number of grants of discretionary leave to remain, suggesting that better case preparation led to a higher recognition of applicants' being people 'of concern' to the UNHCR—see Home Office *Evaluation of the Early Legal Advice Project Final Report* Research Report 70 May 2013.
79. *Odelola v SSHD* [2009] UKHL 25, *MA (Pakistan)* 2019] EWCA Civ 1252, *R (Abidoye) v SSHD* [2020] EWCA Civ 1425,
80. *Reilly (No. 2) & Anor, R (on the application of) v Secretary of State for Work and Pensions* [2014] EWHC 2182 (Admin) (04 July 2014), 2015] 2 WLR 309, [51–54].

81. *HSMP Forum UK Limited* [2008] EWHC 664.
82. *Rhuppiah* [2018] *UKSC* 58.
83. Warren, Richard. 2016. *Private life in the balance: Constructing the precarious migrant*. Journal of Immigration Asylum and Nationality Law, 30 (2).
84. Home Office Nationality Guidance: *Good Character* [48].
85. An amendment on this has been proposed to the Nationality and Borders Bill (November 2021). On 4/2/22 the Free Movement blog reported a Government minister in the Lords as confirming that noone had been refused citizenship solely because of a past lack of comprehensive private sickness insurance. In March 2022 the CJEU finally ruled that eligibility for NHS treatment does count as comprehensive sickness insurance as required by EU free movement law.
86. See *SC & Ors, R (on the application of) v The Secretary of State for Work and Pensions & Ors* [2019] EWCA Civ 615.
87. An ancient aphorism quoted in Kingsley Amis, *Lucky Jim.*
88. *MA (Pakistan)* 2019] EWCA Civ 1252.
89. York, Sheona. 2017. *Deportation of Foreign Offenders—A critical look at the consequences of Maaouia and whether recourse to common-law principles might offer a solution.* Journal of Immigration, Asylum and Nationality Law, 31 (1).
90. *R (Abidoye) v SSHD* [2020] EWCA Civ 1425, especially [41–54].
91. UK Borders Act 2007 (Commencement No. 3 and Transitional Provisions) Order 2008.
92. Application and Supreme Court Order refusing permission to appeal were kindly provided by the appellant and his solicitors DJ Webb & Co.
93. National Audit Office 2020 *Immigration Enforcement.* HC 110 Session 2019–2021, 17 June 2020.
94. Cane, Peter 2010. *Outsourcing administrative adjudication.* Legal Quarterly Review 126 (July). pp. 343–347, discussing the case of *Heald v Brent LBC* [2009] EWCA Civ 930; [2010] 1 WLR 990.
95. Craig, Paul. 2002. *Contracting out, the Human Rights Act and the scope of judicial review.* Paul Craig, Legal Quarterly Review 118 (October). pp. 551–568.

96. *Woodland v Essex County Council* [2013] UKSC 66.
97. Ibid. [7].
98. Ibid. [23].
99. (Other than the fact of unlawful detention, which is directly litigable under far stronger legal principles).
100. Clayton, Richard QC. 2015. *Accountability, judicial scrutiny and contracting out*. UK Constitutional Law Association November 30, 2015.
101. Bales, Katie and Mayblin, Lucy. 2018. *Unfree labour in immigration detention: exploitation and coercion of a captive workforce*. Economy and Society, 47 (2). pp. 191–213.
102. Immigration Act 2014 Part 3 Access to services Chapter 1 Residential Tenancies s20.
103. Immigration Act 2016 Part 2 Access to Services s 39.
104. House of Lords on 12 April 2016 12 April 2016 Volume 771. New guidance was issued in June 2016.
105. Home Office 2018 *A short guide to the right to rent* [9].
106. *SSHD v R (oao) Joint Council for The Welfare of Immigrants* [2020] EWCA Civ 542.
107. Walker, Peter. 2018. *MPs urge Home Secretary to review 'right to rent' policy* Guardian 6/6/18.
108. *Rice v Connelly* [1966] 3 W.L.R. 17 (420).
109. Department of Health. 2012. *2012 Review of overseas visitors charging policy summary report* Department of Health.
110. This requires every applicant (and dependant) to pay an up-front Health Surcharge fee, now £624 per year.
111. York, Sheona. 2018. *The 'hostile environment': How Home Office immigration policies and practices create and perpetuate illegality*. Journal of Immigration, Asylum and Nationality Law, 32 (4).
112. ICIBI. 2019. *An inspection of the policies and practices of the Home Office's Borders, Immigration and Citizenship Systems relating to charging and fees June 2018–January 2019*.
113. Ibid., para 3.11 and footnotes.
114. Smith, Charles et al. 2021. *How do I survive now? The impact of living with No Recourse to Public Funds* Citizens Advice, National Association of Citizens Advice Bureaux.

115. Institute for Government report 2019, House of Commons HAC *The work of the Immigration Directorates Jan–June 2014* HC 712.
116. ICIBI 2019 n112.

7

'In the Light of What We Know'—Immigration Control, Social Cohesion and Citizenship as Common Purpose

1 Introduction

Ever since the 1950s discussion of UK immigration control has focused on *controlling entry* and *enforcement*, aiming to identify 'undesirable' migrants and encourage or force them to leave. The previous chapters have shown that these political priorities have led to long-term degradation in standards of public administration and legal probity. Nevertheless, net migration has not been reduced, and the various goals of enforcement have proved unachievable. This study instead proposes starting from a consideration of *the purpose and content of British citizenship,* not as a tool of immigration control, but understood as *common purpose* and the right to participate fully in society. Then we need to discuss the effects on society of hosting a large precarious population with limited or no social, economic or civic rights, a situation which is contributing to poverty, ill-health and disaffection, which will affect future generations. This is what must underlie consideration of the basis on which we decide who may enter and remain the UK and on what conditions: what kind of society we want to live in, and who we invite to join us. The chapter concludes by identifying the 'elephant in the

S. York, *The Impact of UK Immigration Law*,
https://doi.org/10.1007/978-3-030-98721-3_7

room'—the lack of democratic accountability in immigration control. This is the subject of the final chapter.

2 The Purpose and Meaning of British Citizenship

2.1 Review of the British Nationality Act 1948

Developments in UK nationality law have given wholly insufficient consideration to the democratic desirability for wide public agreement on principles, purpose and content of citizenship. The British Nationality Act 1948 simply 'included everybody' born in the Empire and Commonwealth, without discussion of what they were being included in; what rights and duties were envisaged; what it might mean if 'everybody' had tried to exercise their rights: or whether, if asked, most colonial populations would have chosen sovereign independence rather than citizenship of somewhere else. The British Nationality Act 1981 limited itself to embedding in nationality law the reactive immigration control measures of the previous twenty years, and aroused no democratic discussion about what modern British citizenship should stand for. Home Secretary David Blunkett, in the 2002 *Secure Borders, Safe Haven*[1] promised *an open and constructive debate about citizenship*, which never took place. Arguably it was that lack of democratic discussion which gave room to the Labour government in 2008 to draw up plans for 'earned citizenship', again conceived in narrow immigration control-based terms and which entirely ignored considerations of what citizenship meant for British society. And arguably it has been that same lack of discussion which has given room to subsequent policies and rule changes downgrading the status of migrants without indefinite leave to remain to 'precarious', significantly increasing the price payable, and stretching out the years required to reach settlement and eventual citizenship.

Chapter 1 showed how, under popular pressure for immigration control, the 1948 Act's implementation of full British citizenship rights for all colonial citizens did not last. The proposing and passing of that

Act involved no public discussion, nor even private ministerial consideration, of basic principles on which a citizenship law might reasonably be founded. For modern states, especially those like Germany and Italy which achieved unification in the nineteenth century, achieving independence for the 'nation' generally settled the civil and political rights, reciprocal duties, and a sense of common history and common purpose for those counted as that nation's citizens. In contrast, statehood in Britain had been settled by a small ruling aristocracy some three hundred years previously, and 'citizenship' was long regarded by the British elite as a dangerously radical idea not to be publicly discussed.[2] For most people born in Britain, citizenship can have meant no more than an obligation to serve in the military in time of war, a conditional right to vote and more recently the obligation to sit on a jury. For the majority of those born elsewhere in the Empire, the concept of British subjecthood had meant *subjection*—economic oppression and a grievous lack of political rights *in their own country*, which many had long been organising and fighting to overturn. For most of those, a 'citizenship' which allowed unfettered entry to the territory of 'the mother country' meant nothing whatsoever until the economic possibility arose of emigrating to Britain to find work. For those born in the Colonies but already living in Britain, it was no more than a paper status, ignored in law and practice. A wide public discussion *among the British electorate* about the nature of citizenship and the rights and duties attached to it would probably have led to demands for a legal definition of citizenship restricted to the territory in which the political rights would be exercised. For *those still under colonial domination*, such a discussion must have prompted even more ferocious demands for independence all over the Empire. There were few colonies in which there were no labour revolts or independence campaigns, or in which those were not being met by heavy counterinsurgency operations. Two things are clear. One is that the political and economic demands of the subject peoples in the colonies did not include rights of entry to the metropole. They were more interested in throwing off foreign economic and political domination. The second is that it would have needed the most unprecedented construction of international political solidarity for the 450,000,000 subjects of the Empire to have freely and collectively arrived at the legal position set out in the BNA 1948.

2.2 The Nationality Green Paper of 1977; the British Nationality Act 1981

The conception, presentation and eventual implementation of the new nationality law were again narrow and lacking in legal transparency. There was little debate outside parliament. The Act's likely deleterious effects, both retrospective and into the future, were identified in debate, to no avail.

In the February 1974 manifesto, Labour had included the following aim:

> Review the law of NATIONALITY so that our immigration policies are based on citizenship, and in particular to eliminate discrimination on grounds of colour.[3]

The manifesto did not discuss any other aspect of the meaning and purpose of citizenship. The intention of reform was again mentioned in the October 1974 manifesto, and a working group was set up under Alex Lyon, soon after Labour took office. A Green Paper[4] was published in April 1977. The problems it strove to resolve were that:

> the present citizenship of the United Kingdom and Colonies … relates both to the United Kingdom and overseas territories; it does not identify those who belong to this country and have the right to enter and live here freely; in consequence it prevents the United Kingdom from basing its immigration policies on citizenship. Our citizenship is in these respects different from the citizenships of many other countries including our partners in the European Community.[5]

Home Secretary Merlyn Rees, introducing the Green Paper to the House of Commons, said: *There is no doubt that the sort of nationality that we had in 1948 was based on a concept that was even then outmoded.*[6] The aims of the proposed new law would be to limit British citizenship to those with a close connection with the UK; to eliminate sex discrimination, to ensure that there would be no one remaining in the Commonwealth or colonies who would be without citizenship, while avoiding the creation of future 'pools' of people born overseas acquiring

British citizenship by descent and thereby gaining a right to enter and live in the UK. The Green Paper neither proposed or explored any more fundamental meaning or content of 'citizenship' beyond its comprising who should be allowed to enter and remain in the UK. Speakers agreed with the need to legislate quickly, to avert '*a danger that some groups of people around the world who presently have the right of abode in the United Kingdom will be frightened into trying to exercise their right before legislation is produced*'.[7]

But that Labour government introduced no new legislation on immigration. The Conservatives won the election in 1979, heralding a big change of direction in almost every aspect of public policy. The Conservative election manifesto for the first time[8] included proposed stricter entry control on specific groups, as well as the intention to legislate on nationality. It is worth highlighting the manifesto's assurances to the settled population:

> IMMIGRATION AND RACE RELATIONS
>
> … firm immigration control for the future is essential if we are to achieve good community relations. It will end persistent fears about levels of immigration and will remove from those settled, and in many cases born here, the label of 'immigrant'.
>
> (i) We shall introduce a new British Nationality Act to define entitlement to British citizenship and to the right of abode in this country. It will not adversely affect the right of anyone now permanently settled here. (my emphasis)

A White Paper on nationality was produced in July 1980, and it and the eventual Act closely followed the Labour Green Paper, as confirmed by William Whitelaw, Home Secretary, in the second reading on the Act on 28 January 1981.[9] The Act abolished *ius soli* (i.e. becoming British simply by virtue of being born in the UK or on a British ship or aircraft). Citizenship would henceforth depend not just on place of birth but on the immigration status of the mother or the married father.[10] It dealt explicitly with the 'colonial residue' of CUKCs with 'no connection' to the UK, by creating a series of second-rate citizenships[11] giving no right to enter or remain in the UK.

In debate, no sentimental or pro-imperialist statements were made about the Empire, and very little about what Britain owed to its subjects overseas. Paradoxically, only the declared anti-migrant MPs wanted to discuss the philosophical content of citizenship. Enoch Powell spoke about 'allegiance' and said that citizenship could only be founded on this vague mixture of *ius soli* and *ius sanguinis* (citizenship based on descent), as the Bill proposed, if the population were '*vaguely homogeneous*'; and on being asked what he meant by 'homogeneous' he said *'being the same sort of people who have lived in that territory for years gone by*' [967–8]. Others spoke about the responsibility of those who are '*trustees preserving the essential identity of the nation*' [989]. Harvey Proctor, in considering 'belonging', repeated what he acknowledged to be a 'crude' description from a constituent: '*a dachshund born in a foxhound's kennel may remain a dachshund, but he may feel himself to be more of a foxhound than a dachshund, and if he remains long enough in the kennel may behave so much like a foxhound as to be accepted as such*'—a sharp example of the prevalence and continued acceptability of racial thinking.

Most Labour speakers followed Roy Hattersley [946] and strongly opposed the bill, on the basis that it was racist, sexist, demeaning and illiberal. David Steel, leader of the Liberal Party, agreed that it was all those things, but noted that Hattersley had voted for the Commonwealth Immigrants Act 1968, the forerunner of this legislation [958]. Following Conservative MP John Stokes, who spoke about '*the indigenous people being supplanted by aliens and British people will gradually disappear from these islands*', Stan Thorne, Labour, Preston South, said:

> If national identity was what took us across the world to subjugate the peoples of India, Africa and the West Indies to obtain raw materials and exploit the labour in those countries, I want little or nothing to do with it... we can never repay the debt that we owe to the countries we have exploited... We are certainly not accepting our responsibilities with legislation such as this. [989–990]

Objections were made in particular to narrowly circumscribing who would be British citizens on commencement, leaving many Citizens of the UK and Colonies without effective rights to enter or remain on any territory, and leaving at least some children born in the UK without any citizenship; to the elimination of sex discrimination by 'levelling down' i.e. reducing the rights of men to pass on their citizenship; the potential problems of children being born overseas not being British, and not necessarily finding out until they grew up.

Alex Lyon drew attention to the erosion of rights by retrospective measures, an issue which has since become of great importance. He drew attention to three examples. First, children born abroad to those who are British by birth would be British, but not those born abroad to 'citizens by descent', which was to include those registered and naturalised as British. Secondly, immigration law and procedure was itself changing the nature of people's rights. The status of being 'settled' used to have a clear meaning, but by 1981 settled status, and even citizenship, could be lost following an accusation of 'deception'—*which may be no more than the fact that somebody came in at London airport and did not volunteer information to an immigration officer who never asked the question.* [981].[12] Thirdly, making access to citizenship of spouses dependent on length of residence discriminated against those from the Asian subcontinent simply because of the lengthy queues and delays in deciding applications for entry visas before they could even begin their three years' qualifying period. He among others also wondered how a child's citizenship would be ascertained—would every black woman giving birth be asked about her immigration status? The answer was no, but we have seen subsequently that large numbers of children whose parents came from the Commonwealth or colonies have assumed they were British and not found out the truth until later required to obtain or show a passport. And the other concerns did lead to legal difficulties in the future.

The Act provided what seems now to be a generous transitional period of five years during which a Commonwealth citizen settled in the UK five years before the Act came into force could register cheaply for British citizenship. But the Home Office did not publicise that scheme, and reassured people that their rights to indefinite leave to remain would not be prejudiced if they did not apply.[13] The Windrush debacle shows how those who did not apply eventually fell foul of increasingly restrictive internal controls, which had been introduced in the absence of what the recent *Lessons Learned Review* refers to as 'institutional memory' concerning the legal position of those people.

Looking back, the British Nationality Act 1981 amounted to tidying up and dignifying the racist dog's dinner of the Commonwealth Immigrants Act 1968 and the transparently racist construction of 'patrial' in the Immigration Act 1971. However, even the members of parliament who described the Act as racist and who would vote against it would not have proposed keeping nationality law as in the 1948 Act, nor proposed abolishing the immigration controls introduced after it. By that time, the need for immigration controls was fully accepted by all apart from a few small left-wing groups. During the 1981 debate and outside parliament a few were suggesting a 'non-racist immigration policy'. Church of England bishops had proposed that *'Any new nationality law should state as a matter of principle that our national identity is multi-racial, thereby avoiding the potential racial conception of national identity'.*[14] Instead, as shown in Chapter 2, what took place was the intensification of control on those living in the UK.

2.3 *Encouraging Citizenship*—The 1990 Report

At no point in the passage of either of the British Nationality Acts was there any public or even official consideration of what 'citizenship' meant, or the values, rights and duties it represented, aside from determining rights under immigration laws. But in 1990 a Commission on Citizenship, set up in 1988, reported[15] to the House of Commons. Its purposes included defining citizenship, including active citizenship, and examining the '*advantages and disadvantages of different kinds of recognition*'. Beginning by referencing Magna Carta, it argued that *'citizenship is one of the most important concepts of modern political struggle and social development'* and believes that it needed re-evaluating to take account of recent changes in British society and Britain's position in the world. These included having joined the European Communities, having a '*changed relationship with the Commonwealth*' and having become a multiracial society, as well as changes in income, lifestyle, work, retirement and care in the community, a growth in consumer rights and the '*contested*' changes in role and financing of the public services. The Commission feared that many believe that the *'rights of individuals in this country are regarded as superior to the rights of those in other countries but best left unstated'*, and assert that *'citizenship, whatever it means, is a cultural achievement, a gift of history, which can be lost or destroyed'*, and that *'the challenge to our society in the late twentieth century is to create conditions where all who wish can become actively involved'.*

Looking for a definition of citizenship, the Commission began with Aristotle: *'a citizen is one who has a share in both ruling and being ruled'*. Following TH Marshall's scheme of civil, political and social rights,[16] the Commission decided that a definition must include legal membership of a political community based on universal suffrage, and also membership of a civil community based on the rule of law. The Commission noted that most of those they consulted regarded social rights as essential, otherwise rights *'become an empty constitutional promise without any substance'.*

The main thrust of the Commission's recommendations flows from a view that a citizen's rights and duties are not wholly demarcated by formal requirements and formal state institutions, but are exercised through a multiplicity of political and social associations. *'It is in the area of social existence in which citizens voluntarily cooperate together and sustain their common life and common undertaking'.*[17]

The report then considers wider realms of civil, political and social rights arising from the UK's membership of the European Community and its ratification of various international human rights and similar instruments. It notes that the benefits of some of those rest on residence rather than nationality, and that many people play an active role in more than one legally defined community. It asks whether people knew *'who was, or was not, a member of the legally constituted community of the UK, and whether they were in an equal position'* (The report notes that people did not know these things). Referring to the British Nationality Act 1981 and the Representation of the People Act 1983, the report noted that Commonwealth citizens and citizens of the Irish Republic are eligible to vote—strangely, the report implies, as they are not British citizens; while equally strangely *'the right of residence .... is not enjoyed by a significant number of individuals whose nationality status depends on ... the BNA 1981'*. Nationals of the European Community may live and work in the UK, and have access to social rights, but (in 1990) could not vote. The Commission concluded that *'membership of a political community in the UK and the related question of entitlements and responsibilities is confusing.'* They further decided that *'Legal complexity divides citizens from their rights, and this is accentuated by the cost… such inaccessibility is more than an impediment to citizenship: it is a fundamental denial'.*

The report notes the basis in international law for state sovereignty, including conferring 'nationality' on individuals and protecting them from other states when abroad. The separate term 'citizenship' is held to refer to people's rights and duties inside the territory, which in the UK are not set out in Nationality Acts or in a written constitution but in other legislation. A 'new citizenship' is optimistically described as having arisen from the UK's ratification of various human rights and similar instruments, which *'address the content of the legal relationship between the individual and the state, rather than the form'.* The only problems foreseen were legal complexity and expense of proceedings. It certainly was not foreseen that it would be judges who would be deciding on the value of an individual person's human rights, or Immigration Rules and guidance which would restrict them.

For that Commission, reporting in 1990, the presence in our 'social existence' of those who are not legal citizens, and the strangeness of non-citizens who could vote and citizens who could not enter the territory, were not considered problematic either for them or for the rest of society. We might identify this moment as falling in a period of relative calm in terms of the politics of UK immigration control. Family migration arrivals from the New Commonwealth had slowed following the 1988 repeal of the s1(5) IA 1971 rights of Commonwealth citizens in the UK since 1971 to be joined by their spouses, while it had become accepted, as the Commission noted, that '*Britain had become a multiracial society*' with black and Asian representatives from both main parties on local councils, black senior trade union officials and black and Asian members of parliament. Some, such as Conservative MP Norman Tebbit, did consider the multiracial society a problem. In 1990 he said: '*A large proportion of Britain's Asian population fail to pass the cricket test. Which side do they cheer for? It's an interesting test. Are you still harking back to where you came from or where you are?*'[18] On the other hand the arrivals of hundreds of Somali and other refugees had not yet built up into backlogs of thousands of people surviving in legal limbo, and hysteria about 'asylum-seekers eating our swans' had not yet emerged.

Nevertheless, that 1990 report, referring to the beliefs of 'many' that '*rights of individuals in this country are regarded to be superior*' and to '*citizenship, whatever it means*' as a '*cultural achievement, a gift of history which can be lost or destroyed*', implies real anxiety. In 1993 Prime Minister John Major made his famous speech about 'back to basics'. This, usually ridiculed because reports of Tory sex scandals revealed the emphasis on the traditional family to be hypocritical, is more important for what it said and did not say about the state of Britain at the time.

> We live in a world that sometimes seems to be changing too fast for comfort. Old certainties crumbling. Traditional values falling away. People are bewildered. Week after week, month after month, they see attacks on the very pillars of our society - the Church, the law, even the Monarchy ...
>
> ...It is time to return to those old core values, time to get back to basics, to self-discipline and respect for the law, to consideration for others, to accepting responsibility for yourself and your family and not shuffling off on other people and the state.'[19]

The years from 1979 to 1993 had seen the so-called neoliberal 'restructuring' of old-style capitalist production in the West, including the collapse of Britain's coal, steel, shipping, automotive and chemical industries and the emasculation of the large mining and manufacturing trade unions, an economic destruction which had brought social and political destruction especially in the towns and cities of central Scotland, Wales, the North East, North West and Midlands. Major could see the social disruption. But, politically unable to acknowledge the causes, he could not see that his attempts to recreate a sense of community, whether through educating school students about citizenship or by calling on other declining institutions such as the Church to take up the struggle, could not work. Because through the collapse of those economic activities the institutions, processes and even the ideas of political solidarity were largely shattered, and Britain has not since discovered a new basis for social solidarity.

2.4 *Secure Borders, Safe Haven*: Reimagining Citizenship in a Crisis of Social Cohesion

Neither did Labour, faced in the 2000s with widespread discontent and violence erupting among young black and Asian people, develop any better ideas about social solidarity or national identity. The White Paper *Secure Borders, Safe Haven* highlighted the need to consider national identity. At least accepting that the discontent had economic causes, that government targeted public spending on early years education, youth services, benefits and tax credits for poorer families. But Labour also targeted and singled out migrant communities as the source of dissent and discontent, proposing measures set out to emphasise and perpetuate 'difference' rather than integration. Following 9/11, the basis of public anxiety about 'social exclusion' had changed. Education and social services authorities were encouraged to look out for signs of 'radicalisation'. Government programmes looked to coopt 'faith groups' and 'faith leaders' on the basis of colonial-style assumptions that minority populations were not part of everyday democratic involvement but could only be addressed as part of 'their community', denominated on the basis of race or religion.

In that White Paper, the government approached the purpose, meaning and content of citizenship in an immigration context for the first time:

> …The reports into last summer's disturbances in Bradford, Oldham and Burnley painted a vivid picture of fractured and divided communities, lacking a sense of common values or shared civic identity to unite around. The reports signalled the need for us to foster and renew the social fabric of our communities, and rebuild a sense of common citizenship, which embraces the different and diverse experiences of today's Britain.

Citizenship was by then being taught in schools, following the recommendations of the Crick Report 1998.[20] That had noted that '*cultural diversity raises the issue of national identity*', and stated that *'a main aim for the whole community should be to find or restore a sense of common citizenship, including a national identity that is secure enough to find a place for the plurality of nations, cultures, ethnic identities and religions long found in the United Kingdom'.* As to what might be the elements of a common citizenship, among the questions of technique such as 'the nature and practice of participatory democracy' the report said this:

> Majorities must respect, understand and tolerate minorities and minorities must learn and respect the laws, codes and conventions as much as the majority – not merely because it is useful to do so, but because this process helps foster common citizenship.

The White Paper proposed that settled migrants should be encouraged to acquire British citizenship, which would be granted not just on residence grounds but would require knowledge of the English language and society. Citizenship courses would:

> strengthen the ability of new citizens to participate in society and to engage actively in our democracy. This will help people understand both their rights and their obligations as citizens of the UK, and strengthen the bonds of mutual understanding between people of diverse cultural backgrounds.

There would be a new citizenship ceremony and a new oath of allegiance.

The White Paper further stated that the government would *initiate an open and constructive debate about citizenship, civic identity and shared values.* Noting difficulties facing the 'white working class', alienated from the political process and excluded from newly created wealth, along with racism faced by newly-arrived migrants, the White Paper said this:

> Our values of individual freedom, the protection of liberty and respect for difference, have not been accompanied by a strong, shared understanding of the civic realm. The acquisition of British nationality is a bureaucratic exercise, with almost no effort made to engage new members of the community with the fundamentals of our democracy and society.

Meanwhile the mainstream school citizenship programme was soon strongly criticised on multiple grounds. Besides the problems of lack of time and resources, the programme's aim of fostering a common citizenship was arguably being hindered by a separate government policy of permitting diverging models and structures of education including an encouragement of faith schools and separate 'free schools'. That process, along with the parental choice measures brought in by the previous government, meant that the education system was becoming too fissiparous to be an effective instrument of developing commonality.[21] And neither the White Paper nor these reports did more than brush the surface of the question of national identity in a 'culturally diverse' setting.

2.5 The Borders, Citizenship and Immigration Act 2009—Proposed Downgrading of Settlement and Citizenship Rights

This Bill proposed the complete overhaul of migrants' rights in the UK into three categories: those with 'temporary stay', those with 'probationary citizenship' and those with full citizenship, to be achieved through a process of 'earning' the right to be a citizen by volunteering. This had been set out in a Green Paper—*The Path to Citizenship*.[22]

This paper showed a fundamental change in the way Labour was thinking about those who were not born British. Its influence is later seen in the post-2010 Coalition/Conservative policy developments of even longer 'routes to settlement', the designation of all non-settled migrants as 'temporary', and, indeed, as 'precarious'. First, in contrast to the discussion in *Secure Borders, Safe Haven*, the question of citizenship was not located within a broader discussion about the importance of social cohesion for all residents, British or otherwise. There was no reference to the values of democracy, tolerance and fair play. Secondly, the impulse behind wishing to encourage people to naturalise as British was entirely different. In 1998 *Fairer, Firmer, Faster* had shortened the time needed for successful asylum claimants to obtain indefinite leave to remain, and government policy was to encourage naturalisation as a straightforward aid to integration. Even *Secure Borders, Safe Haven* spoke of encouraging naturalisation as an aid to integration. However, the discourse in *The Path to Citizenship* is directed solely at migrants, and amounts to drawing out, delaying and placing obstacles in the way of migrants even achieving settlement. Citizenship is proposed as a distant and difficult goal, but one which migrants must aspire to, apart from the presumed very few for whom naturalisation would present legal difficulties arising from their own country's nationality laws. Integration is not mentioned. The *Path to Citizenship* repositioned settlement (indefinite leave to remain) as a temporary or probationary status, and citizenship as more or less compulsory but a privilege to be earned—with higher standards than required for those born British. Earning citizenship, for Labour in 2008, did not just mean obeying the law, paying taxes, learning English and passing a 'life in the UK' test, but was to require substantial evidence of having volunteered and served in the community. The Green Paper proposed different examples of volunteering, which would be verified by an acceptable referee. Faced with that Bill in Parliament, many MPs were concerned about the oxymoron of compulsory volunteering. They feared the effect on the voluntary sector of large numbers of people demanding an accredited volunteering experience. MPs objected to the retrospective nature of the legislation—introducing new onerous requirements which would make it difficult for people already here with indefinite leave to become citizens. The proposals also effectively downgraded the status of indefinite leave, which had up till then been an entirely satisfactory and secure position especially for those for whom becoming British may have required them to renounce their own citizenship. The proposals were passed in the Borders, Citizenship and Immigration Act 2009, but have never been commenced.

Those wishing to naturalise were required to take a Life in the UK test, pass an English exam and swear an oath of allegiance to the Queen in a citizenship ceremony. But neither the lessons nor the ceremonies addressed national identity more than superficially, despite its being an important political issue during that period. The frank racism of the National Front and subsequently the British National Party underpinned demands to halt immigration and deport migrants, based on a sentimental dream of a 'white England' with patron saint St George. That was only the extreme edge of an inchoate identification with 'Englishness'. That, paradoxically, was influenced by the rise in Scottish and Welsh nationalism and the successful campaigns for devolution, leading to resentment about the Barnett formula[23] and some demands for an English parliament to match the Welsh and Scottish devolution arrangements. John Denham (2019) writes:

> … 'English nationalism' is not the virulent nationalism of liberal nightmares. This nationalism has no political party or programme. Nor does it boast public intellectuals, cultural expressions or social institutions… [but] these citizens see both of England's unions – the United Kingdom and the EU -as working against the interests of the particular England they see as excluded from power. This clash between the "establishment" and the English is about aspirations for power, representation and democracy that would be taken for granted in any other nation; it's neither necessarily regressive nor inherently right wing. Indeed, it might well have formed the programme of a coherent and democratic political project. But without clear articulation or leadership, the English interest remains inchoate: a powerful yet volatile and unpredictable force.[24]

Labour's legislative programme of 'earned citizenship' has not yet been formally implemented, but it may as well have been. It was the first serious government plan to render precarious an entire cohort of migrants and their descendants who were legally settled and who believed themselves to be socially and politically settled. Though Labour's 'earned citizenship' policies were to work through compulsory 'volunteering', there was little reference to 'values' and no sense of a common purpose.

The Coalition and Conservative governments' immigration policies have achieved a similar effect, by lengthening 'routes to settlement', approving a Supreme Court decision[25] that all migrants not yet settled count as *legally* precarious, and introducing restrictive measures with retrospective effect.

The 2010–2015 Coalition government also pursued the need to combat radicalisation of disaffected Muslim young people, again through the medium of inculcating 'British values'. It is notable that, as with the earlier government discussions about citizenship, the education system provides the context in which these are discussed, including the Prevent strategy. The Coalition government published *Guidance on promoting British values in schools: Strengthened guidance on improving the spiritual, moral, social and cultural development of pupils.* A 2014 press release states:

> All [schools] have a duty to 'actively promote' the fundamental British values of democracy, the rule of law, individual liberty, and mutual respect and tolerance of those with different faiths and beliefs.

The guidance stated that schools were to:

> Develop material on the strengths, advantages and disadvantages of democracy, and how democracy and the law works in Britain, in contrast to other forms of government in other countries.

The move from being told by government to teach 'respect' for these values to having to 'actively promote' them demonstrates unease, an unease *detached* from real political developments in Britain at the time. Persuading people of the need for tolerance and respect for the rule of law has to take place not in school but in real-life democratic settings where the outcomes matter, in relation to representative institutions which have the power to change things. It is not surprising, for example, that involvement in trade union membership has declined along with the limitations in trade union power, and that interest in local government elections has declined with declining autonomy and funding for local authorities.

Problematic also must be the prospect of teaching those ideas in schools where a not negligible proportion of students have insecure immigration status, whether straightforwardly unlawful or as one of the newly-defined 'precarious' population. Once again, a government proposed the creation of 'active citizens' in line with 'British values' while at the same time introducing legislation emphasising and deepening divisions in society—in the Cameron government's case the measures making long-resident migrants 'temporary' and 'precarious', and also with immigration control policies continuing to violate the very rule of law held up as a 'British value'. Imagine the reaction to lessons about 'British values' from children and grandchildren of Windrush families, or children of migrant care workers for whom the visa fees and Immigration Health Surcharge are too high for them to renew those children's visas.

2.6 Citizenship as Common Purpose

The 1990 citizenship report's reference to '*individual rights regarded as superior to those in other countries*' may be referring to the structure of English common law derived from early declarations of rights, in which everything is permitted which is not expressly prohibited. Whether or not such rights are 'superior' to individual rights in other countries, *individual freedom* must be considered a fundamental 'British value'. This is especially important at a time when many seem prepared to give away their own and others' freedoms in favour of asking the State to determine for example what we may say, or what political propositions are acceptable, in a world where the role of the State is seen to be to protect us from 'harm'.[26] Instead of such debilitating ideas depriving all of us of agency, we can also take pride in the progressive demands made in 1647–1649,[27] revolutionary for their time, to inspire us as a people and create solidarity on the basis of something like *common right*. It requires some element of renewal—of hope for the future—even if only at the level of 'once we are out of this mess things need to be different for everyone'.

Then, it requires some inspiring idea of *common* purpose. Arguably, the very beginning of the coronavirus lockdown showed elements of this. The first claims that 'we were all in it together', the first claps for front line workers,[28] the first expressions of solidarity for supermarket shelf stackers, for black and ethnic minority doctors noted to suffer disproportionately in the pandemic, for migrant workers in health care, the first few days of recruitment of volunteers to go shopping for shielded people: all this showed that there is some sense of national solidarity 'out there', which could potentially cut across current social and political divisions. In April 2020, a petition was started demanding immediate citizenship for our coronavirus migrant worker 'heroes', recognising that their loyalty and service shows that they 'belong'.[29] Did we, for a few short weeks, witness a moment of *'social existence in which citizens voluntarily cooperate together and sustain their common life and common undertaking'... 'conditions where all who wish can become actively involved'*?[30]

To the extent that this is true, its importance for this study lies in the fact that the people voluntarily cooperating together *are not all legal citizens.* Some have very few rights indeed, but are able to transcend those real economic and legal differences to achieve social solidarity, and from there, political solidarity might, hopefully, be achieved. Taking up John Denham's suggestion, could his '*aspirations for power, representation and democracy*' be taken up to argue for a better post-coronavirus world, starting from the particular issues which have emerged during the crisis such as the inadequacy of universal credit, the wretched lack of rights for those in rented accommodation, the disproportionately high proportions of black and ethnic minority people with worse jobs, poorer accommodation and poorer health leading to their disproportionate chances of catching the virus and dying, and the unacceptable economic and legal conditions of the many migrant workers on which this country relies.

Besides underpinning our conception of citizenship, 'British values' of freedom, democracy, the rule of law and mutual respect, will all require some resolution of those substantive issues. The next part moves on to consider the barriers to the successful formal inclusion into British social and economic life of the over 2 million migrants whose presence is likely to be permanent but who are legally defined as precarious.

3 The Legal Conditions of Migrants Living in the UK: Precarity and Insecurity

The *legal condition of migrants living in the UK* as a political or social issue, though the subject of many NGO reports,[31] has rarely received formal comprehensive public consideration. The previous chapters have shown that citizenship has on the whole been reductively conceptualised as just an immigration status—the most secure, certainly, but not for everyone, as the Windrush debacle showed—and the recent legal treatment of British ISIS supporters has shown that citizenship can be revoked.[32] Those migrants who are not yet citizens, even those with indefinite leave to remain, have faced and will continue to face erosion of formal status and the social rights that go with them. And alongside that process of erosion of rights of those lawfully present, the paths to regularisation for unlawfully-present migrants have been reduced. This section argues that those legal erosions have significant negative consequences for British society.

Two reports issued by the Mayor of London, one in 2009 on earned regularisation of irregular migrants[33] and a 2020 report *London's children and young people who are not British citizens*[34] have presented formal estimates of the numbers of unlawfully-present migrants in the UK and in particular in London, assessed the economic and social consequences of their presence and their lack of status and considered the impact of granting permission to stay. The current Prime Minister Boris Johnson had supported a recommendation for an amnesty[35] when he was Mayoral candidate in 2006. He has not since pursued that proposal—though an editorial in *The Times* on 19 May 2020 suggested that this should be revisited.[36] For lawfully present migrants, many of whom now determined to be legally precarious, there has been no similar high-level formal consideration of the economic and social effects of their conditions, though, as discussed in Chapter 6, the ICIBI has touched on the issues in its inspection of Home Office fee charging policy,[37] and the 2019 Institute for Government's report[38] suggested that the wider effects of that policy should be examined.

For *unlawfully-present migrants,* the enforcement-based policies of the last 10 years have not worked. Year on year, both removals and voluntary departures have declined.[39] Policymakers are criticised for not properly evaluating the effectiveness of specific enforcement or hostile environment measures. But there has been little official consideration of why people do not leave, other than to justify more impoverishment and more restrictions on regular migrants. Recapitulating the policy impacts on *regular* migrants which *create and perpetuate illegality,* and the long-term lack of legal conscientiousness in asylum determination, this part proposes that *Britain's population of unlawfully-present migrants consists largely of people failed by the system.* Instead of seeing their presence as somehow in and of itself causing harm, we should acknowledge that *harm has been inflicted on them* and on wider society by those failures, which could be ameliorated by a regularisation programme.

The previous chapters have shown how *lawfully present* migrants have faced a mixture of hostility, administrative neglect, lack of legal conscientiousness and unintended consequences. Casework backlogs meant that successive tightening of policies has retrospectively eroded and even annulled onward rights of those already here. Heavy financial requirements and extensions of probationary periods for spouses and partners have enforced the division of families and contributed to the breakdown of relationships, exacerbated by the narrowing of article 8 family life rights to those facing '*insurmountable obstacles*' to living elsewhere, or where it would be '*unduly harsh*' or there would be *unjustifiably harsh consequences* for the family to be divided. The general application of no recourse to public funds (NRPF) and the need to save for the high application fees and Immigration Health Surcharge have made life hard for all migrants present on time-limited visas. This has led to migrants 'becoming illegal' through not being able to make the necessary repeat applications. Other policies have explicitly limited access to settlement for certain categories of worker, so that the policy aim of providing work visas to the brightest and the best has been tarnished by subsequent changes in policies towards family reunion and settlement for them. These are living individuals, in real families, with intricate, valued connections with friends, neighbours, work colleagues and others around them in everyday British communities, and who for better or worse consider that Britain is their home. This is why they generally do not leave: but treat 'enforcement' as something to be endured.

Precarity: Chapter 6 noted how the Supreme Court extended the 2014 'public interest' definition of 'precarious' to all migrants not yet settled, explicitly to make it easy for Home Office decision-making.[40] That 'public interest' definition of 'precarious' represents one of the most pernicious aspects of modern UK immigration control. It cements in law one of UK immigration control's worst consequences: the economic and social insecurity of a significant proportion of the UK population. A 2019 Migration Observatory report[41] gives a figure of 1,560,486 migrants on time-limited visas in April 2017.

'Precarious' migrants include labour migrants whether seasonal fruit pickers or the 'brightest and the best'. Precarious also are family migrants, refugees and those on humanitarian or statelessness leave. Chapters 5 and 6 described how the rights and entitlements of family migrants, a category formally accepted as on a 'route to settlement', have been eroded. Many have already been in the UK for some time, whether on previous visas or with no visa. If circumstances change, the migrant must begin again on a different route, remaining precarious throughout, with no recourse to public funds, and facing ever-tightening definitions of 'continuous residence'. Refugees, those granted humanitarian protection and those granted leave on the grounds of statelessness must currently wait 5 years to apply for settlement. That five-year period excludes the long delay between applying for asylum and being granted, despite the Refugee Convention position that refugee status is declaratory and so should have retrospective effect.[42] The nebulous process of a 'safe return review'[43] of their status hangs over them until settlement is achieved. All these people are legally defined and referred to officially by the Home Office as 'temporary migrants'. The legal effect of this precarity is that if such a person is refused and faces a (non-asylum) 'human rights' appeal, the whole period of their residence may, retrospectively, be given '*little weight*' by the tribunal, and their remaining in the UK will rest on whether there are '*insurmountable obstacles*' to their enjoying family life in the migrant partner's country of origin or there being '*very significant obstacles to the applicant's integration*' in their country of origin.

That legal insecurity and the resulting anxiety were brought to public notice by the Covid crisis. Whether furloughed, placed on short time working or dismissed, those migrants who needed to extend their visas risked falling outside the terms of their 'route to settlement' and having to start again from the beginning. Those needing access to public funds were told to make a formal application to the Home Office—applications which take weeks even in normal times—and which relegate the applicant to the 10-year route. A 2020 Migration Observatory report[44] estimated that around 1.376 million people are subject to the NRPF condition. During the first Covid lockdown, migrants with families who become destitute were told by Robert Jenrick, Communities Secretary,[45] to apply to local authority social services for assistance under s17 Children Act 1989—the public administration equivalent of leaving a child on a neighbour's doorstep.

The second group of precarious and insecure migrants present in the UK are those present unlawfully. Chapter 3 showed how numbers started to increase sharply with the development of the backlogs in asylum processing during the 1990s and especially the 2000s. Many were not included in the amnesties discussed in Chapter 5, or dealt with under the Legacy. Chapter 6 suggested that many of those will have met and may still meet the definition of people 'of concern' to the UNHCR. Other 'failed asylum-seekers' have been in the UK since childhood: many have found settled, British or EU partners and now have British children. However, the courts have decided that long-term 'failed asylum-seekers' have no legitimate expectation in law to be allowed to stay, and that courts should not 'sanction' the Home Office for delays and administrative incompetence. Clearly then, instead of relying on litigation, there would need to be a *political* argument that the delays, incompetence and lack of legal conscientiousness evident in UK asylum determination should be regarded as unacceptable; that those migrants' expectations of being allowed to stay are *politically* legitimate, and should now be met by a regularisation programme.

Other long-resident irregular migrants include overstayers. This category includes visitors who tried to remain as students or who fell in love, students who could not keep up with their studies because their family back home ceased to support them; family members deserted by, thrown out or forced to flee from their sponsor, people on work visas who had to stop work because of illness. However, a woman on a spouse visa whose marriage breaks down, or the young family with children born here who become unlawfully present through filling in the wrong application form, does not simply pack up and go home, but tries to make the best of things here. Many 'failed students' or 'failed marriage partners' cannot face returning home, a disgrace and a failure in the eyes of their families. Many have no home to return to—not necessarily because of war and pestilence, but from everyday causes such as the death of a parent. There are children brought on a visitor's visa by their mother dying of AIDS and left in the care of relatives in Peckham. There are mothers who renew their own visa but can't afford to renew those of their children; EU nationals in love with failed asylum-seekers who have been denied EU residence cards or status under the EUSS because they are undocumented; undocumented irregular migrants with mental health problems, for whom the heavy burden of proof makes formal applications impossible.

Away from central government, there are NGO reports, policy initiatives and political campaigns centred on the human and social as well as economic costs of irregular migration. Towards the end of 2006 a new public campaign was launched, *Strangers into Citizens*,[46] aiming to publicise the plight of the large numbers of irregular migrants present in the UK, whether 'failed asylum-seekers' or 'economic migrants', who because of the intransigence of each government are condemned to living in destitution and exploitation. This was a widely supported campaign of local community groups, religious organisations, trade union branches and student organisations. It led to an Early Day Motion tabled on 27 April 2007 with 94 signatories, gaining the support of both Ken Livingstone and Boris Johnson as candidates in the London mayoral election of 2008. The Greater London Authority 2009 report recommending 'earned regularisation' rejected the pull factor arguments:

> The likelihood of large-scale additional irregular immigration is far lower in the UK, where most irregulars come from much further afield – and could only occur if border controls were ineffective.[47]…
>
> the UK has relatively small numbers of truly illegal migrants and the flow of irregular migrants has been reduced through new border measures; as these improve the chances of large-scale increases is unlikely to be significant.

A London School of Economics study[48] gives numbers of irregular migrants of 525,000 to 950,000. Migration Watch, forcefully rejecting the idea of an amnesty, has suggested over a million as at 2010.[49] A Migrants Rights Network report calculated that on the basis of 2009 UKBA costs and rates of removals it would take over 30 years and cost £8bn to remove them all.[50] The 2020 Mayor of London report[51] gives, as at 2017, a 'middle estimate' of 674,000 undocumented people in the UK, including UK-born children, with 397,000 living in London: of whom 215,000 are children, nearly half of whom, 107,000, live in London, with a further 117,000 undocumented young people 18–25, of whom 26,000 live in London. That report suggests that the numbers of undocumented people *'is slowly increasing, because removals and regularisations account for less than the increase in people becoming undocumented, and babies born to those who are undocumented'* [59].

Remarkably, we don't know the extent to which migrants' precarity contributes to their broader social problems such as poverty and ill-health. So far, precarious immigration status and its effects are not generally included as variables, even in the major 'health of the nation' studies such as carried out under Professor Marmot.[52] But it would seem self-evident that those on low wages who are also subject to the no recourse to public funds (NRPF) condition *and* who are required to save up for application fees and the Immigration Health Surcharge must suffer impacts on diet and health, children's success at school and general family well-being.

On 19 May 2020 the *Times* suggested that the 2006 proposal of an 'earned amnesty' '*may once have been politically impossible. Now, such pragmatic ideas just might work*'.[53] Even a return to the rules, policies and application fees of twenty years ago would resolve the immigration insecurity of well over 2 million people. Many sources of retrospectivity would be eliminated. However, without repealing the 'public interest' declarations of s117A-C NIAA 2002, any simplification or regularisation scheme will face problems if cases reach the tribunal, and deportation would still have retrospective effect, continuing the insecurity of a third category—settled migrants who have committed crimes, however long ago.

Nevertheless, with even the most generous of such measures, we would end up with a British population no larger than present, no longer needing to spy on each other or fear criminalisation for not checking on each other's status. A large cohort of long residents currently hidden from the labour market and general social life are ready, able, willing and even desperate to play their part in society. Money the Home Office would lose through loss of fee income would be saved through reductions to bureaucracy and payments for unnecessary outsourcing contracts, fewer appeals and judicial reviews, less wasted costs of pursuing unremovable failed asylum-seekers and foreign offenders, less expense of collecting bills from NHS patients and so on. And once the legal conditions of migrants wishing and needing to stay in the UK are separated from enforcement, other programmes aimed at tackling labour exploitation, trafficking, forced marriage and so on, losing their immigration enforcement role, may find they receive more public support and become more effective.

4 Reimagining the Purpose and Content of External Control, *'in the Light of What We Know'*

Government and parliamentary discussions of immigration control, as well as much wider political comment, have focused on reducing numbers and enforcement. Discussions of labour migration at least since the 1970s have concentrated on keeping out unskilled workers whether from the 'new Commonwealth' or elsewhere, and attracting the 'brightest and the best'. Family migrants have historically been scrutinised as suspected economic migrants, using sham marriages to get into the UK labour market. Refugees are 'welcomed', but only if 'genuine', and now, only if they have been prepared to wait for several years in a squalid camp before being selected for resettlement. The drive under Labour to attract foreign students always faced a tension based on the 'culture of disbelief'—that especially those from particular countries will be suspected as 'bogus'.

For twenty years both Labour and Conservative **labour migration** policy has aimed to encourage 'the brightest and the best' to come to the UK 'to meet the needs of the UK economy'. Less is said about protecting their legal conditions of stay, or furthering social cohesion with the rest of British society. Chapter 4 showed that neither was much said about the pressure on local communities of arrivals of large numbers of labour migrants undercutting wages and working conditions—a trend considered to have influenced the Brexit vote and more recently the fall of Labour parliamentary seats to the Tories in the so-called 'red wall' areas. Chapter 4 cited a population report from 1948[54] which identified issues still important today. The report stressed that new labour migrants should be chosen on the basis that they would integrate socially, intermarry and become part of British society, and recognised that *'insofar as immigrants are permanently satisfied with lower standards... they constitute a threat to the interests of the British working class....*[55] Many argue that using migrants to fill labour shortages risks failing to address the lack of investment and vocational training in the British economy, based as it is on debt, low wages,[56] stagnant productivity and financialised short-termism. Even if those wider economic issues were addressed, it may be necessary to rely on overseas recruitment to fill vacancies which must urgently be filled. Even before Covid, Britain was short of doctors and nurses, skilled construction workers, experienced social care staff, qualified HGV drivers as well as the people needed to harvest British-grown fruit and vegetables. At the time of writing wages are creeping up in those sectors most under pressure from the departure of EU nationals from the workforce, such as HGV drivers, fruit and vegetable harvesting and processing. But in social care, where currently there is little room for wage increases, recruitment problems are severe. A shift to a higher waged and more productive British economy may be desirable, but in the short term, even more people especially those on benefits will be 'left behind' as prices go up. However, as Chapter 4 argued, trying to solve these problems through a guestworker system raises a multiplicity of contested political issues.

From the wider perspective of *the content and purpose of external control,* the position of ***family migrants*** should be simple. International conventions signed and ratified by the UK propose family unity and the best interests of the child as high-level guiding principles. Entry policies do not have to be limited by the meanest, narrowest conception of right to family life as litigated upon by domestic and European courts. In particular, reducing rights to family unity to concepts such as 'insurmountable obstacles' and 'unduly harsh' should be considered politically unacceptable, as the average British family would undoubtedly be surprised if they understood the implications. The government's December 2021 proposals on human rights[57] focus sharply on curtailing the use of art 8 ECHR to resist deportation of foreign offenders, but litigation since 2012 has shown how deportation cases have driven restrictions in the application of art 8 to all migrant families. These proposals are currently open to a strictly limited multiple choice consultation rather than the wide democratic debate which is needed.

An entry policy aimed at *facilitating* family unity, recognising the validity of a family's wish to settle in the UK rather than elsewhere, applying a shared burden of proof, proper standards of proof and a fee structure designed just to cover the cost of administration, would reduce the wider societal costs of divided families, many of whom are reduced to claiming social benefits precisely because one parent is stuck abroad. That cost is currently not given proper, or any, weight in the performative desperation to avoid every single allegedly sham marriage and every single short period during which a family with a migrant in it may need recourse to social benefits.

Foreign criminals: Few would object to someone's criminal record being considered to weigh against an application to enter the UK, or even weigh against being allowed to remain. And not many would object to the deportation of a person assessed to be likely to reoffend. However, as shown in Chapter 6, the timeless provision *The deportation of foreign criminals* ***is*** *in the public interest,* taken together with the automatic deportation provisions of the UK Borders Act 2007, *with no limit on how long ago the relevant offence was committed,* is leading to the deportation of people who, if British, would have found their crimes long since counted as 'spent'. We are also seeing deportation orders being maintained against people who had already successfully appealed against deportation for the same offence. The current legal position thus renders 'deportable' any migrant who has not yet become a citizen—an especially frightening prospect since Home Secretary Priti Patel has suggested reducing the level of prison sentence triggering 'automatic deportation' from 12 months down to 6 months.

Asylum-seekers and illegal entrants: Though every government asserts that they 'welcome' 'genuine refugees' the current border control aim is to prevent *any* entry by a person without formal permission. Better than a false 'welcome' would be commitments to accept refugees under the Convention and those fleeing countries experiencing war and civil unrest, including a commitment to take more than a trivial number of refugees from refugee camps abroad, rather than already reneging on existing commitments.[58] Emphasising that in the context of continental European and world migration flows the numbers arriving spontaneously in Britain are frictional and manageable, their asylum applications should be assessed efficiently and promptly on the basis of a shared burden and the asylum standard of proof, additionally making a proper assessment of whether, even if not meriting refugee status, they are people 'of concern' to the UNHCR, i.e. fleeing from countries in civil war and armed turmoil.

The question of whether those 'landing on the beaches' should or can be 'sent back to France' should be relegated to a manageable aspect of the reciprocal arrangements being made as part of Brexit between the UK and its neighbours to manage and police the millions of passengers and freight crossing the Channel. The burden of any aspect of those arrangements, whether rescuing small numbers of unaccompanied children from the Calais camps or providing extra funding for the UK's charitably-funded lifeboat service, is a matter of political discussion, available resources and priorities. The treatment of this problem as an operational catastrophe that must be 'stopped' has led to ridicule as well as leaving officials '*not knowing what success could look like*'. It is not a second world war battle, and it is not helpful to treat it as giving rise to some free-floating, unmeasurable moral imperative to protect the British population from 'harm'.

5 Conclusion

This chapter has explored immigration control issues from the standpoint of 'who belongs', and on what basis, beginning with an examination of what the UK and its population might understand to be the values of citizenship. The current legal position of migrants in Britain is contrasted with the security enjoyed by citizens, and their rights and opportunities for social and political participation. Finally, the current concentration on controlling entry and enforcement is critiqued as both ineffective and corrosive of social cohesion. A more purposive, holistic consideration of who may enter, and on what terms, is proposed. The next and final chapter continues this discussion by looking at questions of democratic accountability, before setting out some recommendations.

Notes

1. Home Office. 2002. *Secure Borders, Safe Haven: Integration with diversity in Modern Britain* CM 5387.
2. Porter, Bernard. 2004. *The absent-minded imperialists: Empire, society and culture in Britain* Oxford: Oxford University Press.
3. Labour election manifesto February 1974.
4. *British Nationality Law Discussion of possible changes* Cmnd 6795 April 1977.
5. Ibid [4].
6. HC Deb 27 April 1977 vol 930 cc1227-34.
7. Ibid [1231].
8. The 1974 Conservative manifestos did refer to 'abuse' and the need for restrictions, but there were no specific proposals.
9. HC Deb 28 January 1981 Vol 997 cc 935 -1947.
10. This gender inequality was later abolished, first through the law abolishing illegitimacy and then through abolishing gender bias in the Nationality Act itself.
11. British Overseas Citizenships, British Dependent Territories Citizenship, British Subjects Without Citizenship, etc.
12. referring to *Zamir*, discussed in Chapter 2.
13. Williams, Wendy, *Windrush Lessons Learned Review* HC 93, March 2020 [12].
14. HC Deb 28/1/81 vol 997 col 946 (Roy Hattersley).
15. Commission on Citizenship 1990 *Encouraging citizenship* Report of the Commission on Citizenship, HMSO.
16. Marshall, TH 1950 *Citizenship and Social Class* Cambridge University Press [10, 11].
17. Pateman, Carole, cited in *Encouraging citizenship* n15.
18. Goodhart, David. 2019. Daily Telegraph 13 July 2019.
19. Major, John 1993 Speech to Conservative Party conference http://www.britishpoliticalspeech.org/speech-archive.htm?speech=139 accessed 30/11/21.
20. *Education for citizenship and the teaching of democracy in schools* Final report of the Advisory Group on Citizenship 22/9/1998: Qualification and Curriculum Authority 1998.

21. Faulks, Keith. 2006. *Education for citizenship in England's secondary schools: A critique of current principle and practice*. Journal of Education Policy, 21 (1). pp. 59–74.
22. Home Office Border and Immigration Agency. 2008. *The path to citizenship: Next steps in reforming the immigration system*. This was preceded by two speeches by Gordon Brown, to the British Council on 7/7/2004 and to the the Fabian Society in 2006: and the 2007 report *The Governance of Britain*, CM7170, July 2007 and Lord Goldsmith's report *Citizenship: Our Common Bond* [2007].
23. The Treasury formula governing block grants to Scotland, Wales and Northern Ireland to cover their shares of public expenditure.
24. Denham, John. 2019. *English nationalism is misunderstood* Irish Times 13 August 2019.
25. *Rhuppiah* [2018] UKSC 58.
26. Ramsay, Peter. 2012. *The insecurity state: Vulnerable autonomy and the right to security in the criminal law* Oxford: Oxford University Press.
27. The Levellers, 1647–49 *'An Agreement of the People...'* Sharp, Andrew. 2008. *The English levellers (Cambridge texts in the history of political thought)* Cambridge University Press.
28. This took place every Thursday evening between 26 March and 28 May 2020.
29. https://www.middleeasteye.net/news/coronavirus-petition-demands-british-citizenship-all-foreign-frontline-health-workers 30/4/20 accessed 12/7/20.
30. *Encouraging citizenship* 1990 n15 [xv] and [8] (citing Pateman).
31. For example from the No Recourse to Public Funds network http://www.nrpfnetwork.org.uk/Pages/Home.aspx.
32. *Begum* [2021] UKSC 7.
33. Gordon, Ian et al. 2009. GLA Economics. 2009. *Economic impact on London and the UK Economy of an earned regularisation of irregular migrants to the UK* https://www.london.gov.uk/sites/default/files/gla_migrate_files_destination/irregular-migrants-report.pdf GLA [7].

34. Mayor of London/University of Wolverhampton. 2020. *London's children and young people who are not British citizens* Greater London Authority.
35. *Strangers into Citizens,* Strangers into Citizens campaign 2006 http://london.noborders.org.uk/news/strangers-citizens; accessed 30/11/21: Kevin Smith, *Strangers into citizens—For the regularisation of UK people without status* Race & Class 11/1/07; House of Commons Early Day Motion 27/4/07.
36. The Times editorial *Open Britain—The government should rethink its immigration rules for NHS staff and carers* 19/5/20.
37. ICIBI 2019 *An inspection of the policies and practices of the Home Office's Borders, Immigration and Citizenship Systems relating to charging and fees June 2018–January 2019.*
38. Institute of Government 2019 *Managing Migration after Brexit.*
39. Walsh, Peter William. 2021. *Briefing deportation and voluntary departure from the UK* Migration Observatory, University of Oxford.
40. *Rhuppiah* n25.
41. Migration Observatory. 2019. *Permanent or temporary: How Long do Migrants stay in the UK?* University of Oxford.
42. Immigration Rules para 339R, applying from 2013 [archived Rules as at 30/12/13].
43. Previously 'active review'.
44. Migration Observatory. 2020. *Between a rock and a hard place: The Covid-19 crisis and migrants with No Recourse to Public Funds (NRPF)* University of Oxford.
45. On the daily Covid press conference 18/4/20, in response to a Voice journalist.
46. Strangers into Citizens campaign n35.
47. Ibid [14].
48. Gordon, Ian et al. 2009. *Economic impact on the London and UK economy of an earned regularisation of irregular migrants to the UK* LSE Interim Report, cited in Migrants Rights Network *Irregular migrants—The urgent need for a new approach* May 2009 [8] fn12.
49. Migration Watch 2019 briefing MW 434 https://www.migrationwatchuk.org/key-topics/illegal-immigration.

50. Migrants Rights Network 2009 *Irregular migrants—The urgent need for a new approach* [16].
51. Mayor of London/University of Wolverhampton report n34.
52. Marmot, Professor Sir Michael. 2021. *Build back fairer in Greater Manchester: Health equity and dignified lives*, UCL Institute of Health Equity, June 2021.
53. The Times, cited above, 20/5/20.
54. PEP *Population policy in Great Britain—A report by PEP* April 1948, discussed in Chapter 1.
55. Ibid 110–112, cited in Chapter 2.
56. Migration Advisory Committee 2020 *A points-based system and salary thresholds for immigration*, [16].
57. Ministry of Justice 2021 *Human Rights Act Reform: A Modern Bill of Rights A consultation to reform the Human Rights Act 1998.*
58. Syal, Rajeev 14/12/21 *UK tightens criteria for Afghans to enter despite 'warm welcome' pledge* The Guardian.

8

Immigration Control and Democracy—Who Belongs, and Who Decides?

1 Introduction

This chapter examines democratic accountability for immigration control, pervasively neglected by government, opposition, activists and academics. I begin with the perspective of the 'abstract migrant' not yet on the territory but asserted to possess 'rights' to seek a better life in new lands. That approach usefully reveals the wide gap between those migrants' aspirations and the reality of closed borders. But that perspective takes little account of the views or condition of the host population. Consideration of this contest requires at least a brief reference to the nation-state and the uneven development of modern capitalism.[1]

Central to this study is the lack of democratic accountability *within Britain* for the detailed architecture of UK immigration control. It concludes by noting the current difficulties facing democratic discussion of issues so closely touching our senses of society, identity and mutual responsibility—difficulties arising from the 'fracturing of public space'.

The chapter ends with conclusions from the whole study, and recommendations for the future.

S. York, *The Impact of UK Immigration Law*,
https://doi.org/10.1007/978-3-030-98721-3_8

2 Democracy and the 'Abstract Migrant'

A wide range of academic writing focuses on the 'migrant', and ascribes free-floating 'rights' based on such as human dignity and personhood, discussed without consideration of any particular territory or polity the migrant might be seeking to join. Different justifications are advanced, including *hospitality*, *reparations*, *illegality* and *agency*. Here I also briefly discuss *human rights*, as although the Convention and its caselaw address the position of individual migrants in their specific circumstances, human rights principles are often put forward as if they ought to trump other social and political issues.

Alex Balch (2016)[2] considers whether a migrant's right to enter another territory could be derived from ancient and traditional concepts of ***hospitality***. He contrasts those traditions, based on the idea of the reciprocal receiving of guests, limited by custom so as not to ruin the hosts, with the great religious ideals which hold every human being to be of equal moral value. Examples of the former might be nomadic customs where travellers may drink from a stranger's well, but not for too long. Thus, *on entering someone else's territory*, a desperate survivor or even a tired and hungry traveller can expect something from their hosts, but not in advance, not everything, and not permanently.

There are no modern examples of a truly universal, permanent, unconditional hospitality. And the suggestion that it should apply generally to migrants not yet on the territory lacks any realistic basis for reciprocity, the essential basis for most traditional hospitality. The proposition ignores the immense political struggles needed in the capitalist West to get from Christian universal moral values, everywhere preached in the Christian feudal world but nowhere observed, to even the limited acceptance of redistribution of social and economic goods which has been achieved in the democracies, and which remains under threat. To argue for solidarity between those living in the UK and those outside who currently have no connection with that place, no links of family, friendship, work or political campaigning, would be virtually impossible, as there is nothing solid which is shared, and no possibility of reciprocity, only an aspiration.

Discussion is developing which consider migrants' rights as a form of ***reparations*** for the depredations of empire. Referring to the 2015 European 'migrant crisis', a 2016 press release[3] states *'It is time for Europe to open its borders as a form of reparations for the past injustices that led to the crisis in the first place'*. There can be no disagreement about the enormities of imperial oppression and exploitation. Indian politician and writer Shashi Tharoor spoke at the Oxford Union in 2015 on whether Britain should pay reparations for 200 years during which:

> ...British rule deindustrialised India, created landlessness and poverty, drained our country's resources, exploited, enslaved, exiled and oppressed millions, sowed seeds of division and inter-communal hatred that led to the country's partition into two hostile states, and was directly responsible for the deaths of 35 million people in unnecessary and mismanaged famines as well as of thousands in massacres and killings. That just skims the surface of the havoc wreaked by British colonialism.[4]

But, though he wished the UK to recognise the principle that reparations are owed, he did not argue for any more than a token financial settlement. It is argued here that it is a category mistake to apply tort law concepts to the consequences of the uneven development of capitalism across the world. The brutalities of slavery and imperialism abroad were perpetrated by the same elites who were meting out oppression and exploitation at home, in the form of land clearances, famine and denial of basic economic and political rights. And the spoils of empire were not shared around the home population, but largely squandered in wars and on the private luxuries of a very small upper class. Even the reality of continuing postcolonial capitalist exploitation cannot impose an obligation on the people now living in 'broken Britain', *'a rich country with poorer people in it'*,[5] without presenting cogent arguments about where political responsibility for current economic problems truly lies, and seeking and winning political solidarity *on that basis* from those who would be sharing Britain's social goods with them.

Legality: Bas Schotel (2012)[6] argues that the doctrine of nation-states' sovereignty on immigration is '*legally untenable*'. He proposes that the '*first burden*' of justification for exclusion should fall on the receiving state, and that fully argued reasons must be provided in each case. He applies different theories of jurisprudence, including some which appear directly or indirectly to speak of the legal position of states as distinct from individuals, and concludes that 'the rule of inherent sovereignty', based at its best on 'the exclusion thesis' has no legal validity, and officials who are charged with implementing a state's immigration laws 'should feel uncomfortable'.

But officials do not feel uncomfortable, at least at that general level. They are implementing what has been enacted in Parliament, in an internationally-recognised sovereign state. Such procedures are described by HLA Hart as 'rules of recognition', for which there is no legal 'first cause'.[7] Any particular country's rules of recognition are regarded from outside as facts, and international law is just what states agree to accept.

Schotel conflates what a state can do with what a state official is permitted to do under the laws of that state. He speaks about the 'purpose' of the state. But the state, as such, does not have 'a purpose'. It is an entity which came into being through internal and external political struggle, from time to time constrained internally by lack of resources and political will, and from outside by war, aggression, international treaties and conventions voluntarily entered into. But these treaties and conventions are followed only so far as the government of the day thinks pragmatically necessary. An outstanding recent example was the abandonment of open borders by many Schengen countries at the height of the 2015 'migrant crisis'. Schotel is just wrong. A migrant sleeping rough in Calais, not having claimed asylum in France, undocumented and on French soil, is of no more legal concern to the UK state than if they were still in their own country. They have no legal claim on the UK, let alone a right to full individualised reasons for refusing entry to them. The general rule of customary international law is that no individual may assert a right to enter a state of which they are not a national: and this is normally applied to refugees.[8] By contrast, once that migrant arrives on British territory,[9] officials 'comfortably' may, and must, deal with him under UK laws passed by a democratically-elected parliament.

Tendayi Achiume (2019)[10] argues that, as a matter of international law, an individual migrant who sets out from a previously colonised country and arrives on the shores of the erstwhile imperial oppressor should be recognised and acknowledged as being part of the same *demos* and entitled to the same rights as the residents of that country. The migrant is a citizen of the *co-sovereign entity* made up of the imperial country and its former colony, and is thus exercising the rights of a citizen. For Achiume, the ex-colonies remain in subordination to their erstwhile rulers, both economically and politically, which '*maintains the political association between the First and Third Worlds in a political community of de facto co-sovereigns…'* For Achiume, that continuing economic and political domination means that we are still part of the same *demos*. Further, *given the unlikelihood of third world prosperity or an end to neocolonialism,* a partial exercise of 'corrective distributive justice' is required, which she proposes would consist of a freely-chosen exercise of citizenship of the imperialist country. For Achiume, such a proposed citizenship of the co-sovereignty made up of the ex-colony and the imperialist/post-imperialist state requires a rectification in the international law position concerning (first world) nation-states' right to exclude non-nationals, and a demand for citizenship for those third-world nationals who wish to rectify their weak position as part of an exploited population by migrating to the metropole.

However, to be part of the same *demos* means having or at least aspiring to equal *political* rights. This could mean a right to vote and sit in a joint or federal legislature, and thence participate in a joint political attempt to combat the continuing neo-colonial exploitation. But this was never a demand of any colonial population during their independence struggles, nor is it a current political demand of any of the ex-colonial nations—who rather demand sovereign independence and true economic self-determination. Secondly, in Achiume's scheme, the migrant's arrival and presence on European territory would 'count' for more than the European-resident individuals already present—whose opinion would not be sought. As a proposition of international law, such a scheme can make sense only as a *contrivance* by which to argue that those irregular migrants who happen to make it to Britain should be treated as citizens. It proposes no democratic accountability to either the receiving or the sending part of her 'whole demos'.

Agency: Souter (2014)[11] among others proposes that an individual migrant's decision to enter a country illegally should be regarded as a political act which should stand with some of the great progressive movements in history, from the Diggers and Levellers to the individual acts by such as Harriet Tubman, Mahatma Gandhi and Nelson Mandela. But this view does great harm to the concept of political activity. There is a world of difference between individual acts of resistance as part of, and predicated on, a wide political debate gaining popular support and social weight; and separate individuals making decisions to break the law on their own account. We cannot invest the acts themselves with political significance until discourse about those acts is brought into the *public space* which is an essential feature of a democracy—the space in which the protagonists of those ideas must discuss them with people they do not know, who may have other interests, and who remain to be persuaded of our worldview. A demand that we accord universal moral value to every human being is not enough to bridge the large gap, requiring a massive political struggle to bridge, between that and persuading the population, the *demos*, of the receiving country to accept all irregular migrants. It is the neglect of that gap which leads voters and politicians to talk about the 'cosmopolitan elite' who are 'citizens of nowhere'[12] and who therefore do not mind inviting other citizens of nowhere to share a part of their territory and their public services.

Some writers describe the citizens of the receiving states as 'constituted' by the processes of immigration control, presented as 'controlling *movement*', and thus being *party* to the national and international capitalist and state-sponsored industries of incarceration and deportation along with the ensemble of securitisation and externalisation of border control.[13] The truth is that few of today's citizens could be considered 'parties' in those processes. The vast majority of citizens are descendants of the *other side* of the democratic and political struggles needed to achieve any civil, political and social rights at all. What we have inherited, but are in danger of forgetting, is not a life of ease stolen from the oppressed of Empire, but a sense of being part of the same continuing struggle for political and economic power of millions of people all over the world who are no less entitled to abstract human equality than the 'migrant'. TH Marshall (1950) noted that '*citizenship ... is stimulated by the struggle to win those rights and by their enjoyment when won*'.[14] And the existence of migrants *as migrants* does not arise out of some prehistoric natural need 'to move', inherent in every human being as part of their animal nature, but is driven by the social needs of individuals, private enterprises and governments to deal with the continuing impacts of uneven development across the world. One person's decision to emigrate is inevitably constrained by the democratically-expressed decisions of other people: the very numerous, opinionated, even desperate electorates of the receiving populations, exercising their own hard-won political rights.

Human rights: Like the UN Convention on Refugees, the European Convention on Human Rights (ECHR) is still regarded by many activists and lawyers as providing an international legal framework in which to articulate the needs of the 'abstract migrant'. However, Chapters 2 and 3 showed the limited way European states were prepared to operate the Refugee Convention: and the caselaw of both the European Court of Human Rights (ECtHR) and UK courts has shown how *little* the ECHR has to offer to migrants. At the time of its coming into force in 1953, the aim of the Convention was to signal the kind of behaviour towards individuals to be avoided by democratic states, including the absolute prohibition entailed in art 3 on sending a person back to a place where they might face torture, inhuman or degrading treatment. Otherwise it was not envisaged, and is still strongly resisted by signatory States, that the ECHR would operate as a redistribution mechanism for social goods and services. For example, a homeless person cannot claim a 'right' to housing under the Convention.[15] In the immigration realm, the Convention has long been held not to entitle a person in great need of medical treatment, but with otherwise no claim to remain in the relevant country, to remain and receive any treatment, unless very near death.[16] It was nearly twenty years before *Paposhvili*[17] reconsidered that issue. 'Civil rights,' protected under art 6, and the art 7 protection from retrospective criminal sanctions, are still held not to apply to immigration at all.[18]

And in relation to family and private life, the Commission, and then the Court, early and firmly ruled that the admission of 'aliens' is a prerogative of the state.[19] Article 8 ECHR sets out the extensive interests a state may call on to qualify an applicant's right:

> 2… 'national security, public safety or the economic well-being of the country, for the prevention of disorder or crime, for the protection of health or morals, or for the protection of the rights and freedoms of others.

In the face of those weighty considerations, an individual applicant's circumstances would clearly have to be exceptional. The UK's incorporation of the ECHR into domestic law, the attempts to incorporate art 8 considerations into the Immigration Rules, and the tightening of the law, rules and caselaw have all led to the *narrowing* of UK family and private life provisions. This has driven a foregrounding of litigation and campaigns for the *vulnerable* such as children, trafficking victims, victims of domestic violence. In its turn, this concentration on those consciously identified as victims, and the increased legal reliance on art 8 ECHR, has *reduced* any 'rights' or expectations accorded to individuals and families with no particular claim to exceptionality, but who under previous rules and Home Office policies may have benefited from consideration of a positive—their contribution to the community. For example, in *Oludoyi* (2014) the court decided that the fact of a migrant's working as a nurse—a shortage occupation—*added nothing* to her art 8 right to family life.[20] Neither will a foreign offender's rehabilitation protect from deportation.[21] The 2020 Upper Tribunal case of *RA* states in its headnote:

> Rehabilitation will not ordinarily bear material weight in favour of a foreign criminal.[22]

Along with the 2012 family migration rules and the IA 2014 definition of 'precarious', recent human rights rulings amount to an exercise of a colonial-style right to interfere in family life.[23] Activists' concentration on human rights and on litigation rather than on a more political emphasis on a migrant's place in society has allowed the development of a Home Office and wider political view that most if not all migrants are *temporary*, resulting in their *legal definition* as 'precarious', with the pernicious legal consequences described in this study.

None of this prohibits the signatory states from making humanitarian provision, such as the UK's settlement schemes for vulnerable Syrian refugees, but neither the Refugee Convention nor the ECHR can found an *obligation*. Even the formal human rights milieu is not hopeful. In January 2018 it was reported that the UN human rights chief Zeid Ra'ad al-Hussein would not be seeking a second term in office, noting that '*…reminding governments that they are breaking the [human rights] laws they signed up to is no longer working*.'[24]

Samuel Moyn (2010) argues precisely that 'human rights' emerged as a consciously *apolitical* rallying-cry for people who wanted a better world—'*when Westerners left the dream of revolution behind*'.[25] However, not only does an emphasis on the aspirational rights of an 'abstract migrant' avoid—and in some cases even reject—the idea of democratic accountability,[26] but this position itself risks alienating people who are concerned about the plight of refugees, and grates on the ears of citizens and residents facing real economic hardship and feeling cut adrift in their own country.[27]

We may dislike the politics of the receiving state's current party of government. We may disagree with some of the political theories underlying voters' choices: we may argue that policy choices about immigration control are not based on evidence; are misguided, racist, cruel; breach international human rights norms, and so on. But those contentions must be made to that electorate: and must prevail there. The organised working classes of the main first-world economies did not achieve full civil, political and economic rights and entitlements even within their own polities, let alone in the rest of the whole world. The rallying-cry '*workers of the world unite*' did not prevail, and the twentieth-century workers' revolutions did not succeed in moving the world economy beyond capitalism. The prewar decades of political alliances between international and British black intellectuals and British working-class activists did not manage to achieve colonial independence under socialism—because of the strength of capitalism and of the governments supporting it.[28] And in the UK now, as in many first-world states, we are barely maintaining the advances in rights, entitlements and living standards we achieved.

3 Democratic Accountability and UK Immigration Control

Our collective knowledge and experience of UK domestic history and politics since the Second World War would surely include an overwhelming sense that 'immigration' has been one of a few issues which have dominated political debate and government activity: and that the debate has been often crude, racist, xenophobic and ignorant. It is in that context that this study argues that, nevertheless, UK immigration control lacks democratic accountability, and that migrants themselves and wider society have all suffered because of this.

3.1 Citizenship

First of all, this study has shown how little public discussion there has been about the meaning and purpose of citizenship. I have speculated that if there had been formal public consultation within the UK and throughout the Colonies and Commonwealth, the British Nationality Act 1948 could not have been passed. The UK electorate would probably have demanded a citizenship limited in some way to those born and living in the UK itself. The populations of at least the large Colonies would have intensified their independence demands. Both the future population of the UK, and the political futures of those Colonies, may well have been different. But, beyond speculation, the effects of that Act, passed with almost complete lack of public discussion, must afterwards have contributed to the sense of deception within the UK about immigration issues—a sense that the government was hiding something—which persists to this day. The receiving population of the UK was in no way prepared for the big influxes of people from the Colonies and Commonwealth. It was years before formal political demands were made for assistance to local areas for housing, schools and medical facilities for the new arrivals. The prevalence of racial thinking, at every level of society, was for years not met by any formal attempts whether through education or political discussion—even despite the existence of campaigns for colonial independence and to fight racism *in the Colonies.*

It is evident from formal Parliamentary debates and other political discussions, including within the Labour Party and in the trade union movement, that politicians and campaigners were embarrassed about the prevalence of racial thinking in Britain, but had inadequate theoretical and practical arguments and insufficient courage for public debate.

These fundamental unresolved political questions can be seen to have infected every debate on immigration law since that time. Chapter 2 showed that, in the 1970s and 1980s, published reports began to look at the social cost of racism and discrimination in society. Chapter 7 pointed to two separate moments, under very different governments in very different political situations, in which the questions of British citizenship, 'British values' and 'inclusion' were afforded serious consideration. The 1990 report *Encouraging Citizenship*[29] drew on contributions from historians and philosophers to arrive at principles which they believed underlay what is understood by citizenship in Britain. But they noted that those principles were not widely known or understood. Neither was the legal status of citizenship clear, nor its attendant rights and duties, as scattered between different areas of legislation. Relevant here is that the Commission noted that the rights and duties of citizens were not even clearly or directly related to immigration status—though they did not feel that that was important. We saw how, at that same time, schools had been given responsibility to teach citizenship, explicitly as a way of inculcating a sense of inclusion in young people, but that, partly because the local authority education system had begun to break up under the Thatcher governments, it was difficult to ensure common practice among schools, or assess the effectiveness of that programme. No other public discussion was proposed.

The second significant formal attention to citizenship, in Home Secretary David Blunkett's 2002 White Paper *Secure Borders, Safe Haven*[30] promised *an open and constructive debate about citizenship,* which never took place. And, as I suggested in Chapter 7, it was arguably that lack of discussion which permitted Labour to contemplate the 'earned citizenship' proposals, included in the Borders, Citizenship and Immigration Act 2009, never commenced, but arguably forming an intellectual basis for the Conservative measures rendering migrants 'temporary' and 'precarious' over long periods of time.

Since as a matter of immigration law the question of citizenship appears settled, it is unlikely that any government would now initiate a formal discussion. However, I argue that until there is a discussion, of the *meaning and purpose of citizenship,* what values it embodies and who should therefore be invited to hold that status, it will be difficult to address comprehensively any of the issues of social inclusion which are touched by problems arising from insecure immigration status.

3.2 Legislation, Rules and Guidance

Chapter 6 argued that a key breach of rule of law principles in the world of immigration control is the passing of legislation and introduction of Immigration Rules which obscure their true purpose, for example using contrivances such as 'patrial' to disguise a racial purpose. This illustrates a different aspect of lack of democratic accountability. Yes, the Commonwealth Immigrants Acts 1962 and 1968, and the Immigration Act 1971 were passed in parliament: the 1968 Act in particular after widespread and frantic public discussion. But, as with many subsequent examples, poorly-drafted and obscure measures then drove the need for changes to patch up errors and close loopholes, and often that was done through the Immigration Rules. Other very significant measures passed in primary legislation have been slipped into bills on their way through parliament and enjoyed almost no debate.[31] Crucially, the clauses introducing the concept of 'precarious', and the timeless *The deportation of foreign criminals is in the public interest* clause, into the Immigration Act 2014 faced no discussion of the consequences and so benefit from no transitional provisions or other safeguards. This is discussed in the next section.

The Immigration Rules require only negative resolution: they come into force as soon as issued, but are laid before parliament for 40 days to give time for the changes to be 'prayed against'. There is no detailed scrutiny. Significant changes in immigration law, from the 'primary purpose' rules of the 1970s to the significant changes to family migration introduced in 2012, have been introduced in this way, enjoying no or very limited debate in parliament.[32] Chapter 6 noted that the entire regime of application fees was introduced without debate, and the onerous front-loading of increases in those fees, not unlawful but surely controversial, were merely noted in an impact assessment attached to a statutory instrument and received no general publicity. Subordinate legislation is currently being used to impose digital-only proof of immigration status from 6/4/22, in a world where especially elderly and disabled migrants have limited access to the internet.[33]

In a significant shift away from any recognition of integration or contribution to the community, again made in an unheralded rule change, decisions on refusal, removal and deportation decisions no longer needed to consider a person's age, length of residence in the UK, family, work and other associations with the UK, or domestic or compassionate circumstances.[34] A new para 353B limited consideration to 'character, conduct and associations including any criminal record...' and 'compliance with any previous conditions'.

The 2014 case of *Oludoyi*,[35] mentioned above, stated:

> the notion that a good immigration history on the part of an individual somehow reduces (at all or to any significant extent) the weight that would ordinarily attach to the state's interests in immigration control [is misconceived] ...

The tribunal stated that Ms Oludoyi's being a nurse, which was formally classed as a shortage occupation, did not count as an exceptional circumstance—though to the public at large it might well have done.

The 2019 Institute for Government report on immigration control questioned the wide use of secondary legislation. It recommended that rule changes should be scrutinised by a committee similar to the Social Security Advisory Committee, to consider the impact of each new rule and precisely how it would be put into practice.[36]

This stricture must apply even more strongly to the Home Office practice of making significant changes by way of guidance and procedural changes. Chapter 6 described how the good character requirements for citizenship have recently been extended in guidance to requiring 10 years of lawful residence rather than five, ruling out even those whose unlawful residence was later overlooked by a grant of leave, and those EU nationals with periods of residence during which they were not working or self-employed, but held no comprehensive private sickness insurance *even though* another government department, the Department of Work and Pensions, may have deemed the applicant to have the right to reside. The impacts will be profound,[37] for a change in policy not placed before parliament.

The Institute of Government report noted also that immigration and asylum operations display an important feature not seen in any other caseworking department: the significant decision-making done by ministers in person.[38] This has undesirable legal and political consequences. First, this introduces discretion even beyond the published guidance, in an apparently rule-based system. Secondly, knowing that ministers may be concerned about politically controversial decisions (such as on deportation of a foreign offender) officials may apply rules more strictly to avoid ministerial criticism. And release of decisions may be held up, to manage political fallout.

3.3 Legal Changes Through the Courts

Finally, big developments have taken place in immigration law through restrictive judicial interpretation of legislation and rules. This process is simply part of the UK legal system. But where the results are so startling and surely controversial, the lack of parliamentary review must be disquieting.

In response to the welter of litigation following the passing of the Human Rights Act 1998, (and in particular response to foreign criminals winning appeals on art 8 ECHR grounds), the Immigration Act 2014 brought in a new Part 5A Nationality, Immigration and Asylum Act 2002,[39] which set out at s117A-C a statement of the '*public interest considerations*' to which a court or tribunal 'must' have regard in deciding a claim based on art 8 ECHR. These include

> (4) Little weight should be given to—
>
> (a)a private life, or
>
> (b)a relationship formed with a qualifying partner,

that is established by a person at a time when the person is in the United Kingdom unlawfully.

(5) Little weight should be given to a private life established by a person at a time when the person's immigration status is precarious.

After decisions in the Upper Tribunal appearing to some commentators[40] to be out of line with ECtHR jurisprudence on the meaning of '*precarious*', the Supreme Court, in *Rhuppiah*[41] in 2018 decided to provide a 'bright line' for Home Office decision-makers: all those without indefinite leave to remain must count as '*precarious*'. That decision is condemning many more than just that appellant, already resident 20 years in the UK, to a further 10 years of 'precarious' life on a 'route to settlement' whose requirements might change at any time. It is surely controversial that a legal precedent which will require people to remain 30 years in the UK before qualifying for settlement would not be reviewed or discussed in parliament.

In another retreat from the leading judgments of the 2000s, the Supreme Court in *Agyarko*[42] again required couples to show '*insurmountable obstacles*' to their enjoying family life in the migrant's own country of origin. A further retreat from pre-2010 human rights caselaw was demonstrated in the 2020 case of *SD*,[43] in which the Tribunal decided that neither domestic nor ECHR jurisprudence, '*nor the Rules nor any current Home Office policy expressly identifies the fact that an entry clearance applicant has children with British citizenship as a factor of any particular weight*'. In relation to the children's dual citizenship, '*...There is nothing in the Strasbourg or domestic jurisprudence that requires the respondent or a tribunal, as a general matter, to ascribe greater significance to the child's European/British citizenship than to the citizenship of the other country. That is unsurprising, since any such requirement risks being seen as a form of Eurocentric arrogance*'. This determination on its own looks like a cackhanded attempt to 'decolonise' the law which resulted in British children being kept out of the country. But it also represents a significant legal backtracking from previous established caselaw and Home Office policy. Again, it is surely controversial that this legal shift would not be reviewed by parliament.

These court and tribunal decisions are dividing families in the UK—and are a source of shock not just to the affected families themselves, but to the wider world, every time such a case reaches the media. But the cumulative effect of these legal judgments is not widely known.

Those types of court and tribunal decisions have intensified the legal need to find something exceptional in *any* family or private life application. In practice it now requires DNA evidence of relationship to win refugee family reunion cases. It now requires individualised medical or social worker evidence to show that splitting a family would have an 'unduly harsh' effect on a child; that a child would not thrive in a household faced with destitution; or that a very sick person will not survive long in a country with no public health service. And, undiscussed anywhere in the public realm, every family and private life application, whether formally meeting the requirements of the Rules or not, now requires a full statement of why the applicant cannot return to his or her own country to live, and why they cannot return there to pursue an appeal if refused. This requirement was not introduced even through a change in the Immigration Rules, but in the drafting of online application forms.

In relation to asylum law and procedure, in particular the question of whether the UK's asylum determination regime operates as a pull factor, Mayblin (2019) argues that government failure to present countervailing evidence is 'not fulfilling democratic values'.[44]

All these processes, which are driving a desperate retreat to the 'exceptional' in 'human rights' cases, have barely been exposed to democratic scrutiny, or even much public discussion. We only need to look at the wide public debate in 2012 around the introduction of the 'bedroom tax' and in 2017 on the 'two child limit' on child benefit, and the strenuous political debate in 2021 on whether the Covid-related £20 increase in Universal Credit should be retained, to see how comparatively little scrutiny is given to equally significant changes in immigration control policy. The recent proposal for an 'interpretation bill' to deal with court judgments to which the government takes exception has been heavily criticised. But those seeking better conditions for migrants arguably need a procedure like this.[45]

4 Difficulties of Democratic Discussion

It is not suggested that the kind of democratic discussion we need would be easy. Zygmunt Bauman (2000)[46] described a new phase of 'light' or 'liquid' capitalism in which the institutional bases of old class solidarities have disappeared. For Bauman, the individual has finally been cut loose from social bounds, released to an experience of life as a perpetual personal struggle to survive and achieve personal meaning, and in which other people even suffering the same problems cannot be applied to or relied on to provide personal support, let alone wider political solidarity. We use chat shows, radio phone-ins and revelations about the lives of public figures to find out how to navigate our own problems, increasingly named, medicalised and discussed in public but more often endured in private. Actual public issues, such as the impact of precarity on UK-resident migrants' families, can become almost incomprehensible presented at that level. Presented as a problem facing an individual, the audience is given no context in which to assess how serious it is. In this world, the *public space* needed to discuss problems conceived of as being society's problems, capable of collective solution, is diminishing. There is a declining ability even to speak to strangers with civility as there are fewer opportunities to do so, and fewer public spaces in which to do this. Often, debate, especially on social media, has become reactive, unstable and unpredictable, and public disagreement has become problematic. In those conditions, the longing for 'community' is often limited to the construction of small enclaves (whether territorial, intellectual or social) in which we meet people like ourselves, among whom virtue-signalling is practised, and in which we can feel 'safe'. However, as a society, as a *demos*, we need somehow to reach beyond these barriers to ensure that *public* debate takes place which properly presents the *social* harm arising from such immigration policies.

5 Conclusions on Democratic Accountability

This study has noted global trends and forces including global movements of capital and national demands for overseas labour. It has noted the growth in a human concern about world economic and social conditions, operating at the level of the universal and tugging at both our individual sympathy and our progressive desires to express political solidarity with the widest possible number of people, including those not yet on the territory. The study has also emphasised the need to acknowledge the many various and different concerns within the receiving country about culture, economic security, social cohesion, belonging and citizenship. These strands of valid political and moral concern exist in tension *because of the material fact of the onward march of capitalist economics in a world of uneven economic development,* and that tension cannot simply be wished away.

The political tension surrounding issues of immigration control, and the importance of the rights and entitlements under consideration, thus demand the most intense democratic accountability for policy changes. Major changes in migrants' rights and entitlements require full parliamentary scrutiny and should not be introduced by means of changes in the Immigration Rules, Home Office guidance or changes to online forms. Close parliamentary attention to outcomes of legislative and rule changes, including unforeseen outcomes and the consequences of developments in caselaw, need a combination of accurate measures to monitor and evaluate them but which also question outcomes in a wider context, such as the costs and impacts on different parts of British society of government policies and legal decisions.

This study now presents some proposals for discussion. First, a **solidarity-based approach to the 2 million insecure migrants present in the UK.** The Legacy process 2006–2011 and even the efforts to rectify the Windrush debacle (still continuing) foundered on the rocks of inadequate resources, the burden of proof falling on the applicant and, in relation to criminality, retrospective measures. Even a return to the terms of the pre-2012 Immigration Rules would provide a shorter and easier path to settlement and citizenship for a large proportion of insecure migrants, including many who are unlawfully present. The repeal of the hostile environment is supported by many, but it is not widely understood how far back, and how embedded, internal controls have become. Repeal would have to consider not just the measures contained in the Immigration Acts 2014 and 2016, but all the internal control measures introduced since the 1980s.

It is acknowledged that there would be significant opposition to any regularisation scheme. On the other hand, the political contestation required in arguing for such an amnesty represents a politically realistic chance of identifying common interests among those who live, work and survive in the UK and building solidarity between them. It also provides a necessary basis for combating the continued strength of racial thinking which still affects not just the politics of immigration but wider concerns in society.

Secondly, on **labour migration policy**, concerns for social and economic solidarity might argue, as argued in 1948, that *'provided the contract is freely entered into, there is no injustice ... [but]' insofar as immigrants are permanently satisfied with lower standards... they constitute a threat to the interests of the British working class...*[47] The scourge of employers relying on illegal workers or cheap temporary migrants to keep wages down can far better be confronted if migrant workers are free to change jobs and employers, and if migrant workers were able to organise and speak out against abuse and not be afraid of any immigration consequences. The space for racism and xenophobia to flourish would be diminished, since where everyone has equal political, social and economic rights the irrationality of trying to treat people differently on the basis of colour, nationality, accent, etc. would become clearer. Fewer differences for capitalism to exploit. No room to say 'go home' because it would be clear that they are already 'home'.

Lastly, on **citizenship**, a democratic discussion about immigration control requires the fullest consideration of what we understand by 'belonging' and solidarity. Progress to citizenship, for many people who have made their home in the UK, is currently an 'over the rainbow' status dangled out many years in the future, and for those who committed criminal offences never attainable. To achieve any kind of solidarity, for them and for everybody else, requires that they be able to enjoy the right to participate as fully as possible in the society in which we are all living. Citizenship based on birth on the territory would avoid the situation of children suffering because of the immigration problems of their parents. Citizenship for settled migrants should be available on clear legal pathways requiring no more than the 5-year period of legal residence provided for in the BNA 1981 and an assessment of good character that accepts the 'rehabilitation of offenders' criteria applied to British people. Those who think citizenship should be 'earned', or is a 'privilege' which should be paid for, should bear in mind that for people who are born British there are no requirements of residence, or good character. We are not even required to participate. We don't have to be 'good' citizens. We can be lazy, *'feckless, unemployable and uncultured'*.[48] That 'right' to behave badly is curtailed by our communal political discussions about what should and should not be accepted. We can surely demand that naturalised British citizens fit in, to the extent that they obey the law. But there appears to be no good argument why someone who is settled in the UK, living and working amongst citizens, can be required to live at a higher moral, economic or cultural level than those born here, before gaining access to citizenship, the gateway to democratic participation.

6 Concluding Summary

This study has looked at the development of post-war immigration control, and identified four major impacts, on migrants, on wider British society and on the law itself: and makes a number of proposals, set out at the end as Recommendations.

The study bases its conclusions on the examination of three principal periods and categories of migration. Chapter 2 analysed the social and legal impacts of policies intended to control the arrival (and return) of colonial-born and Commonwealth British subjects, invited to fill Britain's acute labour shortages: followed by thirty years of Commonwealth labour migration and the slow process of admission for colonial and Commonwealth spouses and families. Chapter 3 analysed the impact of measures controlling the arrivals and processing of a new type of migrant: the 'spontaneous' or 'irregular' arrivals of asylum-seekers.

Chapter 4 considered the conceptualising and treatment of labour migrants, from the post-war European resettlement schemes through the downgrading of overseas British subjects into labour migrants, to the later expansions of work-based migration and the opening of complete free movement for nationals of the newly-acceded A8 EU nations in 2004.

Even in the face of the 2010 Coalition government's major policy shift towards restriction, increasing numbers of work migrants, both EU nationals and others, continued to arrive. Growing opposition to this fed into wider political concerns about membership of the European Union, leading to Cameron's 2015 attempts to renegotiate the terms of the UK's membership, the vote for Brexit in 2016 and the long and politically lacerating process, including changes of party leaders, court cases examining constitutional issues and two general elections, leading to the UK's withdrawal from the EU on 31 December 2019 and the 2020 relaunch of the points-based scheme for selecting labour migrants.

Chapter 5 noted the restrictive responses of the Coalition and Conservative governments from 2010 onwards: stringent new entry requirements, applications fees and charges, and the formal hostile environment. Then it examined, in the light of the above narratives, the secular poor public administration of control, amounting to a *policy, arguably based on racial thinking*, of neglect of migrants and their rights. It proposes the intellectually simple remedies, echoed in many official and independent reports, of significant simplification of legislation, rules and application procedures and a significant increase in resources, to end delays and administrative incompetence.

Chapter 6 identified and examined the immigration control function's long-standing indifference to the rule of law and lack of legal conscientiousness, demonstrated at every stage of the exercise of immigration control, from planning and implementing legislation, administration and decision-making through to the appellate structures and enforcement machinery. In that chapter, this study considers and proposes a less legalistic and more political understanding of issues affecting hundreds of thousands of UK-resident migrants, including delay, legitimate expectation and the retrospective effect of decades of introducing changes with no or inadequate transitional provisions. It concludes that without moving to a shared burden of proof, and without significant efforts to avoid retrospective effects of legal changes, the odious legal consequences of immigration control will continue.

Finally, in Chapter 7 this study directs us to consider what are the real issues in immigration control today. Not some list, always restrictive and always contentious, of who should or should not be permitted to enter and remain. Nor the presence of a few non-national offenders on British soil. Nor even the asylum-seekers having the temerity to arrive on British beaches in small boats. The major issues are: first and fundamentally, what should be the meaning and purpose of British citizenship, seen as the political right to participate as full members of our democracy. Next is the need to reduce the precarity and insecurity in which over 2 million residents are expected to live, work and bring up their children; the need to agree on what moral, political and social considerations should guide decisions about external control, such as what should be the rights and entitlements of labour migrants and of family members: and what would count as a moral and efficacious welcome to asylum-seekers and refugees. Measures of control and enforcement should *emerge from those discussions*, rather than dominating political discourse on immigration.

7 Recommendations

The following specific proposals are advanced, without which no immigration policy could free itself from the criticisms advanced in this study.

a. The introduction of a shared burden of proof in the immigration and asylum jurisdiction
b. The eradication of retrospective effects from immigration control legislation, rules and procedures
c. The provision of sufficient resources for the immigration and asylum function in public administration, without reliance on prohibitive fees or exploitative and malfunctioning outsourcing contracts
d. A restatement of the entire legal architecture of control, whatever its substantive content, in a form that is simple, coherent and transparent

e. A generous scheme for the regularisation of long-resident irregular migrants and their children, based on a shared burden of proof and adequate resources
f. An official campaign to encourage immigrants including labour migrants, to seek permanent residence and eventual citizenship, emphasising *common purpose*, with simple requirements and without prohibitive fees

These recommendations are offered firstly as practical measures that seek to address the immediate circumstances of those who wish to enter or remain in the UK, and secondly to prompt the engagement of the public in a discussion about the meaning of citizenship and the integration of immigrants where that is desired. It is only on the basis of improved procedures for immigrants and asylum-seekers, and fuller participation by the *demos* in their design, can we begin to repair the social corrosion exacerbated by the long since 'broken' UK immigration control system.

Notes

1. This Part has drawn on the following works among others: Harvey, David. 2011. *The enigma of capital and the crises of capitalism* Profile Books; Anderson, Benedict. 1983. *Imagined communities* Verso; Gellner, Ernest. 1982. *Nations and nationalism* Basil Blackwell; Hobsbawm, Eric. 1992. *Nations and nationalism since 1970* Cambridge: Cambridge University Press; Nairn, Tom. 1977. *The breakup of Britain—Crisis and neo-nationalism* London: Verso; Calhoun, Craig. 2007. *Nations matter—Culture, history and the cosmopolitan dream* London: Routledge.
2. Balch, Alex. 2016. *Immigration and the state: Fear, greed and hospitality* Palgrave Macmillan.
3. https://www.versobooks.com/blogs/2900-europe-s-migration-crisis-or-open-borders-as-reparations advertising Reece Jones *Violent borders, refugees and the right to move* Verso 2016.
4. Shashi Tharoor, *Does Britain owe reparations to India and other former colonies?* https://www.scmp.com/week-asia/opinion/article/

2050394/does-britain-owe-reparations-india-and-other-former-colonies
5. Pabst, Adrian. 2015. *Britain's broken economy*, in *Blue Labour—Forging a new politics* ed Pabst, Adrian and Geary, Ian, IB Tauris 5.
6. Schotel, Bas. 2012. *On the right of exclusion* London: Routledge.
7. Riddal, JG. 1999. *Jurisprudence* Oxford: Oxford University Press.
8. Macdonald, Ian, Blake, Nicholas. 1991. *Immigration Law and practice* 3rd edition. London: Butterworths [288 n3], citing Oppenheim *International Law* Lauterpacht 7th edition [616].
9. The current (December 2021) Nationality and Borders Bill seeks to exclude British territorial waters from this definition.
10. Achiume, E. Tendaye. 2019. *Migration as decolonization.* Stanford Law Review, 71 (June).
11. Souter, James. 2014. *Towards a theory of asylum as reparation for past injustice.* Political Studies, 62. pp. 326–342.
12. May, Theresa, 2016 Conservative party conference.
13. See for example the contributions in Nicholas de Genova and Nathalie Peutz eds 2010 *The deportation regime: Sovereignty, space and the freedom of movement* Duke University.
14. Marshall, TH. 1950. *Citizenship and social class.* Cambridge University Press [28–29, 40–41].
15. *O'Rourke v United Kingdom* [2001] Application no. 39022/97 (unreported) 26 June 2001 ECtHR.
16. *D v United Kingdom (Application no. 30240/96), N v United Kingdom* [2008] ECHR 453.
17. *Paposhvili* ECHR 412 (2016).
18. Decided in the truly cursory *Maaouia* judgment: York, Sheona. 2017. *Deportation of foreign offenders—A critical look at the consequences of Maaouia and whether recourse to common-law principles might offer a solution.* Journal of Immigration, Asylum and Nationality Law, 31 (1).
19. Dembour, Marie-Benedict. 2015. *When Humans become migrants: A study of the European Court of Human Rights with an inter-American counterpoint.* Oxford Scholarship Online [104].

20. *Oludoyi & Ors, R (oao) v SSHD (Article 8 – MM (Lebanon) and Nagre) (IJR)* [2014] UKUT 539 (IAC).
21. *Danso v SSHD* [2015] EWCA Civ 596.
22. *RA (s.117C: "unduly harsh"; offence: seriousness)* [2019] UKUT 123.
23. *SD (British citizen children – entry clearance) Sri Lanka* [2020] UKUT 00043(IAC) [#90], discussed in 2.3 below.
24. Betts, Alexander. 2018 Guardian 21/1/18.
25. Moyn, Samuel. 2010. *The last utopia—human rights in history* Harvard: Belknap Press.
26. Arguments that social and welfare services in the metropole were an act of theft from colonial peoples, have been advanced by Nadine El-Enany in *(B)ordering Britain* University of Manchester Press 2020. She refers to *'the Leave vote's embodiment of a rejection of anyone considered to be a migrant'* and proposes reliance on scholars and academics as agents for political change [218].
27. See for example the discussions in *Blue labour—Forging a new politics* Ed Adrian Pabst and Ian Geary IB Tauris 2015.
28. Gopal, Priyamvada. 2019. *Insurgent Empire* London: Verso.
29. *Encouraging citizenship* Report of the Commission on Citizenship, HMSO 1990.
30. *Secure Borders, Safe Haven: Integration with Diversity in Modern Britain* Home Office 2002 CM 5387.
31. Sections 9–11 Asylum and Immigration Act 1966, and s55 Nationality, Immigration Act 2002, were both slipped quickly into legislation, engendered little debate and had severe consequences, discussed in Chapter 3.
32. Home Secretary Theresa May called a debate on the 2012 Rules: but most of the debate was taken up with the issue of foreign criminals.
33. Restrictions on Employment and Residential Accommodation (Prescribed Requirements and Codes of Practice) and Licensing Act 2003 (Personal and Premises Licences) (Forms), etc., Regulations 2022 (SI 2022 No. 242). Laid before parliament March 2022.
34. Para 395C of the pre-2012 Rules.
35. *Oludoyi*, n19 [43].

36. Institute for Government 2019 *Managing migration after Brexit* https://www.instituteforgovernment.org.uk/publications/managing-migration-after-brexit [52].
37. Many of the over 5m EU nationals will be forced to wait up to 5 extra years to qualify to apply for British citizenship. Many will nevertheless apply, as not understanding the legal position, wasting thousands in application fees.
38. Institute of Government 2019 n34.
39. Brought in by s19 Immigration Act 2014.
40. Richard Warren's article *Private life in the balance: Constructing the precarious migrant.* Journal of Immigration, Asylum and Nationality Law 2016, 3 (2) was put before the Supreme Court in *Rhuppiah.* Unfortunately, the court did not prefer his argument.
41. *Rhuppiah* [2018] UKSC 58.
42. *Agyarko* [2017] UKSC 11. The facts of both cases were weak indeed and the dismissal of the appeals was not that surprising.
43. *SD* n22.
44. Mayblin, Lucy. 2019. *Imagining asylum, governing asylum seekers: Complexity reduction and policy making in the UK Home Office* Migration Studies, 7 (1), pp. 17, 18.
45. The Conversation 9/12/2021 https://theconversation.com/why-the-uk-governments-plan-to-overturn-court-decisions-is-a-bad-idea-173441.
46. Bauman, Zygmunt. 2000. *Liquid modernity* Cambridge: Polity Press.
47. PEP report 1948, cited in Chapters 2 and 4.
48. Hayter, Theresa Hayter, *Open borders.*

Index

S. York, *The Impact of UK Immigration Law*,
https://doi.org/10.1007/978-3-030-98721-3

The manufacturer's authorised representative in the EU is Springer Nature Customer Service Centre GmbH, Europaplatz 3, 69115 Heidelberg, Germany. If you have any concerns regarding our products, please contact ProductSafety@springernature.com

Printed and bound by CPI Group (UK) Ltd, Croydon, CR0 4YY

30/09/2026

02225499-0011